Simple Real-time Operating System
A kernel inside view for a beginner

 www.trafford.com

North America & international
toll-free: 844-688-6899 (USA & Canada)
fax: 812 355 4082

In loving memory of my Grand Father

Satyanarayana Penumuchu

who loved me most, financed my education and blessed me the ability to write this book

4

CONTENTS

6

Preface

The first motivation for writing this book is to teach my colleagues about RTOS (Real-Time Operating System) concepts and the proprietary RTOS developed for our project by me. I realized that the same material with some extension can be useful to most embedded engineers who are beginners in learning about RTOS. I came across many embedded engineers who are not comfortable to use real-time operating system. A significant fraction of these people have taken operating systems course during their undergraduate or graduate studies! The unease obviously even more aggravated for those embedded engineers who do not take operating systems course during their college level studies. I think this is the main reason that some companies still use tricky, messy workarounds to solve their scheduling problems in their simple and moderately complex projects. The operating systems course the engineers studied during their undergraduation is too broad which only cover theoretical aspects of all kinds of systems, and mostly devoid of practical training that students can not gain the ability to develop one!.

RTOS market share surveys show a significant fraction of companies use their proprietary operating systems. The proprietary RTOS has the advantages of leanness, higher efficiency and much more configurability as it is entirely open. Even though the market share for proprietary RTOS is slowly declining, the fraction of the companies that use proprietary RTOSes will be significant for many more years. This book can be a great resource for the engineers who are developing and maintaining a proprietary RTOS for his/her company.

This book address the needs of the people who want to learn about RTOS and also those who want to develop one. This book gives in-depth understanding of RTOS, make the reader comfortable in understanding a code written using RTOS, make the reader comfortable using RTOS to develop a new piece of code. This book explains all basic RTOS concepts starting from scratch in detail. So a beginner or a person only with little experience with RTOS can significantly benefit from this book. This book discusses most of the RTOS concepts and implements them in a piece of code and develops one simple RTOS kernel, named as SROS (Simple Real-time Operating System). All the features for SROS kernel are developed one at a time in an evolutionary manner. So this book can also benefit an experienced person who wants to know more about RTOS kernel. As this book develop feature by feature in a piece meal fashion, this book can greatly benefit the people who want to develop a proprietary RTOS for their projects. As this book covers the kernel of RTOS and point out some short term projects a reader can do, this book can also be used by students who want to know about the kernel of RTOS and want to do some short term projects on RTOS.

This book introduces the RTOS concepts one by one and shows their implementations in C code, or pseudo C code together with ARM assembly code when C implementation is not possible (i.e. in case of Hardware Abstraction Layer functions). Every piece of code shown as example in this book has either C code or pseudo C code so readers with out the knowledge of ARM architecture and instruction set can also understand the functionality of the code easily. (The ARM code given in this book and CDROM is developed for ARM architecture V5 and tested on ARM9 platform). Allover the book when we mention ARM processor, it means we are referring to an ARM core that implement ARM V5 architecture. The RTOS code developed in the book is named as SROS (Simple Real-time Operating System). The SROS kernel implementation is on similar lines to many commercially available RTOSes. The SROS kernel features are added chapter after chapter. At any level of development, SROS code available in the accompanied CDROM can be readily used in an ARM based system and can be ported easily to other processor platforms. SROS features are implemented incrementally so that user has the choice of using it at any level of complexity. SROS with minimal features provide minimum code, execution time overheads and vice versa. The code size and execution complexity of SROS is less in the initial version compared to the later version even after unused functions are removed by linker. The accompanied CDROM provides 2 versions of SROS which were incrementally developed and finished by the end of 2nd and 3rd chapters.

The author assumes that the reader is familiar with C programming, and simple data structure - linked lists. No knowledge about assembly programming of ARM processor is assumed, even though the accompanying CDROM provide the SROS implementation on ARM platform, which is auxiliary.

The readers of this book after reading it can have the comfort of working/evaluating any RTOS, can have the comfort of knowing the internals of RTOS, can use highly simple and optimal SROS without any royalties with the flexibility of customizations, or can develop a simple proprietary real-time operating system in a few days.

Note: In some distributions of this book, CDROM is not attached. In such cases reader can download the CDROM contents by visiting this book webpage at the publishers website at www.trafford.com/07-0194 . If this do not work for the reader for any reason, He can request the author through E-mail with the subject "Request for SROS CDROM contents" in the subject field at author's mail address chowdary_penumuchu@yahoo.com

P.V.Chowdary

1 What is RTOS and why do we need it?

Coding a single job on a micro processor does not need complex time scheduling or time sharing methods required to share the CPU time among multiple jobs. For example take the simple job of reading the measurement of a physical quantity from a transducer[1], processing the measurement, and displaying the result on the LCD. The pseudo code in Figure 1-1can do this job.

```
While(1)
{

        read the measurement from transducer.
        Process the measurement.
        Display the result on LCD.

}
```

Figure 1-1

But unfortunately most of the real world applications are not as simple as the one shown in Figure 1-1. Most of the applications need to do many jobs involving a variety of input/output devices, many independent periodic jobs, and many aperiodic jobs, which may depend on one another in a complex way.

Let us take a moderately complex application video-ip-phone. Video-ip-phone operates on IP (Internet Protocol) network, transmits and receives video along with audio (i.e. speech) using IP packets. Video-ip-phone during its operation sends and receives audio, video, call control packets through IP network. The video-ip-phone need to capture audio, video of near end and render the audio, video of far end smoothly. In addition it has to process call control packets and respond to inputs from user interface appropriately.

A simple pseudo code implementation of video-ip-phone is shown in Figure 1-2. For simplicity, establishment and release of the call is ignored and not shown.

---

[1] Transducer is a device that converts a physical quantity like temperature, pressure etc.. into electrical signal for measurement.

12

```
While(call established)
{
        if (packet(s) received from IP network)
        {
                Place audio packet(s) in audio jitter buffer*.
                Place video packet(s) in video jitter buffer.
                Place call control packet(s) in call control packet buffer.
        }
        if(audio playout of audio playout ping pong buffer* is finished)
        {
                Decode next audio packet. Place decoded audio data which
                has to be played out, into audio ping pong buffer.
        }
        if(video frame rendering of video playout ping pong buffer is finished)
        {
                Decode next video frame. Place decoded video frame data
                into video ping pong buffer for rendering.
        }
        if(control packet available in call control packet buffer)
        {
                Process call control packet.
        }
        if(user interface input available)
        {
                Process input from user interface.
        }
        if(capture of audio samples into audio capture ping pong buffer is finished)
        {
                Encode captured audio samples. Send encoded packet(s) over IP
                network.
        }
        if(capture of video frame into video capture ping pong buffer is finished)
        {
                Encode captured video frame. Send encoded packets over IP network.
        }
}
```

Figure 1-2

*⁻The Jitter buffer is a large buffer used to tackle the bursty nature, out of order arrival of IP packets on an IP network.

*⁻The ping pong buffer is the word used to denote a buffer in a set of two buffers used to work with real-time capture/playout devices. While Input device is capturing data into first buffer, previously captured data in the second buffer is processed by the

processor. The processing of second buffer data will be complete before the capturing device can fill the first buffer. After the first buffer is filled, the role of the buffers is exchanged. (i.e. second buffer is being written by the capture device while first buffer data is being processed). This way of operation resembles the ping-pong game so the two buffers collectively called ping pong buffers. The same operation and naming is possible with playout device as well. In the video-ip-phone example audio capture need a set of ping pong buffers, audio playout need a set of ping pong buffers, video capture need a set of ping pong buffers, video rendering need a set of ping pong buffers.

One may think, the code in Figure 1-2 can work in the system. But in practice it has lot of limitations to work properly. The limitations stem from its assumptions

- It assumes audio, video ping pong buffers are capturing and playing for the same amount of time.

- It assumes encoding/decoding of audio video takes constant time.

- It assumes call control processing time, user response processing time is very small and can be done in a fraction of one audio/video ping pong buffer playing/rendering time.

- It assumes lot of packets can be buffered in network interface. In the above example it is (peak network receive rate)*(audio/video ping pong buffer rendering time).

In practice usually none of the above assumptions can be easily satisfied. Some assumptions are not feasible to implement in practice. Let us see the implementation feasibility of each assumption one at a time.

- Audio and video ping pong buffers are usually associated with different capture/playout times. Usually audio requires short length (i.e. in time) ping pong buffers to shorten the end to end delay. Usually audio ping pong buffers size is such that it can capture/play 10 msec, but the amount of video frame rendering time is few tens of milliseconds. For a video frame rate of 30frames/sec, the video frame rendering time is 33.33msec. For 10frames/sec rate it is 100msec. To worsen the things video frame rate is usually negotiated during the call setup to accommodate bandwidth limitations of networks and we do not know the video frame rendering time in advance.

- Audio/video encoding/decoding algorithms complexity peak to average ratio is as high as 10 or more depending on the algorithms used. Even though decoding algorithms usually takes constant time, complex audio/video encoding algorithms which try to represent the compressed signal as closely as possible to the input signal, make repeat calculations. So the peak to average ratio of processing time can be very high. Silence and simple audio signal takes less processing time where as complex audio signal takes high processing time. In the same way less video processing time when the video is a still image and high processing time when the video is fast moving.

- There can be a variety of call control processing, user input processing functions. Some of these functions can be very complex. Completing even one at a time with in a fraction of audio/video ping pong buffer rendering time is almost impossible.

- Usually all the packets can not be buffered at the network interface when we wait for long time and when they are arriving at peak rate because of small buffer space limitations.

The limitations look formidable. How to over come these limitations?

Theoretically it should be possible to build the system when the average processing complexity of one while loop in Figure 1-2 is lower than processing capacity of the micro processor.

What wrong we are doing?

The first mistake of code in Figure 1-2 is, it is processing real-time functions(for example decoding audio, video and updating ping pong buffers) and non real-time functions(for example call control/user inputs processing) in a rigid sequence and imposing the real-time functions dead-lines on non real-time functions as well!.

The second mistake is the code is doing all the jobs in a single thread (thread will be discussed soon) i.e. in a single sequence at same urgency level. Even though some tasks like decoding of audio is more urgent (i.e. inherently have more priority) than user input processing, both were done at same urgency (priority) level. The urgency level of a function is not at all taken into consideration. Similarly considering the small amount of audio ping pong buffers capture/play out time compared to the video ping pong buffers capture/render time, audio encoding/decoding is more urgent than video encoding/decoding. But both are done at same urgency level.

So the obvious solution is to divide the functions according to their priority and executing the highest priority functions first. When a higher priority function is waiting for some input we can process next high priority (i.e. lower priority) functions. If required input is available after some time for the waiting high priority function when we are processing a low priority function, we have to abandon temporarily low priority function in the middle and start executing high priority function. After finishing high priority functionality with the available input and when high priority function is again waiting for next input, we can resume the abandoned low priority function.

The division of monolithic video-ip-phone functionality in Figure 1-2 according to their priority levels is shown below in Figure 1-3 through Figure 1-9. Each divided piece of code shown in Figure 1-3 through Figure 1-9 is called thread of the application.

```
While(1)
{
    Wait till a packet is received.
    If(received packet is video packet) then place packet in video jitter buffer.
    else if (received packet is audio packet) then place packet in audio jitter buffer.
    else if (received packet is call control packet) then place packet in call control
                                                                    packet buffer.

}
```

Figure 1-3 Network receive thread

```
While(1)
{
    Decode audio packets after removing them from audio jitter buffer and make one
    audio frame.
    Wait till previous audio ping pong buffer is played.
    Update audio playout ping pong buffer to play the decoded audio frame.
}
```

Figure 1-4 Audio decode thread

```
While(1)
{
    Decode video packets after removing them from video jitter buffer and make one
    video frame.
    Wait till previous video ping pong buffer is rendered.
    Update video playout ping pong buffer to render the decoded frame.
}
```

Figure 1-5 Video decode thread

```
while(1)
{
    Wait till a call control packet is available.
    Process call control packet.
}
```

Figure 1-6 Call control processing thread

```
while(1)
{
   Wait till a user input is available.
   Process user input.
}
```

Figure 1-7 User Input processing thread

```
while(1)
{
   Wait till capturing of audio frame into audio capture ping pong buffer is finished.
   Encode the captured audio frame and keep the encoded audio packet(s) in the
   network output packets queue.
}
```

Figure 1-8 Audio encode thread

```
while(1)
{
   Wait till capturing of video frame into video capture ping pong buffer is finished.
   Encode the captured video frame and keep the encoded video packets in
   the network output packets queue.
}
```

Figure 1-9 Video encode thread

In all the above threads "wait till the occurrence of some event", is a synchronization method(will be discussed soon) which convey some information to a special program about its input/resource needs, and the special program will decide to continue execution of the thread or not.

Now we have reached the appropriate time to define 'thread'. A thread is nothing but a sequence of instructions to be executed by a processor, for doing a specific job. Each thread has its own independent program start address and hence a separate program counter, stack pointer and stack space. Each thread has a status. The status of the thread is the processor registers, program counter, stack pointer, all flags and any other control registers. When ever a thread is executing, its status is changing continuously. (i.e. executing instructions continuously change the registers, program counter). When ever a thread has stopped executing (i.e. waiting for CPU, or for a resource, or for an input), its status is frozen. i.e. all the status information is saved into memory. With the saved status information which is available in the memory, we can start executing (running) a thread again at a later point of time. (i.e. with the status information saved to memory when the thread is stopped, we can start executing the thread again at any point of time with out worrying about any loss of context of the thread). The status of the thread is also called "context". The memory area where the context and all other information regarding the thread is stored is called "thread control block" (TCB) or "thread object" or simply "context space". So we can say the applications in Figure 1-1, Figure 1-2 are single threaded applications. Where as the application consisting of all the threads shown in Figure 1-3 through Figure 1-9 make one multi threaded application. Figure 1-3 through Figure 1-9 show different threads designed for doing a specific job in the video-ip-phone system. In a uni-processor environment, one and only one thread can be in the running state. The rest of the threads in the system should have their context saved in the memory, and waiting for the CPU time or availability of resources or inputs needed for the threads to continue their execution. A thread is a basic unit for CPU utilization in a multi threaded application.

In a general purpose computer, the operating system can load and execute many applications simultaneously. Each application is also called a process. A process is a group of threads making up an application. So a process is also boiled down to threads. We do not discuss much about multi process concepts in this book as this book is focusing on single multi threaded embedded application running on a processor. Nevertheless, most of the concepts discussed in this book can also be used when developing an application to be loaded and executed by a general purpose operating system.

When we have divided our system into many threads, consequences of this division pops up. Initial requirements are answers to the questions

- Who will load the thread context into the processor for executing the thread?

- Who will stop the running thread at appropriate time and start executing new thread?

- How the running thread will get stopped?

- How the stopped threads resume execution?

- Who will maintain the thread status information of all the threads efficiently and consistently?

The answers to all the above questions involve "a special program". The "special program" should take care of all the requirements we raised with the above questions. The "special program" should act as a manager for the threads in the system. That "special program" is called "Real-time Operating System (RTOS)".

RTOS is a program that does no useful work by itself. It creates an environment in which threads can do the useful work. RTOS is just like a boss of a big company who does not produce any goods (useful work) by himself. But he direct/coordinate the work of his subordinates/workers who do the actual work.

Let us specifically answer to the questions raised in the earlier paragraph. Answering those questions should give the specifications for RTOS design.

Question: Who will load the thread context into the processor for executing the thread?

Answer: RTOS should identify which thread is the most urgent thread ready for execution among many threads (i.e. highest priority ready thread) in the system. Then it should load the context from highest priority ready thread's TCB (Thread Control Block) into the processor and jump to the starting address in TCB to start execution of the highest priority ready thread.

Question: Who will stop the running thread at appropriate time and start executing new thread?

Answer: RTOS stops the running thread at appropriate time by saving running thread's context to its TCB memory space. RTOS starts a new thread by loading its context from the TCB. Stopping the running thread and starting a new thread is called context switch. Context switch is always done by RTOS.

Question: How the running thread will get stopped?

Answer: A thread always switches between the states as shown in Figure 1-10. (Some commercial RTOSes keep more arrows and more states to the diagram in Figure 1-10. The states and arrows shown in the diagram are basic and sufficient to most applications).

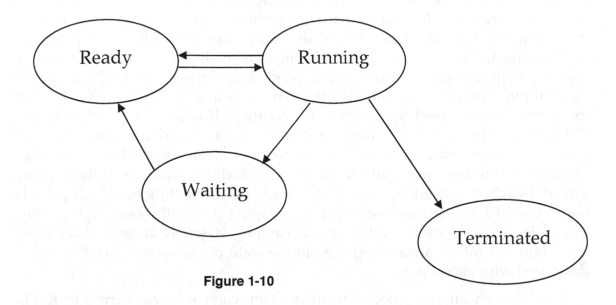

Figure 1-10

When ever a currently running thread needs certain events/resources necessary to continue its execution, it asks RTOS by making a RTOS call with the events/resources it need, to continue its execution. When a running thread make a RTOS call, RTOS has the opportunity to decide whether to continue running the running thread by returning from the RTOS call, or to save the running thread's context to its TCB in memory and make the thread go into waiting or ready state(See Figure 1-10). RTOS check for the necessary events/resources the running thread asked for it to continue execution. If the events/resources asked by the running thread to continue its execution are available, its execution is not stopped and the running thread continue its execution as RTOS call return immediately granting the resources to the running thread. If the events/resources asked by the running thread to continue its execution are not available, RTOS decide to stop the execution of the running thread and make the running thread go into waiting state. To switch the running thread into waiting state, RTOS freeze the context of the running thread i.e. save context to TCB space of the running thread in memory and mark the events/resources which the running thread has asked for. After switching the running thread into waiting state, RTOS load the context of next most urgent thread which is in ready state for execution. i.e. when a running thread go into waiting state, next high priority ready thread will be switched from ready state to running state. As stated above any number of threads can be in any state except one and only one thread can be in running state.

The required event needed for the running thread to continue its execution is communicated to RTOS through a synchronization object. The resource a thread needs for it to continue execution will also be associated with a synchronization object when a thread shares the resource with the peer threads. For example in Figure 1-7 we need "user input availability event" before starting user input processing. The user input processing thread asks RTOS about the "user input availability event". If the event is available, RTOS allow the user input processing thread to continue its execution. If the event is not available, RTOS saves the context of user input processing thread into memory thus making the user input processing thread go into waiting state. The waiting state of the thread is associated with the event for which it is waiting. If the running thread switched to waiting state, RTOS loads the context of next high priority ready thread into the processor to start executing it. (i.e. the next high priority thread is switched from ready state to running state). Note that "user input availability event" is always reflected in the state of the synchronization object associated with user input.

When an interrupt occurs in the system, control is transferred to RTOS. RTOS calls the appropriate interrupt service routine. The interrupt service routine can trigger some events, and triggering events can move threads from waiting state to ready state. i.e. when a thread is waiting for an event and the event is triggered by other thread or interrupt service routine, the waiting thread will be moved to ready state. When the interrupt service routine returns, control is again transferred to RTOS . RTOS has the opportunity for a context switch after interrupt service routine. When a higher priority thread (compared to the priority of the running thread) is moved to ready state from waiting state(during interrupt service routine), RTOS has the opportunity to move the running thread from running state to ready state and to resume the high priority thread which came to ready state during interrupt service routine. Even after interrupt service routine, if the running thread is the highest priority ready thread in the system, there is no need for context switch and the RTOS transfer control back to running thread (the thread during whose execution the interrupt occurred) and running thread continue execution.

The running thread can post an event in to the system using a RTOS call. When the running thread makes an RTOS call, RTOS has the opportunity to stop the thread. The event posted by the running thread can trigger (i.e. move) waiting thread from waiting state to ready state, if the waiting thread is waiting for the posted event. When a thread is waiting for an event and the event is posted in to the system, the waiting thread will be moved from waiting state to ready state. If a thread of higher priority than the running thread comes to ready state due to the posting of event, RTOS decides to stop the running thread and start the higher priority thread that became ready. To stop the running thread

RTOS saves the context of running thread in to its TCB. The new thread (which became ready) TCB will be loaded in to the processor for running by RTOS. Even after posting the event by the running thread, if the running thread is the highest priority ready thread in the system, there is no need for context switch and the RTOS transfer control back to running thread and running thread continue execution.

In summary

1. A running thread can go to waiting state by itself by making a RTOS call for an unavailable event/resource.

2. A running thread can be forced from running state to ready state if an interrupt service routine trigger higher priority thread(s) to ready state from waiting state.

3. A running thread can be forced to ready state from running state, if it posts an event, which can make a higher priority thread than itself, become ready.

Question: How stopped threads resume execution?

Answer: All the waiting threads in the system are waiting for a certain event to happen in the system. For example user input thread is waiting for user input availability event. Audio encoding thread is waiting for a filled audio capture ping pong buffer availability event. All these events are associated with RTOS synchronization objects. Interrupt service routines or the running thread can post the events in to the system. When ever the event needed for a waiting thread to continue its execution is available in the system, the waiting thread is moved from waiting state to ready state. When an event occurs in the system, control is always with RTOS. After all, the events production and consumption is always done with RTOS calls!. So RTOS always has the opportunity to make a context switch to start running highest priority ready thread, as highest priority ready thread can be different from time to time as events are generated and consumed from time to time. i.e. Till the availability of required event a thread will be in waiting state, when event is available the thread move to ready state. RTOS always run highest priority thread which is in ready state. So after a thread moved to ready state, the thread still wait till no other thread has higher priority than itself. When a thread achieves the designation of highest priority thread in ready state, the thread's context will be loaded by RTOS into the processor and the thread move to running state. (See Figure 1-10).

Question: How the events are generated in to the system?

Answer: All events generation and consumption is through RTOS calls only. The events are generated in to the system through RTOS calls by interrupt service routines, or through the RTOS calls by the threads themselves (ofcourse when

22

they are in running state). For example user input availability event is triggered from the user interface interrupt service routine (such as keypad or touch screen interrupt service routine). Audio input availability event is triggered from audio capture interrupt service routine. The user input interrupt is generated by user interface peripherals (such as keyboard, remote controller or touch screen etc...). Audio input interrupt is generated by audio interface unit (such as serial port which is connected to analog-to-digital converter which in turn connected to mic). Note that not only interrupt service routines, but also the threads can generate events and consume when they are in running state.

Question: Who will maintain the thread status information of all the threads efficiently and consistently?

Answer: Obviously our special program (RTOS) has to maintain the thread status information (i.e. TCB) of each thread.

Question: How the interrupts are handled?

Answer: Whenever an interrupt occurs, control is always transferred to RTOS. RTOS calls appropriate interrupt service routine. The interrupt service routine is implemented by the application, not by the RTOS. RTOS just intercept the interrupt and call the interrupt service routine. Interrupt service routine can generate some events. When ever any thread is waiting for a generated event that thread is moved to ready state from waiting state. (For example user input interrupt service routine will generate "user input availability event". So if the user input processing thread is waiting for the "user input availability event", the user input processing thread is moved to ready state from waiting state). After interrupt service routine, control is returned back to RTOS. Interrupt service routine will never go into waiting state (as interrupt service routine is not a thread). RTOS can decide after each interrupt service routine whether to stop the currently interrupted thread and start executing the new thread or to continue the interrupted thread. So if a high priority thread than the running thread (i.e. interrupted thread) is triggered to ready state in the interrupt service routine, context switch occurs. Context switch means switching the contexts in the processor. i.e. moving the running thread to ready/waiting state and loading another ready thread context into the processor for execution (thus brining it to running state).

Question: When all the threads are waiting for some events in the system what will be run by the processor?

Answer: When all the threads are waiting for some events, RTOS run special "idle thread". Idle thread is created by RTOS during its initialization and has lowest priority in the system. When no work has to be done by processor, idle thread will be scheduled by RTOS to keep the processor busy, till any other thread becomes ready to run.

Question: When a thread finishes its execution where it will return?

Answer: When a thread finishes its execution it returns control to RTOS. When ever a thread is created, the return address given to it is a module address of RTOS. That RTOS module take care of any clean up needed and start running the next higher priority ready thread in the system. When ever a thread returns control to RTOS, it is said to have entered into Terminated state. (See Figure 1-10). A terminated thread is not active in the system.

So after learning about the introduction of RTOS and the method of interaction between RTOS and the threads in the system let us see the software structure of the video-ip-phone in Figure 1-11

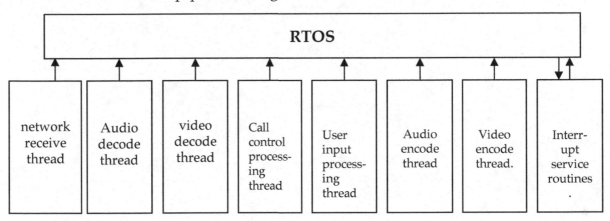

Figure 1-11

In the diagram in Figure 1-11 rectangular box denote a module. The interface between two modules is through the function calls. Arrows denote function calls. Base of the arrow denote the caller module, head of the arrow denote callee module. If we observe in the diagram all the modules make RTOS calls. But RTOS never call a user module to implement its functionality. i.e. RTOS is independent/ignorant about the functionality of user threads but provide the environment for the threads to function properly. RTOS calls appropriate interrupt service routine when an interrupt occurs. The interrupt service routine should be implemented by the application and can not be implemented by the RTOS itself. RTOS just intercept the interrupt, and call the interrupt service routine. Usually all RTOSes provide a way to configure the user interrupt service routines into RTOS. Interrupt service routine can make RTOS calls to generate events in the system.

2 Mutual exclusion, thread synchronization and scheduling

An important ramification when dividing a single threaded application into multiple threads is satisfying the requirement of mutually exclusive usage of inherently non sharable resources.

When we have divided the application into many threads, two threads may want to use the same hardware device simultaneously, which is inherently non sharable. But non sharable devices should be controlled by only one thread at a time. For example assume thread A, thread B both use a serial port in the system. When thread A is using the serial port, thread A might be preempted by an interrupt. (Preemption is the process of forcibly moving a thread from running state to ready state when a higher priority thread become ready to run). If thread B has higher priority than thread A and ready to run after interrupt, thread B come to running state and may start using the serial port. This disrupts the operation on serial port by thread A, as thread B tries to access the serial port in the middle. So we some how, have to make sure that a shared device shall be controlled by only one thread at a time. (i.e. we have to ensure mutually exclusive access to non sharable hardware devices).

Similar to sharing a hardware resource, two or more threads might share some memory space (i.e. some global variables in the application). The memory sharing might be for communication among the threads, or for any other purpose. In that scenario two or more threads might want to update the shared memory at the same time. For example assume thread A generate a packet of data one at a time, thread B consume a packet of data one at a time. Thread A, thread B use a shared variable named *"packetCount"* to count the number of packets outstanding which have to be consumed by thread B. Thread A increment the *"packetCount"* whenever a packet is generated. Thread B decrement the *"packetCount"* whenever a packet is consumed. The *"packetCount"* variable is stored in memory. To increment or decrement a memory location usually the variable is brought to a processor register, appropriate modification is done to the register and the register is written back to memory. (Many modern RISC processors do not support updating memory directly). The pseudo code for modification of *"packetCount"* by thread A, thread B is shown Figures 2-1, 2-2.

```
LDR R0, packetCount          (1)

ADD R0, R0, #1               (2)

STR R0, packetCount          (3)
```

Thread A operation

Figure 2-1

```
LDR R0, packetCount          (1)

SUB R0, R0, #1               (2)

STR R0, packetCount          (3)
```

Thread B operation

Figure 2-2

In Figure 2-1 all the three instructions correspond to incrementing the *packetCount*. Statement (1) loads the *packetCount* from memory into a processor register R0. Statement (2) increments the register R0 by 1. Statement (3) stores the register R0 back into *packetCount* variable in memory. The same comments hold to Figure 2-2 except that statement (2) decrement the register R0 instead of incrementing it.

For example *packetCount*=4 and thread A is the running thread. Assume thread B has higher priority than thread A, Thread A got the packet and it is executing the code shown in Figure 2-1. Assume that statement (1) got executed, and immediately after statement (1) thread A unfortunately got preempted by an interrupt and thread B is ready to run. Thread B want to consume a packet and executed all the code shown in Figure 2-2. After thread B execution of code in Figure 2-2 the *packetCount* in memory is 3. After some time thread A will be scheduled to run, and after thread A executed statements (2), (3) in Figure: 2-1, the *packetCount* in memory is 5!

After all in summary, we have produced a packet and consumed a packet when *packetCount*=4. So the *packetCount* should not get changed from its value 4.

But we have inconsistent result at the end; *packetCount* is 5, not 4 which is the correct value.

Now let us start with thread B having lower priority than thread A. Let us assume thread B is running in the system. If thread B is preempted after statement (1), and thread A execute all the 3 statements, and later thread B finishes its remaining two statements, the *packetCount* will be 3 in memory, not 4 which is the correct value.

The problem here is that one thread has read *packetCount* into register, it was preempted before it update the *packetCount* in memory, and by the time it has the opportunity to start executing again, the value it has in its register (i.e. context) is wrong!.

The above problem with the shared variable will not be present when the processor has the capability to update the memory with one atomic operation. (atomic operation is the operation which will not be divided into two or more instructions as in Figure 2-1 and Figure 2-2. All atomic operations will be performed with one processor instruction). But if the shared memory consists of multiple variables, the problem pops up again because no processor can update arbitrary number of variables in memory in one atomic operation.

The pieces of code which access the shared resource is called "critical sections" of the resource. The shared resource can be either a non sharable hardware device or a shared memory. The code shown in Figure 2-1, Figure 2-2 are critical sections for the shared memory "*packetCount*" variable.

To avoid the inconsistent operation involving a shared resource, we have to make sure that two or more threads can not be in critical section of a resource at any point of time.

One simple way to avoid the critical section problem is to make sure that a thread in critical section can not be preempted! This can be done by disabling the interrupts at the entry of a critical section and enabling at the exit of a critical section! But if the critical sections are large chunks of code, the interrupt response time will suffer, and in some cases system may not work properly if we disable interrupts for longer time periods.

To avoid the critical section problem we have to implement a flag that can be tested and updated atomically. The flag is called mutex (to denote mutual exclusion). The mutex has two states either 1 or 0. 1 denotes no thread is in critical section. 0 denotes one thread is in critical section. Any thread want to enter the critical section need to test the flag for 1, and if the flag is 1, set the flag to 0 and enter the critical section (All these operations are done in one atomic operation). If the flag is 0, the thread has to wait for mutex to be turned to 1. When a thread leaves the critical section, the thread has to set the mutex back to 1.

Setting the mutex to 0 when it is 1, is called mutex lock operation. Setting the mutex back to 1 when it is 0 is called mutex unlock or release operation. Many processors support testing and setting a flag in memory atomically with some special instruction.

ARM processors support swap instruction which exchanges register and memory atomically, which can be used to implement the mutex operation.

For example,

SWAP R0, R0, [R1]

This instruction writes the register R0 into memory location pointed by R1, and simultaneously updates R0 with the content available at memory location pointed by R1. i.e. it swaps the register and memory location. If R1 points to the mutex and R0 holds 0, the above instruction try to lock the mutex. If the mutex already got locked by a different thread (i.e. mutex=0), this instruction does not effect the mutex anyway. But if the mutex is in unlocked position mutex will be locked. If R0 initially holds 0 and holds 1 after swap instruction, mutex is successfully locked by the running thread and no other thread had previously locked the mutex. If R0 still holds 0 after swap instruction, locking the mutex is unsuccessful as the mutex already got locked by some other thread and the running thread has to wait till swap operation get her 1, before proceeding into the critical section.

The same SWAP instruction as shown above can be used after the exit from critical section with R0=1, R1= "address of mutex" to unlock the mutex.(to set the mutex back to 1).

So as an initial thought, the code around critical section should look like Figure 2-3 !.

```
do
{
        Try to lock the mutex in one atomic operation.
}while (mutex not locked)
critical section
unlock the mutex.
```

Figure 2-3

The implementation of the code in Figure 2-3 using SWAP instruction is shown in Figure 2-4.

```
MOV R0, #0
LDR R1, #address of mutex
While(R0 == 0)
{
        SWAP R0, R0, [R1]
}
critical section.
MOV R0, #1
LDR R1, #address of mutex
SWAP R0, R0, [R1]
```

Figure 2-4

One may think the above piece of code can solve the critical section problem that is associated with multi-threading. This kind of solution is called "busy-waiting" solution. The obvious problem with busy waiting solution is it wastes the CPU time when mutex already got locked by a different thread. This solution may only work although inefficiently when OS allocate each thread a constant amount of time (irrespective of priority). The busy waiting solution can not solve the critical section problem if the RTOS run highest priority ready thread for an indefinite amount of time till that go to waiting state (which most RTOSes do). If a low priority thread locks the mutex, a higher priority thread can be stuck in busy-waiting for the mutex. The high priority thread will be busy for ever waiting for the mutex! So busy-waiting is the worst solution and should not be used.

The solution for the critical section problem is to make any thread not able to acquire the mutex be forced to move to waiting state i.e. freeze its context, and schedule the next highest priority ready thread to run in the processor.(scheduling is the process of deciding which thread has to be given CPU time and loading the context of that lucky thread into CPU and let it run). In such a case the thread in running state move to waiting state and, another thread in ready state move to the running state (See Figure 1-10). As stated earlier this operation is also called context switch. When ever the mutex got unlocked, RTOS has to make the waiting thread (which is waiting for the mutex) has to be woken up and move it to ready state. So to implement this functionality mutex locking and unlocking has to be done by RTOS at the request of threads, instead of by threads themselves. Mutex locking and unlocking are events in the system and they have to be generated only with RTOS calls. When ever an RTOS call is made, RTOS has the opportunity for context switch.

We now got RTOS a responsibility in ensuring mutual exclusion. All functions related to mutex have to be implemented by RTOS, and not by the application threads. Application threads will request RTOS by making a RTOS call to lock or unlock a specified mutex. RTOS has to grant the mutex (i.e. lock the mutex) if it is available (i.e. in unlocked state). If the mutex is not available RTOS has to freeze the context of the thread which requested locking the mutex, move the thread to waiting state and load the context of next highest priority ready thread and let the next highest priority thread run by the CPU. Similarly application threads will request RTOS by making RTOS call to unlock the mutex. In such a case RTOS has to unlock the mutex, move any waiting thread (which was kept into waiting state when it tried to lock the mutex which was already locked) to ready state. If the thread in the running state has lower priority than the thread which became ready to run, RTOS has to make a context switch. (i.e. move the running thread to ready state and load new highest priority ready thread context into the CPU and let it run). If the running thread has higher priority than the thread which is moved to ready state from waiting state, context switch should not take place.

2.1 Mutex implementation in SROS

It is time to see an example implementation of functions that manipulate the mutex. Let us see the mutex implementation in SROS. The memory area that holds the mutex and its associated variables is called "mutexObject" in SROS.

```
typedef struct
{
        int32 mutex;
        listObject_t waitList;

}mutexObject_t;
```

Figure 2-5

The simplest definition of the mutexObject used in SROS is shown in Figure 2-5. In SROS all structures are type defined and the type definition name end with _t (as in mutexObject_t, listObject_t) to denote it as a structure tag name. When we are speaking we just spell it with out _t (as mutexObject) for convenience.

The variable *"mutex"* in the mutexObject is just a binary flag (though declared as int32 to make the size of mutexObject a multiple of 4 bytes). The value of the *"mutex"* as mentioned earlier is either 0 or 1. 0 indicates the mutex is locked by some thread in the system, 1 indicates the mutex is not locked by any thread in the system. Mutex can be locked by only one thread at any point of time. When the thread that locked the mutex release the mutex, then another thread can lock the mutex.

The *"waitList"* is of type listObject which is a linked list. This linked list hold contexts of threads that are waiting to lock the mutex. This mean threads that go to waiting state due to the unavailability of mutex will have their contexts in the *waitList*. Each node of this linked list hold address of a threadObject (i.e. address of the context space) and some auxiliary information about the waiting thread. (See listObject definition, operations on listObjects in the sections 2-8, 2-9).

2.1.1 threadObject

The context of a thread is stored in memory and that memory space is called as threadObject of the thread. The definition of threadObject depends on the processor architecture and also on RTOS as it need to maintain some book keeping information about the thread. For example the simplest definition of threadObject that is used in initial version of SROS on ARM platform is shown in Figure 2-6

```
typedef struct _threadObject_
{
        int32 R[16];
        uint32 cpsr;
        uint32 priority;
        char   *threadObjectName;

}threadObject_t;
```

Figure 2-6

The ARM processor contains 16 registers R0-R15 and a current program status register(CPSR). The variables *R, cpsr* variables hold all registers, current program status register respectively (i.e. context). *priority* field stores the priority of the thread. In SROS highest priority thread has *priority* value of 0. A thread become low in priority as the priority field value increases. *threadObjectName* just used to note the name of the thread for debugging purposes. (When threadObjects are in a list one can easily identify the thread by looking at its name in this field during debugging). It has no other use. The definition of threadObject will take more space than the context if RTOS support many features. We can see the evolution of threadObject as we add more features for SROS.

In this book the term threadObject mean a thread's threadObject. For example "running threadObject" mean running thread's threadObject. Similarly "waiting threadObject" mean "waiting thread's threadObject". threadObject is also used as a synonym for thread. From the context it is always clear whether we are referring to thread or threadObject(i.e. context space).

2.1.2 mutexObjectInit()

The *mutexObjectInit()* function initializes the mutexObject data structure. It initializes the *mutex* to some initial status (either 1 or 0) and initializes the *waitList*.

The C code that initializes the mutexObject is shown in Figure 2-7.

```
void mutexObjectInit(mutexObject_t *mutexObjectPtr,  int32 initialFlag)          (1)
{
        assert(initialFlag == 0 || initialFlag == 1);                            (2)
        mutexObjectPtr->mutex = initialFlag;                                     (3)
        listObjectInit(&mutexObjectPtr->waitList);                               (4)
}
```

Figure 2-7

Statement (1) shows the prototype. This SROS call takes address of the mutexObject and the initial status of the *mutex*. (i.e. either 0 or 1 to denote the locked position or unlocked position respectively) and return nothing.

Statement (2) is just an assert statement to catch errors in the debug version of SROS.

Statement (3) initializes the initial status of *mutex*.

Statement (4) initializes the *waitList*. After initialization, *waitList* shows that no thread is waiting for the mutex. (See listObject definition, operations on listObjects in the sections 2-8, 2-9).

2.1.3 mutexObjectLock()

Mutex is a lock to a resource (resource is either a non sharable hardware device or a shared memory). From our earlier discussion it is clear that RTOS has to lock or unlock the mutex at the request of application threads. All RTOSes provide a RTOS call to initialize, lock and unlock mutex. Usually RTOS request to lock the mutex, provide an option to the requesting thread what to do when the mutex is not available. This option will be applicable only when the mutex is already locked by a different thread. This option let the requesting thread to be returned immediately indicating failure to lock the mutex(i.e. without going to waiting state), or to move the requesting thread into waiting state and to wake it up when mutex is available. This option in SROS is called *waitFlag*, is an input argument to the SROS call that lock the mutex. *waitFlag* indicates whether to wait or not to wait when mutex is not available. When mutex is not available and *waitFlag* is 1 then the requesting thread will wait till the mutex is available. When mutex is not available and *waitFlag* is 0 then control is returned immediately to the requesting thread indicating failure to lock the mutex.

Thus the SROS function locking the mutex has to do as mentioned below:

1. If the *mutex* is in unlocked state, lock the mutex and return "success".

2. If the *mutex* is in locked state, check for the *waitFlag*. If the *waitFlag* is 1, go to step 3. If the *waitFlag* is 0 return "failure".

3. Save the context of the running thread, which should be functionally equivalent to the context at the start of the mutexObjectLock() function, into the running thread's threadObject. Insert the running thread's threadObject into mutexObject *waitlist*. Jump to *scheduler* to start running the next high priority ready thread. *Scheduler* is the module in SROS which start running the highest priority ready thread in the system. See *scheduler* in sections 2.1.7 and 2.1.8.

The pseudo code in Figure 2-8 shows the SROS implementation of mutexObjectLock(). This pseudo code is the basis for the assembly implementation on the target platform.

Statement (1) shows the function prototype. This function takes mutexObject address, and *waitFlag* as inputs, and return success (i.e. 1) or failure (i.e. 0) in locking the mutex.

Statement (2) tries to lock the *mutex* atomically. If locking the *mutex* is successful, then success (i.e.1) is returned.

If the mutex locking is unsuccessful, statement (4) check the *waitFlag*. If the *waitFlag* is 0 , failure is returned in statement (9).

If the *mutex* locking is unsuccessful, and *waitFlag* is not 0, the context which is functionally equivalent to the starting of the *mutexObjectLock()* function is saved into the running thread's threadObject in statement (6). So at a later point of time the current thread start executing from the beginning of the *mutexObjectLock()* function trying to lock the mutex again. The running threadObject is inserted into the *waitlist* of the mutexObject in statement (7). Note that *runningThreadObjectPtr* is a global variable in SROS which always hold the address of the running threadObject.

```
int32 mutexObjectLock(mutexObject_t *mutexObjectPtr, int32 waitFlag)        (1)
{
        if(swap(0, mutexObjectPtr->mutex))                                  (2)
        {
            return 1;                                                       (3)
        }
    else
    {
        if(waitFlag)                                                        (4)
        {
                interruptDisable();                                         (5)
                get the context which should be functionally equivalent to
                starting of this function and store that context in the running
                thread's threadObject i.e. context space of running thread.  (6)
                listObjectInsert(&mutexObjectPtr->waitList,
                                    runningThreadObjectPtr);                 (7)
                jump to scheduler;                                          (8)
        }
        else
        {
                return 0;                                                   (9)
        }
    }
}
```

Figure 2-8

It is worth while to elaborate on what is "context" that is functionally equivalent to the start of the *mutexObjectLock()*? Is this context is the identical context that existed when we have entered the *mutexObjectLock()*?

It is not necessarily the absolutely identical context (all the registers with same value). If a context that produce functionally identical result when we rerun the *mutexObjectLock()* and do not have any side effects on the thread that made the RTOS request, that context is called functionally equivalent context. Please see the assembly implementation of *mutexObjectLock()* function in section 2.1.4 to have more clear idea about "functionally equivalent context".

Statement (8) make a jump to the *scheduler* to start running the next high priority ready thread.

Statement (5) disables interrupts. This step is necessary because during context switch interrupts can occur and mess up the code flow. All RTOS data structures can be thought of as shared variables with no mutex object to protect them from inconsistent updating. So any change in originally intended flow of

RTOS code when updating the RTOS variables will be fatal. So no interrupts should be allowed when we are updating RTOS variables. So disabling interrupts in statement (5) is a must. When the *scheduler()* load the context of next high priority thread, interrupts will be automatically enabled. Interrupt latency time is one of the bench marks for RTOSes. Interrupt latency time is the maximum time that can elapse between rising of an interrupt and servicing it.

The C implementation is not possible for *mutexObjectLock()* function, because this function collects the context which should be done at processor register level, which is not possible in high level language like C. This function also make a jump to outside of the function (jump to *scheduler* which is difficult to implement in C). So assembly implementation of this function (with the above pseudo code in Figure 2-8 as basis) is necessary when porting this function to any processor platform. This function is one of HAL (Hardware Abstraction Layer) functions for SROS.

The HAL layer is the set of functions with all or part of their implementation underlying machine dependent.

The HAL layer position with RTOS in an embedded application is shown in Figure 2-9.

Application
RTOS
HAL
Processor Hardware

Figure 2-9

From the figure it is apparent that only HAL layer is Processor dependent. Changing the processor platform needs only changing the HAL layer.

2.1.4 mutexObjectLock() assembly implementation

The author has the intention to keep no ARM assembly code in the main part of this book, so that users without the knowledge of ARM architecture can follow the concepts of the book with out much difficulty. Nevertheless to explain what is functional equivalence of context more clearly, the author has kept the assembly code for *mutexObjectLock()* function in the main part of the book. Readers who understood the concept of "functional equivalence of the context" mentioned in the earlier section and do not know the ARM architecture may skip this section.

When we are going to keep the running thread in to waiting state, we should save the correct context of the thread so that we can start executing the thread again at a later point of time. *mutexObjectLock()* call is made by running thread to lock the mutex. So the control should be returned to the running thread only after locking the mutex. So at a later point of time when we start executing the currently running thread, we should try to lock the mutex again (as we have not locked the mutex yet in the current run). So we should start the thread from the beginning of the *mutexObjectLock()* function and hence we should save context available at the beginning of *mutexObjectLock()*.

The context we should save depends on the calling convention of the C compiler. The calling convention of the compiler clearly define:

- How all arguments of a function are passed from calling function to called function?

- Which registers the called function is allowed to destroy and which registers the called function has the obligation to preserve.

- How the called function send return value to calling function.

According to simple ATPCS (Arm Thumb Procedure Call Standard) of ADS (Arm Developer Suite) tools:

- The calling function has to pass the first 4 function arguments to the called function through R0, R1, R2, R3 registers, and the rest of the arguments have to be pushed on to the stack. i.e. if there is only one argument, that argument is passed in R0. If there are two arguments the arguments are passed in R0, R1 respectively and so on. If there are 5 arguments calling function should pass the first 4 arguments in R0, R1, R2, R3 registers, 5th argument should be pushed to the stack. The called function should assume the same about the function arguments and work accordingly.

- The called function is free to destroy R0-R3, R12 registers. The called function should not destroy any other general purpose registers. If the called function want to use registers R4-R11, they have to be saved to the stack at the beginning of the function and should be restored back when returning to calling function.

- R13 is used as stack pointer; R14 is used as return address register. The stack pointer has to be preserved. (The value at the function entry should be same at exit).

- The called function should send the return value to calling function through R0 register.

```
mutexObjectLock
MOV   R2, #0              ;R2=0;                                              (1)

SWP           R2, R2, [R0]    ;lock the mutex atomically.                    (2)

CMP           R2, #1          ;if(mutex == 1)                                (3)

MOVEQ         R0, #1          ;if(mutex == 1) return value=1                 (4)

BXEQ  LR                      ;if(mutex == 1) return 1.                      (5)

CMP           R1, #0          ;if(waitFlag == 0)                             (6)

MOVEQ         R0, #0          ;if(mutex == 0, waitFlag == 0) then return value = 0  (7)

BXEQ  LR                      ;if(mutex == 0, waitFlag == 0) then return 0.  (8)

;waitFlag != 0 and mutex is locked by some other thread.
;So keep the current thread in waitList of this mutex and
;jump to scheduler.

;interruptDisable()
INTERRUPTS_SAVE_DISABLE oldCPSR, R2, R3                                      (9)

              ;creating context for the current thread.
LDR    R3, =runningThreadObjectPtr ;R3=&&running thread Object              (10)

LDR           R3, [R3]                                                      (11)

STMIA R3, {R0-R14}    ;save R0-R14 in the running threadObject              (12)

ADR           R4, mutexObjectLock  ;get the starting address of this function. (13)

STR           R4, [R3, #(15*4)]        ;saved into PC of running threadObject.  (14)

LDR           R4, =oldCPSR                                                  (15)

LDR           R4, [R4]        ;get the original CPSR of the running thread. (16)

STR           R4, [R3, #threadObject_t_cpsr_offset] ;save the original CPSR in the
                                                     ;running threadObject.  (17)
```

```
;insert the running thread into waitList of mutexObject.
ADD    R0, R0, #mutexObject_t_waitList_offset  ;R0=&mutexObject->waitList.     (18)


MOV            R1, R3    ;R1=&runningThreadObjectPtr                            (19)


BL             listObjectInsert;                                               (20)


;jump to scheduler
B              scheduler                                                       (21)
```

Figure 2-10

So our *mutexObjectLock()* function has to expect the two arguments it need in registers R0, R1 respectively. The contents in R3-R12 registers are of no concern to the function *mutexObjectLock()*. The *mutexObjectLock()* function should use R0, R1 as its input arguments. The *mutexObjectLock()* function is free to destroy R0, R1, R2, R3 and R12. The *mutexObjectLock()* function need to preserve R4-R11.

To start the *mutexObjectLock()* function correctly (after taking the thread into waiting state and restarting at a later point of time), we need correct R0, R1 (i.e. function arguments), R4-R11 (*mutexObjectLock()* function has the obligation not to destroy these registers). The R13, R14 anyway need to be stored properly due to their special purpose. So the registers R2, R3, R12 can be of any value in the context. We have no need to save them correctly (i.e. no need to save identical values available at the beginning) into running threadObject, and still the function *mutexObjectLock()* work correctly. So any context which locks the mutex correctly and returns control properly to the parent function is called functionally equivalent context.

Let us see the functionality of the assembly function in Figure 2-10. (A brief note on ARM architecture and instruction set is presented in Appendix-A).

At the beginning of the function, according to the discussed calling convention of ADS tools, R0 hold the *mutexObjectPtr* (i.e. address of the mutexObject) and R1 hold the *waitFlag*.

Statements (1) (2) try to lock the mutex atomically. Statement (3) check whether the mutex got locked successfully. If mutex locking is successful, statements (4) (5) return control with success flag. If the mutex did not get locked successfully, statement (6) checks the *waitFlag*. If the waitFlag is 0, the control is returned with failure flag in statements (7) (8). Note that EQ condition at the end of the instruction denotes the instructions will be executed only when equality condition is satisfied.

If the mutex locking is unsuccessful and *waitFlag* is 1, statement (9) disable interrupts. Statement (9) is a macro and after its expansion it looks as shown in Figure 2-11.

MRS	R2, CPSR	(1)
MOV	R3, R2	(2)
;disable 6th (F), 7th (I)bits to disable interrupts by setting 1.		(3)
ORR	R2, R2, #0x000000C0 ;set F, I bits to mask interrupts.	(4)
MSR	CPSR_c, R2 ;write control field to mask interrupts	(5)
;Now only after masking interrupts change SROS global variable oldCPSR		
LDR	R2, =#oldCPSR	(6)
STR	R3, [R2]	(7)

Figure 2-11

One important note that has to be observed in Figure 2-11 is that *oldCPSR* (a SROS global variable to store the old program status register value when disabling interrupts) shall be changed only after disabling the interrupts. Any SROS variables can be touched only after disabling interrupts. Note that Interrupts will not happen after the execution of statement (5) in Figure 2-11. oldCPSR is written in statement (7) only after effectively disabling the interrupts. One may write into oldCPSR after statement (1) itself, which can be disastrous if interrupts happen after writing into oldCPSR. (As code executed during interrupts can modify oldCPSR!!).

Let us go back to Figure 2-10. Statement (10) gets the address of the *runningThreadObjectPtr* into R3 and statement (11) gets the address of the running threadObject into the R3. Statement (12) stores all the registers R0-R14 into the running threadObject. Note that R2, R3 do not contain the identical values at this position compared to the beginning of the function. But functionally R2, R3 values do not effect the operation at a later point of time. Statement (13) get the starting address of the *mutexObjectLock()* function into R4 and statement(14) stores R4 into the running threadObject PC register (R15 register). Statements (15) (16) (17) save the CPSR into the running threadObject. Statements (18) (19) (20) insert the running threadObject into the mutexObject *waitList*. Statement (21) jumps to the scheduler to start the next high priority ready thread in the system.

2.1.5 SROS data structures in the first version

It is time to have a look at SROS book keeping global variables. The book keeping global variables used in SROS initial version are surprisingly simple (Just 3 variables).

listObject_t *readyList* :

This is a linked list that holds the information about all the threads that are in readyState. (Each node of the linked list holds threadObject's addresses and some information about that thread). All the threadObjects are stored orderly in the list with their priority as key. The highest priority threadObject is at the beginning of the list. (See listObject definition, operations on listObjects in sections 2-8, 2-9).

threadObject_t **runningThreadObjectPtr*:

This is an address variable that always holds the address of the running threadObject.

threadObject_t *idleThread*:

This is a threadObject that holds the context of idleThread in the system. The idleThread in the system will run when no other thread can occupy the system. (i.e. all threads are in waiting state). The idleThread execute an idle loop and always in ready state or running state. It never goes to waiting state as it does not depend on any resource other than CPU.

2.1.6 mutexObjectRelease()

The mutexObjectRelease() functionality:

1. It has to release the *mutex*.

2. It has to move any thread waiting for the *mutex* from waiting state to ready state. i.e. if there is any thread waiting for the *mutex* in the mutexObject *waitList*, then it has to be moved from *waitList* of the mutexObject to *readyList*. If more than one thread are waiting for the *mutex*, the highest priority waiting thread has to be given the *mutex*. So only the highest priority waiting thread has to be moved to *readyList* from the mutexObject *waitList*.

3. If the waiting thread has higher priority than the running thread, and this function is called from a thread (and not from interrupt service routine) running thread has to be preempted. The waiting thread which becomes ready has to be loaded into the processor for execution. If the running thread is preempted, its threadObject has to be kept in ready State. In summary when a higher priority thread becomes ready to run due to the release of mutex, context switch has to be done.

Note that if mutexObjectRelease() is called from an interrupt service routine and if it trigger a higher priority thread to ready state, context switch should not be done in the mutexObjectRelease() function. Note that interrupt service routine is not a thread to make context switch. All RTOSes (including SROS) has provision to do context switch after interrupt service routine. If RTOS decide to do context switch after interrupt service routine, it keeps the interrupted thread into ready state and start the highest priority thread which just became ready because of interrupt service routine. (See interrupt handling in sections 2.2 and 2.3).

The pseudo code for the mutexObjectRelease function is shown in Figure 2-12.

Statement (1) shows the prototype of the function mutexObjectRelease(). This function just expects the address of the mutexObject and returns nothing.

Statement (3) disables interrupts. As RTOS data structures may get updated in this function, interrupts has to be disabled to prevent inconsistent updating. More over, the execution flow change by interrupts can be fatal. So interrupts shall be disabled.

Statement (4) releases the mutex.

Statement (5) checks if there are any threadObjects waiting for the mutex to be released. The *listObjectCount()* function return the number of nodes in the *waitList* of the mutexObject. In each node one waiting threadObject exist.

Statement (6), (7) move a waiting thread from *waitList* of mutexObject to *readyList*.

Statement(8) check if the priority of the waiting thread which is now ready to run in the *readyList* is higher than the running thread priority, and this function is not called from interrupt service routine. If both conditions are satisfied, context switch has to take place. The context of the running thread with program counter as return address of this function, and all other registers are saved to threadObject in statement(9). The running threadObject is inserted into *readyList* in statement (10). Jump to *scheduler* is made to start the highest priority thread. (Highest priority thread is the thread, which is previously waiting for this mutex release). Note that lower the *priority* number, higher the thread priority in SROS.

Statement (12) restores the interrupts and return. This function return happen when one of the three conditions is met. 1. No thread is waiting for the mutex. 2. One or more threads are waiting for the mutexObject release, but the highest priority waiting thread in the *waitlist* of the mutexObject has priority lower or equal to the running thread Priority. 3. This function is called from interrupt service routine.

```
void mutexObjectRelease(mutexObject_t *mutexObjectPtr)                    (1)
{
        threadObject_t *waitingThreadObjectPtr;                          (2)
        interruptsDisable();                                            (3)
        mutexObjectPtr->mutex = 1;                                      (4)
        if(listObjectCount(&mutexObjectPtr->waitList))                  (5)
        {
                waitingThreadObjectPtr=
                        listObjectDelete(mutexObjectPtr->waitList);     (6)
                listObjectInsert(&readyList, waitingThreadObjectPtr);   (7)
                if(waitingThreadObjectPtr->priority < runningThread.priority &&
                This request is not made from interrupt service routine) (8)
                {
                        get the context functionally equivalent to the end
                        this function and save that context into running
                        threadObject.                                   (9)
                        listObjectInsert(&readyList,&runningThread);    (10)
                        jump to scheduler.                              (11)
                }
        }
        interruptRestore();                                            (12)
        return;
}
```

Figure 2-12

Note that context switch should not happen when this function is called from interrupt service routine. Interrupt service routine is the unblockable kernel code (i.e. interrupt service routine is not a thread) and program flow change should not occur. In the case even when a higher priority thread is ready to run the control has to be returned to SROS. SROS anyway check for possible context switch at the end of interrupt service routine. So higher priority thread will always run when it become ready after the interrupt. (See interrupt handling in sections 2.2 and 2.3).

The code corresponding to some of the statements in Figure 2-12 can not be implemented in C language. Statements (9) and statements (11) can not be implemented in C easily. So the assembly implementation of this function is necessary. See Appendix-B or accompanying CDROM for assembly implementation on ARM platform. This function is one of the HAL functions.

2.1.7 scheduler

One important function any RTOS has to implement is to schedule one thread to running state among many threads which are in ready state and competing for CPU time. Usually RTOSes maintain a linked list that holds all threadObjects in the ready state. SROS also maintain a linked list of all threadObejcts which are ready to run. The linked list is called *readyList* in SROS. The scheduler runs some algorithm to pick one threadObject from this readyList. Simple RTOSes just run the highest priority thread in this readyList indefinitely till it goes to waiting state or get preempted by another even higher priority thread. If there are more than one thread having the same highest priority level in the readyList, simple RTOSes just pick one highest priority thread and run it indefinitely (as if it is the only highest priority thread in the system). Some RTOSes execute all the highest priority threads in round robin fashion. i.e. CPU time is sliced among all the highest priority threads. If there is only one highest priority thread, the highest priority thread occupies CPU all the time till it goes to wait state or till it get preempted by even higher priority thread. If there are two highest priority threads, each thread get 50% of CPU time. CPU time is given to one after another in round robin fashion (i.e. one after another in a repeated manner). How much time one thread can continuously execute before getting preempted forcibly by the scheduler to start running another highest priority thread which is at the same priority level, when there are multiple highest priority threads is configured by the user. To implement such scheduling algorithm hardware timer support is needed. (See timer support in chapter 3). Obviously the simplest scheduling method is to execute one of the highest priority thread indefinitely till it goes to wait state or get preempted by even higher priority thread.

2.1.8 Scheduler Implementation in SROS

The simplest method of scheduling is implemented in SROS. The scheduler algorithm in SROS is "just get the highest priority ready threadObject available from *readyList* and load the context from that threadObject and run". As mentioned earlier only two possibilities will exist when a thread is running. It will go to waiting state when requested a busy resource or will get preempted by even higher priority thread. *readyList* maintains the threadObjects in the order of descending priority i.e. highest priority threadObject is at the beginning of the linked list, so scheduling is just removing the threadObject at the beginning of the linked list and loading the context into the processor. The *readyList* has *idleThread* in it. When all the application threads are in waiting state *idleThread* will be moved to running state. (idleThread is always in ready State or running state). So there is no possibility of invoking the scheduler when *readyList* is empty. The pseudo code of scheduler in SROS is shown in Figure 2-13.

```
void scheduler(void)
{
        interruptsDisable();                                              (1)
        runningThreadObjectPtr = listObjectDelete(&readyList);            (2)
        load the context available at  runningThreadObjectPtr and jump to program
        counter in the context.                                          (3)
}
```

Figure 2-13

It may be little tricky to load the context and jump to the starting address in the context depending on the processor architecture. If the processor has two or more modes of operation (one privileged and one user mode) it may be straight forward to load the context in privileged mode and jump to program counter and start running user mode thread.

If the processor has two or more privilege modes and RTOS is designed to run in privileged (kernel) mode and application is designed to run in user mode. In such cases, we can use SWI (software interrupts) to make a specific RTOS call from user mode. SWIs enable to make a RTOS request and simultaneously turn the processor mode into kernel mode.

But for simplicity, SROS and its embedded application is designed to run in privileged mode all the time. So mutexObjectLock(), mutexObjectRelease() and other SROS calls run in the same mode as the application. So making SROS request using SWIs is not implemented. SROS on ARM platform use system mode for running the application threads, and IRQ mode during scheduling to make step (3) in Figure 2-13 easier.

Allowing the interrupts when updating on the RTOS variables is fatal. So interrupts should be disabled and Statement (1) in Figure 2-13 does that. Statement (2) removes the highest priority threadObject from the *readyList*. Statement (3) loads the context into the processor and makes a jump to the program counter address available in the context. When the status of the user thread is loaded into the processor (current program status register on ARM platform), the interrupts will be enabled automatically.

This pseudo code can not be implemented in C language. This function is also one of HAL functions. The ARM assembly implementation can be found in Appendix-B or in accompanying CDROM.

2.2 Interrupts handling in RTOS

The processor may have different kind of hardware interrupts. Some processors support just one hardware interrupt and all interrupts are multiplexed externally. Some processors support more than one hardware interrupt and each interrupt vectored to a different predefined location. The handling of interrupts in an embedded application with RTOS is implemented in two layers.

The second layer (application layer) is implemented by the application and called by the first layer (RTOS layer).

When ever an interrupt occurred, the control is transferred to the RTOS interrupt handler (first layer). The RTOS interrupts handler calls the interrupt service routine corresponding to the interrupt (in the application layer). i.e. the RTOS layer calls application layer interrupt service routine. After the application layer interrupt service routine return control back to the RTOS layer, the RTOS layer will do context switch if any higher priority thread is ready to run after interrupt service routine, otherwise it just return control to the interrupted thread. In this way RTOS always has the opportunity for context switch after every interrupt.

In this book RTOS layer is referred as "interrupt handler", application layer is referred as "interrupt service routine". A specific RTOS interrupt handler (as one RTOS interrupt handler is defined for each hardware interrupt) is invoked when ever an interrupt occurs. The typical processing done in all interrupt handlers is shown below.

1. Execute the interrupt service routine (application layer function) corresponding to the interrupt.

2. Check if context switch is needed. i.e. after executing interrupt service routine (application layer function), some threads might have moved from waiting state to ready state. If a thread of higher priority than running thread moved to ready state from waiting state, context switch is needed.

3. If the context switch is not needed, just return to the interrupted thread.

4. If the context switch is needed, save the context of interrupted thread into running threadObject, insert running threadObject into readyList, and schedule the highest priority ready thread (which became ready to run due to interrupt) to run in the system.

Note that no new interrupt shall be allowed when handling an interrupt.

The RTOS layer functionality can not be implemented in C. So all RTOS layer functionality (i.e. interrupt handlers) need to be implemented in assembly. These functions are also HAL functions. On the other hand all interrupt service routines of an application layer can be implemented in C, as they do not have any dependency on the processor architecture.

2.3 Interrupt Handler in SROS

The interrupt handling in SROS is similar to the steps we have mentioned in the previous section. SROS assumes only one externally multiplexed interrupt request in the system to simplify the implementation. It is simple matter to extend the implementation for multiple interrupts as mentioned in the earlier section. The interrupt handler in SROS is named as *irq_interrupt_handler()*. Whenever any kind of interrupt happens in the system, control is transferred to *irq_interrupt_handler()*. SROS calls *irq_interrupt_service_routine()*. This function is implemented by the embedded application. So it is up to *irq_interrupt_service_routine()* responsibility to check for the interrupt type and service the peripheral that caused the interrupt. After *irq_interrupt_service_routine()* returns control back, *irq_interrupt_handler()* check to see if context switch is needed. If any thread of higher priority than running thread (i.e. interrupted thread) priority, came to ready state due to *irq_interrupt_service_routine()*, context switch will take place. To make context switch the exact context when the running thread is interrupted will be saved to running threadObject and the running threadObject is kept into *readyList*. The new higher priority threadObejct which is ready to run will be brought to running state by loading its context into processor. If running thread is still the highest priority ready thread in the system after the interrupt service routine, context switch will not takes place and control is returned to the interrupted thread. The pseudo code of *irq_interrupt_handler()* in SROS is shown in Figure 2-14.

Statement (1) shows the prototype. Interrupt handler should not expect an input argument and should not return any thing. Statement (1) shows the same.

Statement (2) calls the application defined interrupt service routine. This function may trigger some events through the SROS synchronization objects. *irq_interrupt_service_routine()* should not make any blocking SROS calls (for example trying to lock a mutex that was already locked by different thread with *waitFlag* = 1). *irq_interrupt_service_routine()* may trigger moving waiting threads to ready state through SROS calls (for example by releasing a resource lock for which some thread are waiting). SROS calls will never make context switch when SROS call is made from interrupt service routine. After all RTOS interrupt handler is not a thread to make context switch. *irq_interrupt_handler()* do context switch anyway if needed after *irq_interrupt_service_routine()* finished servicing the interrupt.

```
interrupt void irq_interrupt_handler(void)                              (1)
{
        irq_interrupt_service_routine();                               (2)
        if (running thread priority >= highest priority
                        thread's priority in the readyList)            (3)
        {
                return to the running(i.e. interrupted) thread.       (4)
        }
        else
        {

                Get the context exactly equal to the position when interrupt happened
                in the running thread, Save that context into the running threadObject.
                                                                       (5)
                listObjectInsert(&readyList, runningThreadObjectPtr).  (6)
                Jump to Scheduler.                                     (7)

        }
}
```

Figure 2-14

Statement (3) checks if context switch is needed after interrupt service routine. If any higher priority thread compared to the interrupted thread is moved to ready state due to the *irq_interrupt_service_routine()*, context switch is needed. Other wise context switch is not needed. If context switch is not needed, statement (4) returns control to the running (i.e. interrupted) thread.

If context switch is needed, statement (5) gets the context of interrupted thread and keeps that into the running threadObject. The context should be identical to the position where the running thread got interrupted. There is no other functionally equivalent contexts as we have mentioned in some SROS calls (See *mutexObjectLock()*, *mutexObjectRelease()*). Statement (6) inserts the running threadObject into the *readyList*. Statement (7) jumps to the *scheduler* to start the highest priority ready thread.

This *irq_interrupt_handler()* need to operate at processor register level and can not be implemented in C. This function is one of the HAL functions. The assembly implementation of *irq_interrupt_handler()* for SROS on ARM platform is available in Appendix-B and in accompanying CDROM.

2.4 Creation of thread in RTOS

It is time to see how a thread can be created in the system. A new thread is created in the system by making a RTOS call that create the thread. The creation of thread in the system is done by allocating and initializing the thread control block (i.e. threadObject), allocating stack space for the new thread and keeping the TCB in to the list of ready state TCBs. A valid context is obtained from the arguments passed to the RTOS call that create the thread in the system.

The inputs to the RTOS call should include a function pointer (i.e. initial program counter), arguments that should be given to the function when the new thread start executing (The function should expect a limited number of arguments and should not expect more than the RTOS call supports), new thread priority, and the amount of stack space the new thread needs. The return address after the thread finishes execution is initialized such that it invokes the routine that deallocates the threadObject, stack space and invoke the scheduler. The way a valid context is created with these inputs depend on how function expects its input arguments. This is governed by the compilation tools used to develop the function and same for all the functions in the system. Note that all the functions developed with C compiler adhere to C calling convention. As mentioned in section 2.1.4 earlier, calling convention is the protocol of C compiler that specifies how the arguments are expected by the called function and register usage/preservation guidelines.

When we create a high priority thread from the low priority thread we have to make the context switch if context switch is allowed. Context switch is allowed when the scheduler has already started and RTOS call is not made from the interrupt service routine. So after inserting the new threadObject in to the list of ready threadObjects, this RTOS call do context switch if necessary. i.e. it collects the context equivalent to the end of the RTOS call into the running threadObject, placing the running threadObject in to the readyList, and starting the higher priority thread that just got created in the system.

2.5 Creation of thread in SROS

The pseudo code for the threadObjectCreate() function is shown in Figure 2-15. In SROS initial version, to avoid dynamic memory management the threadObject, stack space for the new thread are expected to be allocated by the caller.

Statement (1) shows the prototype of the SROS call that creates the new thread into the system. This SROS call takes the address of threadObject (whose memory should be allocated by the caller), starting program counter as a function pointer, a total of 4 arguments to the function associated with the new thread, initial stack pointer for the new thread (stack memory is allocated by the caller), thread priority, initial status (in case of ARM it is CPSR) and the name of thread respectively. This function returns nothing. (Many commercial RTOSes usually return a valid thread ID in case of successful creation of thread or NULL if the memory allocation for threadObject or stack space fail. In case of SROS, as the threadObject, stack space are supplied to the SROS request, such cases do not arise).

Statements (2) to (10) initializes the threadObject. Note that the context is initialized according to the ATPCS (ARM Thumb Procedural Call Standard) which is a calling convention for ADS (ARM Developer Suite) tools. Also note that statement (7) initializes the return address of the function as *scheduler* as no deallocations of memory necessary after the newly created thread finishes execution and before starting the next higher priority ready thread.

Statement (11) disables the interrupts as interrupts should not be allowed when updating the SROS variables.

Statement (12) inserts the new threadObject into the *readyList*.

Statement (13) checks if the priority of the new thread is higher than the running thread and whether context switch is allowed (context switch is allowed if scheduler is started and the new thread is not created from interrupt service routine). If so statement (14) gets the context of the end of this SROS function into the running threadObject and statement (15) inserts the running threadObject into the *readyList*. Statement (16) makes a jump to *scheduler* to start running the higher priority thread just got created.

If the context switch is not necessary or not allowed, statement (17) restores the interrupts status and control is returned to the running thread.

This function depends on the threadObject definition and also may block the calling thread. So this function can not be implemented in C. The assembly implementation of this function can be found in the Appendix-B and in the accompanying CDROM.

```
void threadObjectCreate(threadObject_t *threadObjectPtr,
                        void (*functionPtr)(...),
                        int32 arg1,
                        int32 arg2,
                        int32 arg3,
                        int32 arg4,
                        int32* stackPointer,
                        uint32 priority,
                        uint32 cpsr,
                        int8 *threadObjectName)                          (1)
{
    threadObjectPtr->R[15] = (int32)(functionPtr);                       (2)
    threadObjectPtr->R[0] = arg1;                                        (3)
    threadObjectPtr->R[1] = arg2;                                        (3)
    threadObjectPtr->R[2] = arg3;                                        (4)
    threadObjectPtr->R[3] = arg4;                                        (5)
    threadObjectPtr->R[13] = (int32)(stackPointer);                      (6)
    threadObjectPtr->R[14] = schuduler;                                  (7)
    threadObjectPtr->priority = priority;                                (8)
    threadObjectPtr->cpsr = cpsr;                                        (9)
    threadObjectPtr->threadObjectName = threadObjectName;               (10)
    interruptDisable();                                                 (11)

    listObjectInsert(&readyList, threadObjectPtr);                      (12)

    if(priority < runningThreadObjectPtr->priority && context switch is allowed)
                                                                        (13)
    {
        get the context of running thread equivalent to the end of the function
        into running threadObject.                                      (14)
        listObjectInsert(&readyList,   runningThreadObjectPtr);         (15)
        Jump to schuduler()                                            (16)
    }

    interruptsRestore();                                               (17)
}
```

Figure 2-15

2.6 RTOS initialization and starting

RTOS initialization is the initialization of RTOS global book keeping variables and creation of the idle thread and any other system threads. The system starts working when a jump is made to scheduler to start running the highest priority ready thread. The jump to scheduler will not return. The scheduler starts running the highest priority thread in the system. RTOS initialization should be done as part of system initialization before making any RTOS calls. After all the system got initialized, a jump to scheduler will be made to start the highest priority ready thread in the system to start RTOS.

2.7 SROS initialization and starting

The initialization of SROS is simple as it does not have many global book keeping variables and any system threads other than idleThread. SROS is doing simple memory management of list nodes for linked list operations (See section 2-8). So initialization need to be done for the memory management. *readyList* need to be initialized and idle thread need to be created.

The C code in Figure 2-16 do SROS initialization. SROS has fixed block *listNode* memory allocation, deallocation scheme (See section 2-8). For this system a pool of unallocated *listNode* addresses have to be created. Statement (1) does that.

Statement (2) initializes the *readyList*. After initialization *readyList* is empty.

Statement (3) initializes the running threadObject address (*runningThreadObjectPtr*) to NULL as no thread is running during RTOS initialization.

Statement (4) calls a function which does any initializations that can not be done at C level (i.e. need to be done at processor register level). For SROS on ARM platform it changes the processor mode to IRQ mode and initializes the stack for IRQ mode. (As SROS on ARM platform always run in IRQ mode during scheduling, interrupt handling. Note that whenever an interrupt occurs in ARM processor, mode changes to IRQ mode). See brief note on ARM architecture in appendix-A.

Statement (5) creates idleThread in the system. The idle thread keeps the processor busy when all application threads are waiting for some event to happen. The idleThread executes idleFunction, which is an infinite loop. The C code for idleFunction is shown in Figure 2-17. Some processors support special "IDLE" instruction to keep the processor core in suspended state (i.e. processor core instruction fetch, decode, execution pipeline will be halted) till an interrupt occurs. If the target processor platform supports such "IDLE" instruction, we can place such instruction in the while loop of idle function in Figure 2-17. Using the IDLE instruction in the *idleFunction* conserve power when no thread needs CPU.

The *scheduler* is called after all initialization is complete to start the operation of the system by start running the high priority thread in the system. A simple main function to initialize the system and start the *scheduler* is shown in Figure 2-18.

```
void rtosInit(void)
{
        listObjectModuleInit();                                       (1)
        listObjectInit(&readyList);                                   (2)
        runningThreadObjectPtr = 0;                                   (3)
        rtosInitAsm();                                                (4)
        threadObjectCreate(&idleThread,
                        (void *)idleFunction,
                        0,
                        0,
                        0,
                        0,
                        &idleStack[5],
                        127,
                        INITIAL_CPSR_ARM_FUNCTION,
                        "idleThread"
                        );                                            (5)

        return;
}
```

Figure 2-16

```
void idleFunction(void)
{
        while(1)
        {
                ;
        }
}
```

Figure 2-17

```
void main(void)
{
        rtosInit();
        //Initializing any SROS objects, creating threads can be done here.
        //do any other system initializations here. (Other than SROS initializations).
        scheduler();    //jump to scheduler to start running the high priority thread
                        //in the system. This call will not return.
}
```

Figure 2-18

2.8 List node, memory management of list nodes in SROS

The thread in running state, threads in ready state and waiting state are active threads in the system. The threads in the ready state have their threadObjects in the *readyList*. Each synchronization object (for example mutexObject) in the SROS (infact in any RTOS) has a linked list called *waitList*. The threads in waiting state, which will be waiting for an event through a synchronization object, have their threadObjects in the *waitList* of the synchronization object. So all the active threads in the system except the thread in the running state have their threadObjects in one linked list (either in *readyList* or in *waitList* of a synchronization object). To avoid copying the whole threadObject into the nodes, when moving the threadObjects across the lists, only address of the threadObjects are stored in the linked list nodes.

The list node definition is shown in Figure 2-19.

```
struct _listObject_;

typedef struct _listObject_
{
        threadObject_t *element;
        int32 auxInfo;
        struct _listObject_ *nextListNode;

}listNode_t;

typedef listNode_t listObject_t;
```

Figure 2-19

The list node holds the address of a threadObject in the field *"element"*, some auxiliary information about the threadObject in the field *"auxInfo"*, address of the next list node in the field *"nextListNode"*.

During the operation of SROS, the listNodes are inserted into and deleted from *readyList* and *waitLists*. So allocation and deallocation of list nodes is necessary. As listNode size in memory is fixed, it is simple to allocate and deallocate fixed size listNodes. So a simple fixed size memory blocks management, for allocation and deallocation of list nodes is implemented in SROS.

Initially SROS creates a pool of list nodes (the number of list nodes needed is equal to maximum number of threads in the system at any point of time). The allocation and deallocation will happen from this pool. The programs in Figure 2-20 shows the memory management scheme for listNode allocation and deallocation.

SROS maintains a pool of unallocated list node addresses in a buffer. When ever an allocation is required, one pointer is returned from the buffer i.e. removed from the pool. When ever a list node is freed, the pointer is added to the buffer. i.e. added to the pool.

Statements (1) to (3) includes the necessary include files. Statement (4) defines the maximum number of list nodes that can be allocated.

Statement (5) allocates the memory for MAX_LIST_NODES list nodes statically. Statement (6) declares the counter *listNodesAvailableCount* which always holds the number of unallocated list nodes in the pool. The unallocated listNode addresses are kept in *listNodesAvailable* array.

Statement (7) declares the *listNodesAvailable* array which is a pool of unallocated listNode addresses. The number of valid entries in this array is counted with *listNodesAvailableCount*.

Statements (8) to (13) implement *listObjectModuleInit()* function. This function notes all the addresses of unallocated listNode blocks into the *listNodesAvailable* array i.e. This function creates the pool of all valid unallocated listNode memory blocks. This function should be called before any *listNodeAlloc(), listNodeFree()* functions and only once during initialization.

Statements (14) to (16) implement the *listNodeAlloc()* function. Statement (15) is just an assert statement to catch any errors in debug version. Statement (16) returns the last pointer available in the pool and decrement the count *listNodesAvailableCount*.

Statements (17) to (19) implement the *listNodeFree()* function. Statement (18) notes the pointer to be freed into the pool of unallocated listNode addresses and increment the *listNodesAvailableCount*. Statement (19) is assert statement to catch any errors in debug version.

```
#include <stdlib.h>                                                  (1)
#include <assert.h>                                                  (2)
#include "listObject.h"                                              (3)

#define MAX_THREADS_IN_THE_SYSTEM          100
#define MAX_LIST_NODES    MAX_THREADS_IN_THE_SYSTEM                  (4)
listNode_t listNodes[MAX_LIST_NODES];                                (5)
uint32    listNodesAvailableCount;                                   (6)
listNode_t *listNodesAvailable[MAX_LIST_NODES];                      (7)

void listObjectModuleInit(void)                                      (8)
{
        int32 i;                                                     (9)
        assert(MAX_LIST_NODES > 0);                                  (10)
        listNodesAvailableCount = MAX_LIST_NODES;                    (11)
        for(i=0; i<MAX_LIST_NODES; i++)                              (12)
        {
                listNodesAvailable[i] = &listNodes[i];               (13)
        }
}

listNode_t *listNodeAlloc()                                          (14)
{
        assert(listNodesAvailableCount > 0);                         (15)
        return listNodesAvailable[--listNodesAvailableCount];        (16)
}

void listNodeFree(listNode_t *listNodePtr)                           (17)
{
        listNodesAvailable[listNodesAvailableCount++] = listNodePtr; (18)
        assert(listNodesAvailableCount <= MAX_LIST_NODES);           (19)
}
```

Figure 2-20

2.9 Insertion and deletion of list nodes in the linked lists used in SROS

The functions discussed in this section are simple linked list initialization, insertion and deletion routines.

```
void listObjectInit(listObject_t *listObjectPtr)                        (1)
{
        //The list object has the dummy head at the beginning of the
        //linked list. It is an invalid node.
        //It holds the no of list nodes in auxInfo field.
        listObjectPtr->element = NULL;                                  (2)
        listObjectPtr->auxInfo = 0;                                     (3)
        listObjectPtr->nextListNode = NULL;                            (4)
}
```

Figure 2-21

The linked list is called as listObject in this book. The listObject has same definition of listNode(See definition of listNode in Figure 2-19). The first node in the linked list is referred as listObject. The address of the linked list is the address of the first node in the linked list. The listObject has a special dummy node at the beginning of the list. The first node of the linked list is not a valid listNode in SROS implementation. It is a dummy node (some times called as "dummy head node" or simply "dummy head") which is used only to count the number of listNodes in the list and to limit the programming complexity during insertion and deletion of listNodes. The dummy head in the list holds the number of valid listNodes in its auxInfo field.

The C code for initializing the linked list is shown in Figure 2-21. This function should be called before inserting any element into the listObject. Statement(1) show the prototype. This function takes the address of the first node (dummy head) and return nothing. The auxInfo field in the dummy head counts the number of valid nodes in the list. So the auxInfo field of dummy head is initialized to 0 in statement (3). The first node should not contain any element. So the element is initialized to NULL in statement (2). There are no valid elements in the linked list during initialization. So statement (4) initializes the nextListNode to NULL.

```
void listObjectInsert(listObject_t *listNodePtr,
                             threadObject_t *newThreadObject)          (1)
{
        listNode_t *newListNodePtr;
        uint32 newThreadObjectPriority;
        newThreadObjectPriority = newThreadObject->priority;          (2)
        //listObject first element is dummy head. Its auxInfo hold the
        //number of list nodes available in the list.
        //So the auxInfo is increased when inserting an element.
        listNodePtr->auxInfo++;                                       (3)

        while(listNodePtr->nextListNode != 0 &&
        listNodePtr->nextListNode->auxInfo<=newThreadObjectPriority)  (4)
        {
                listNodePtr = listNodePtr->nextListNode;              (5)
        }

        //allocate and initialize the new node.
        newListNodePtr = listNodeAlloc();                             (6)
        newListNodePtr->element = newThreadObject;                    (7)
        newListNodePtr->auxInfo = newThreadObjectPriority;            (8)

        //insert into the list.
        newListNodePtr->nextListNode = listNodePtr->nextListNode;     (9)
        listNodePtr->nextListNode = newListNodePtr;                   (10)
}
```

Figure 2-22

listObjectInsert() function is shown in Figure 2-22. The new element is inserted in to the list according to descending order of priority. (Note that in SROS lower the priority number, higher the priority. So lowest *priority* field threadObject reside at the beginning of the list).

Statement(1) show the prototype of listObjectInsert. This function takes the listObject address and the address of the threadObject that has to be inserted into the listObject.

Statement (3) increment the counter (*auxInfo* field) in the dummy head which holds the number of elements in the linked list.

Statement (4), (5) implement the while loop such that *listNodePtr* is the last node in the linked list or all the listNodes after the *listNodePtr* contain low priority threadObjects.

Statements (6) to (8) implement the code to allocate and initialize the node with the element passed to the function.

Statements (9) to (10) connect the new node into the linked list appropriately.

Note that *auxInfo* field of listNode is copied with the *priority* of threadObject it holds. This is done only to fasten the execution of *listObjectInsert()*, *listObjectDelete()* functions.

```
threadObject_t *listObjectDelete(listObject_t *listObjectPtr)              (1)
{
        threadObject_t *element;                                          (2)
        listNode_t *freedListNodePtr;                                     (3)

        assert(listObjectPtr->nextListNode != 0);                        (4)
        listObjectPtr->auxInfo--;                                         (5)
        freedListNodePtr = listObjectPtr->nextListNode;                   (6)
        element = freedListNodePtr->element;                              (7)
        listObjectPtr->nextListNode = freedListNodePtr->nextListNode;     (8)
        listNodeFree(freedListNodePtr);                                   (9)
        return element;                                                  (10)
}


int32 listObjectCount(listObject_t *listObjectPtr)                        (11)
{
        return listObjectPtr->auxInfo;                                   (12)
}
```

Figure 2-23

The *listObjectDelete()* function is shown in Figure 2-23. The listNode deletion happens at the beginning of the list. The beginning of the linked list Node element has highest priority threadObject in it.

Statement(1) shows the prototype. This function takes the listObject address and return the threadObject address available in the first valid node of the linked list. Statement (4) is assert statement to catch errors in the debug version. Statement (5) decrement the counter that counts the number of elements in the linked list. Statement (6) notes the first valid listNode as the node to be deleted. Statement (7) notes the element from the list node to be deleted. Statement (8) connects the dummy head to the second valid list node. Statement (9) frees the node deleted from the list. Statement (10) return the element (threadObject address) noted from the deleted node.

listObjectCount() function is shown in Figure 2-23. This function returns the number of valid list nodes in the list. This function simply returns the *auxInfo* field in the dummy head of the linked list, which counts the number of valid listNodes in the linked list.

2.10 semaphore

Some times a resource can be sharable by a limited number of threads. For example a serial port entity that has two physical connections can be shared by two threads simultaneously. In such a case the mutexObject we have discussed previously will not work. But it is simple idea to extend the mutex concept. Mutex is a binary flag intended to indicate the on going access of one thread. A counter can be used instead of a flag to indicate the on going access of many threads. So a semaphore functionally similar to the mutex except it is a counter instead of flag. A semaphore is initialized with the number of simultaneous accesses that are possible at one time. This is analogous to mutex which is initialized with 1, indicating only one simultaneous access. A binary semaphore (where counter has values of only 0 and 1) is identical to the mutex.

Threads decrement the semaphore counter and enter the critical section and increment the counter at the end of the critical section. The control of semaphore is done through RTOS calls similar to the mutex. A typical section of the code involving the semaphore is shown in Figure 2-24

```
SemaphoreObjectPend()

Critical section()

SemaphoreObjectPost()
```

Figure 2-24

Semaphore or mutex can be initialized with 0 and can be used for thread synchronization as shown below.

```
Code section A;

SemaphoreObjectPost(syncSemaphore);
```

Thread A

```
SemphoreObjectPend(SyncSemaphore);

Code section B;
```

Thread B

Figure 2-25

In the Figure 2-25 when semaphoreObject is initialized with 0, (Initialization not shown in the figure and is done in a different thread which is of higher priority than thread A and thread B or before the scheduler has started) Code section A will always execute before code section B.

2.11 Semaphore implementation in SROS

The SROS implementation of semaphoreObject and its associated functions are analogous to the mutexObject. The semaphoreObject is shown in Figure 2-26.

```
typedef struct
{
        uint32 count;
        listObject_t waitList;

}semaphoreObject_t;
```

Figure 2-26

The *"count"* variable counts the number of sharable resources available. *"waitlist"* is the linked list that keeps all the threadObjects which are waiting for the resource associated with the semaphore. When the count is greater than 0, the *"waitList"* is always empty. All the waiting threadObjects are stored in *"waitList"* nodes in descending order of priority. By keeping the threadObjects in descending order of priority it is easy to identify and move the highest priority waiting thread from waiting state to the ready state. (i.e. moving the threadObject from *waitList* to *readyList*).

2.11.1   semaphoreObjectInit()

The *semaphoreObjectInit()* function initializes the data structure of the semaphoreObject. It initializes the semaphore *count* to some initial value and initializes the *waitList*.

The C code that initializes the semaphoreObject is shown in Figure 2-27.

```
void semaphoreObjectInit(semaphoreObject_t *semaphoreObjectPtr,
                                uint32 initialCount)                          (1)
{
        semaphoreObjectPtr->count = initialCount;                            (2)
        listObjectInit(&(semaphoreObjectPtr->waitList));                     (3)
}
```

Figure 2-27

Statement (1) shows the prototype. This SROS call takes the address of the semaphoreObject and the initial value for the semaphore *count* and returns nothing.

Statement (2) initializes the initial value of semaphore *count*.

Statement (4) initializes the *waitList*. After initialization, *waitList* shows that no threadObject is waiting for the semaphore.

2.11.2   semaphoreObjectPend()

The pseudo code of *semaphoreObjectPend()* is shown in Figure 2-28

SemaphoreObjectPend() tries to decrease the semaphoreObject count by 1.

When the semaphore *count* is greater than 0, *count* is decremented by 1 and the control is immediately returned to the requesting thread with return value of 1(success).

When the samaphoreObject *count* is 0, the *waitFlag* is considered. If the *waitFlag* is 0, the control is returned immediately to the calling thread with the return value of 0 (failure).

```
int32 semaphoreObjectPend(semaphoreObject_t *semaphoreObjectPtr,
                          int32 waitFlag)                           (1)
{
    interruptsDisable();                                            (2)
    if(semaphoreObjectPtr->count > 0)                              (3)
    {
        semaphoreObjectPtr->count--;                               (4)
        returnValue = 1;                                           (5)
    }
    else
    {
        if(waitFlag)                                              (6)
        {
            get the context functionally equivalent to start
            of the thread into runningThreadObject.               (7)
            listObjectInsert(&semaphoreObjectPtr->waitList,
                             runningThreadObjectPtr);              (8)
            jump to scheduler();                                  (9)
        }
        else
        {
            returnValue = 0;                                      (10)
        }
    }
    interruptsRestore();                                          (11)
    return returnValue;                                           (12)
}
```

Figure 2-28

When the samaphoreObject *count* is 0, and the *waitFlag* is not 0, the functionally equivalent context to the starting of the function is stored into the running threadObject. The running threadObject is kept into the semaphoreObject *waitList*. A jump to *scheduler()* is made to start running the next higher priority ready thread. When the *waitFlag* is not 0, the *semaphoreObjectPend()* SROS call always return 1, as the calling thread was put to wait till semaphore is available.

Statement (1) in Figure 2-28 shows the prototype of *semaphoreObjectPend()* function. This function takes the semaphoreObejct address and the *waitFlag*. It returns 1 on successfully decrementing the count, and 0 if failed to decrement the count.

Statement (2) disables interrupts. This step is necessary as interrupts can cause disruption in the program flow when updating the RTOS variables, which can be fatal.

Statement (3) checks for the semaphoreObject *count*. If the semaphoreObject *count* is greater than 0, *count* is decremented in statement (4), and *returnValue* is noted as 1 (success) in statement (5) which is retuned in statement (12) after restoring interrupts in statement (11).

Statement (6) checks for *waitFlag* whether semaphoreObject *count* is 0. If *waitFlag* is false, the *returnValue* is initialized to 0 in statement (10), which is returned in statement (12) after restoring the interrupts in statement (11).

Statement (6) checks for *waitFlag* whether semaphoreObject *count* is 0. If *waitFlag* is true, the context which is functionally equivalent to the beginning of the function is saved to running threadObject in statement (7). This step is necessary as we need to decrement the semaphore when we restart the thread at a later point of time. The running threadObject is kept into the *waitList* of the semaphoreObject in statement (8). A jump to *Scheduler()* is made in statement (9) to start running the next high priority thread.

This function can not be implemented in C language. So this function is implemented in assembly for SROS on ARM platform. This is also one of HAL functions in SROS. The assembly implementation of this function on ARM platform can be found in appendix-B and accompanying CDROM.

2.11.3   semaphoreObjectPost()

The pseudo code of *semaphoreObjectPost()* is shown in Figure 2-29.

SemaphoreObjectPost() increments the *count* of semaphoreObject by one. If any (one or more) thread is waiting for the semaphore *count* to be greater than 0, the highest priority threadObject among them is moved from the *waitList* of semaphoreObject to the *readyList*. If the waiting threadObject has higher priority than running threadObject and the current request is not made from interrupt service routine then context switch has to take place. So the context functionally equivalent to the end of the *semaphoreObjectPost()* function is saved to running threadObject and running threadObject is inserted into the *readyList*. The *scheduler* is jumped to start running the highest priority ready thread. (Highest priority ready thread will be the thread which was previously waiting for the semaphoreObject *count* to be greater than 0).

```
void semaphoreObjectPost(semaphoreObject_t *semaphoreObjectPtr)      (1)
{
        threadObject_t *waitingThreadObjectPtr;                       (2)

        interruptsDisable();                                          (3)

        semaphoreObjectPtr->count++;                                  (4)

        if(listObjectCount(&semaphoreObjectPtr->waitList) > 0)        (5)
        {
                waitingThreadObjectPtr =
                        listObjectDelete(&semaphoreObjectPtr->waitList);  (6)

                listObjectInsert(&readyList, waitingThreadObjectPtr);  (7)

                if(waitingThreadObjectPtr->priority < runningThread.priority
                && this function not called from interrupts service routine)  (8)
                {
                        get the context functionally equivalent to the end of this
                        function into the running threadObject.        (9)

                        listObjectInsert(&readyList, runningThreadObjectPtr);  (10)

                        jump to scheduler();                           (11)
                }
        }
        interruptsRestore();                                          (12)
}
```

Figure 2-29

Statement (1) in Figure 2-29 shows the prototype of *semaphoreObejctPost()* function. This function takes just the address of semaphoreObject and returns nothing.

Statement (3) disables interrupts. This step is necessary as disruption in the program flow by interrupts can be fatal. When we are updating RTOS variables, interrupts should be disabled as a thumb rule.

Statement (4) increments the *count* of semaphoreObject.

Statement (5) checks for number of threads in the *waitList* of semaphoreObject. If the *count* is equal to 0, interrupts are restored by statement (12) and the control returns to the running thread.

If there are one or more threadObjects in the semaphoreObject *waitList*, the condition check in statement (5) succeeds. Statement (6) removes the highest priority threadObject among the waiting threadObjects. The removed threadObject is inserted into the *readyList* by statement (7). Statement (8) compare the priorities of the waiting threadObject (which became ready to run and got inserted into the readyList) and the running threadObject, and whether context switch is allowed? If the running threadObject has less priority (i.e. higher priority number, as higher priority number represent lesser priority in SROS) and *SemaphoreObjectPost()* is not called from interrupt service routine, context switch has to takes place. The context which is functionally equivalent to the end of the *semaphoreObjectPost()* is saved to the running threadObject in statement(9), running threadObject is inserted into *readyList* in statement(10), Jump to *scheduler* is made in statement(11) to start executing the higher priority thread that became ready. In short, semaphoreObjectPost() can cause context switch if a higher priority thread than the running thread is waiting for the semaphore, when not called from interrupt service routine.

The semaphoreObjectPost() can not be implemented in C language. This function is also one of HAL function. The assembly implementation of this function on ARM platform can be found in Appendix-B and in accompanying CDROM.

2.12 Mailbox

In Many situations two are more threads need to communicate among themselves. (i.e. one thread send some information/message to other thread) and also synchronize the execution based on sending and receiving the message. For example in our video-ip-phone application in chapter 2, user input processing thread need actual user input and the synchronization mechanism with user input. The execution has to stop to get user input and proceed when user input is available. i.e. unlike semaphore which provides only synchronization, we also need to pass some information, which is user input in this example.

Passing information from one thread to another can be achieved with a shared buffer. Let us call the thread that fills the buffer as producer thread, and call the thread that empties the buffer as consumer thread. Shared buffer needs to be updated by these threads mutually exclusively. So a mutex is needed for mutually exclusive access. The consuming thread need to wait when the buffer is empty. So a semaphore is needed which counts the number of messages in the shared buffer. When there are no messages in the shared buffer (semaphore count is 0), the message consuming thread wait pending on the semaphore. In the example we have mentioned in the previous paragraph, user input processing thread is the consuming thread. After pending on the semaphore is successful, the consuming thread can lock the mutex which guards the shared buffer for mutually exclusive access to remove one input from the shared buffer. The shared buffer is shared among the producing thread and the consuming thread. This method of sharing the messages assume infinite buffer size (i.e. producer will never wait), and removing this assumption further complicates the things. (For finite buffer size, two semaphores and one mutex are needed, one semaphore counts the number of empty slots in the buffer, and one semaphore counts the number of filled slots, one mutex for mutually exclusive access of the buffer!!).

This is very common scenario in embedded systems, so many RTOSes provide mailbox object which simplifies this kind of scenario. The mailbox object is used to send/receive fixed size messages among the threads. Usually the mailbox has fixed size buffer and can hold integer number of messages. One message can be posted at a time to the mailbox, and similarly one message can be removed at a time from the mailbox. A posting thread will wait if the mailbox is full. Similarly a thread which wants to consume a message will wait if the mailbox is empty. Posting a message moves any thread which is waiting for message from waiting state to ready state. Similarly consuming a message will move any thread which is waiting for space in the mailbox from waiting state to ready state.

2.13 Mailbox implementation in SROS

The mailboxObject in SROS is shown in Figure 2-30.

```
typedef struct
{
        int8 *mailboxBuffer;
        int32 readIndex;
        int32 writeIndex;
        int32 mailboxBufferSize;
        int32 emptyBufferSize;
        int32 messageSize;
        listObject_t waitList;

}mailboxObject_t;
```

Figure 2-30

The *mailboxBuffer* holds the address of the memory where messages are stored. *readIndex* is the byte number from the start of the *mailboxBuffer* from where next message can be found. *WriteIndex* is the byte number from the start of the mailboxBuffer from where new message has to be written. *mailboxBuffferSize* is the total size of the *mailboxBuffer* in bytes. *emptyBufferSize* is the number of empty bytes in the *mailboxBuffer*. *messageSize* is the number of bytes in one message. The *mailboxBuffferSize* should be integer multiples of *messageSize*.

waitList is the linked list of threadObjects which are waiting to post a message into the mailbox when the mailbox is full. It also holds the list of threadObjects which are waiting for a message from the mailbox when the mailbox is empty. These two scenarios are mutually exclusive. So all the threads will be waiting to remove a message from the mailbox(when the mailbox is empty) or space to post a message(when the mailbox is full) at one point of time, but not for both(i.e. never some threadObjects waiting to post a message and some other threadObjects waiting to remove a message).

2.13.1   mailboxObjectInit()

The initialization of mailboxObject can be done in high level language like C as it never need to be blocked and do not need any processor details to implement it. The C code for *mailboxObjectInit()* is shown in Figure 2-31.

Statement (1) shows the prototype of *mailboxObjectInit()*. This function takes the address of the mailboxObject, the mailbox buffer address, mailbox size in bytes, size of each message in bytes respectively. (Note that this function expects the memory for the mailbox buffer. Memory need to be allocated by the calling thread itself either statically or dynamically. This way simplifies SROS as SROS do not allocate memory dynamically.

Statement (2) initializes the *mailboxObjectPtr->mailboxBuffer* with the memory address passed to the function. The allocation of the memory for mailboxBuffer has to be done by the calling thread. (Many commercial RTOSes dynamically allocate memory for mailbox buffer with out requiring the memory allocated by application thread. In such cases passing the mailbox size is enough).

Statement (3), (4) initializes the *readIndex*, *writeIndex* in the mailboxObject.

Statement (5) notes the *mailboxBufferSize* (in bytes) into the mailboxObject.

Statement (6) notes the *emptyBufferSize* (in bytes) initially as the *mailboxBufferSize*.

Statement (7) notes the *messageSize* (in bytes) into the mailboxObject.

```
void mailboxObjectInit(mailboxObject_t *mailboxObjectPtr,
                       int8 *mailboxBuffer,
                       int32 mailboxBufferSize,
                       int32 messageSize)                              (1)
{
    mailboxObjectPtr->mailboxBuffer = mailboxBuffer;                   (2)
    mailboxObjectPtr->readIndex = 0;                                   (3)
    mailboxObjectPtr->writeIndex = 0;                                  (4)
    mailboxObjectPtr->mailboxBufferSize = mailboxBufferSize;          (5)
    mailboxObjectPtr->emptyBufferSize = mailboxBufferSize;            (6)
    mailboxObjectPtr->messageSize = messageSize;                       (7)
    listObjectInit(&mailboxObjectPtr->waitList);                       (8)

    assert(mailboxObjectPtr->mailboxBufferSize % messageSize == 0);    (9)
}
```

Figure 2-31

Statement (8) initializes the *waitList*. The *waitList* is used to keep either the threadObjects which are waiting for a message (i.e. message consuming threads when no message is there in the mailbox) or the threadObjects which are waiting to post a message (i.e. message producing threads when the *mailboxBuffer* is full).

Statement (9) is the debugging statement to catch errors when SROS is built in the debug mode. This statement make sure that the *mailboxBufferSize* is integer multiple of *messageSize*.

2.13.2 mailboxObjectPost()

This SROS call is used to keep a message in the mailbox.

When there is a space for at least one message in the *mailboxBuffer*, the message is kept in the *mailboxBuffer* and the data structure of mailboxObject is updated and the control is returned with a return value of 1(denoting success) to the requesting thread.

When there is no space in the *mailboxBuffer*, two possibilities exists. Returning immediately with 0 (denoting failure) or to keep the thread in the waiting state. What action needs to be selected among these two possibilities is determined by *waitFlag*, which is input argument to the *mailboxObjectPost()*.

The pseudo code for the *mailboxObjectPost()* is shown in Figure 2-32.

```
int32 mailboxObjectPost(mailboxObject_t *mailboxObjectPtr,
                        int32 waitFlag,
                        void *message)                                  (1)
{
      int32 returnValue;
      interruptDisable();                                               (2)
      if(mailboxObjectPtr->emptyBufferSize >=
                              mailboxObjectPtr->messageSize)             (3)
      {
            memcpy(&mailboxObjectPtr->mailboxBuffer[writeIndex],
                       message, mailboxObjectPtr->messageSize);         (4)
            mailboxObjectPtr->writeIndex += mailboxObjectPtr->messageSize;(5)
            mailboxObjectPtr->emptyBufferSize -=
                              mailboxObjectPtr->messageSize;             (6)
            if(mailboxObjectPtr->writeIndex ==
                              mailboxObjectPtr->mailboxBufferSize)       (7)
            {
                  mailboxObjectPtr->writeIndex = 0;                     (8)
            }
            returnValue = 1;                                            (9)
            if(listObjectCount(&mailboxObjectPtr->waitList) > 0)        (10)
            {
                  waitingThreadObjectPtr =
                        listObjectDelete(&mailboxObjectPtr->waitList);  (11)
                  listObjectInsert(&readyList, waitingThreadObjectPtr); (12)

                  if(waitingThreadObjectPtr->priority < runningThread.priority
                  &&
                  this function not called from interrupt service routine) (13)
                  {
                        get the context functionally equivalent to the end
                        of the function and keep that into the running
                        threadObject.                                  (14)
                        listObjectInsert(&readyList,
                                    runningThreadObjectPtr);            (15)
                        jump to scheduler;                             (16)
                  }
            }
      }
      else
      {
            if(waitFlag)                                               (17)
            {
```

```
                    create context functionally equivalent to the starting of
                    this function and keep it in the running threadObject.        (18)
                    listObjectInsert(&mailboxObjectPtr->waitList,
                            runningThreadObjectPtr);                               (19)
                    jump to scheduler();                                          (20)
            }
        else
        {
                    returnValue = 0;                                              (21)
        }
    }
    interruptRestore();                                                           (22)
    return returnValue;                                                           (23)
}
```

Figure 2-32

Statement (1) shows the prototype. This SROS call takes mailboxObject address, the *waitFlag* (to indicate the intention of whether to get blocked when the *mailboxBuffer* is full) and address *message* where the message was kept. The success or failure to keep the message in the mailbox is indicated through the return value. When the *waitFlag* is 1, always success (i.e. 1) will be returned as the thread will be kept into waiting state till the space for the message is available.

Statement (2) disables interrupts. This SROS call updates mailboxObject and other RTOS variables. Disruption of program flow by interrupts when doing these operations will be fatal. So interrupts should be disabled.

Statement (3) checks whether the *mailboxBuffer* has enough space to keep the new message. If the mailboxBuffer has enough space, statements (4) (5) (6) (7) (8) keep the message in the *mailboxBuffer* at appropriate place and update the mailboxObject. (Note that *mailboxBuffer* is written circularly).

Statement (9) notes the return value as 1 (to indicate success).

Statement (10) checks if any thread is waiting for a message. (Note that when *mailboxBuffer* has space for a message, no thread wait for space. If any thread is waiting, that should be for a message only.).

Statement (11) (12) move the highest priority waiting threadObject from the *waitList* to *readyList*. The waiting thread can avail the new message that was kept into the *mailboxBuffer* when it starts running.

Statement (13) checks if the context switch is necessary. If the waiting threadObject has higher priority (i.e. lower *priority* field number) than running threadObject and the current SROS request is not made from interrupt service routine, context switch is necessary. If context switch is necessary, context which is functionally equivalent to the end if the SROS call is kept into the running threadObject in statement (14), and the running threadObject is inserted into the *readyList* in statement (15) and a jump to *scheduler()* is made in statement (16). *Scheduler* starts the highest priority ready thread. (which is the thread previously waiting for the message).

When there is no space in the mailboxBuffer, statement (17) checks for the *waitFlag*.

If the *waitFlag* is zero, the *returnValue* is initialized to 0 (to indicate failure) in statement (21), interrupts are restored in statement (22) and the *returnValue* is returned in statement (23).

If the *waitFlag* is not zero, context which is functionally equivalent to the start of the SROS call is stored into the running threadObject in statement (18) and the running threadObject is inserted into the *waitList* of the *mailboxObject* in statement (19) and jump to *scheduler()* is made in statement (20). The *scheduler* starts the next highest priority ready thread in the system (i.e. in *readyList*) (as the running thread is moved to the waiting state).

This function need to block the requesting thread in some situations. So collection of context is needed which should be done at processor register level. So this function can not be implemented in high level languages like C, and qualifies as one of HAL functions. The assembly implementation of *mailboxObjectPost()* for SROS on ARM platform can be found in Appendix-B and in accompanying CDROM.

2.13.3   mailboxObjectPend()

The *mailboxObjectPend()* SROS call retrieves one message from the mailbox.

If the *mailboxBuffer* is not empty, the oldest message is removed from the *mailboxBuffer* and 1(indicates Success) is returned.

If the *mailboxBuffer* is empty, there exist two possibilities. To wait till a message arrives or to return immediately with 0 (indicating failure). One of the possibilities is chosen by the thread that is making SROS request using the *waitFlag* which is an input argument of the SROS request.

The pseudo code of the *mailboxObjectPend()* is shown in Figure 2-33.

```
int32 mailboxObjectPend(mailboxObject_t *mailboxObjectPtr,
                        int32 waitFlag,
                        void *message)                                    (1)
{
    int32 returnValue;                                                    (2)
    interruptsDisable();                                                  (3)
    if(mailboxObjectPtr->emptyBufferSize <=
    mailboxObjectPtr->mailboxBufferSize – mailboxObjectPtr->messageSize)  (4)
    {
        memcpy(message,
            &mailboxObjectPtr->mailboxBuffer[readIndex],
            mailboxObjectPtr->messageSize);                              (5)
        mailboxObjectPtr->readIndex += mailboxObjectPtr->messageSize;   (6)
        mailboxObjectPtr->emptyBufferSize +=
                                mailboxObjectPtr->messageSize;          (7)
        if(mailboxObjectPtr->readIndex ==
                                mailboxObjectPtr->mailboxBufferSize)    (8)
        {
            mailboxObjectPtr->readIndex = 0;                            (9)
        }
        returnValue = 1;                                               (10)
        if(listObjectCount(&mailboxObjectPtr->waitList) > 0)           (11)
        {
            waitingThreadObjectPtr =
                listObjectDelete(&mailboxObjectPtr->waitList);         (12)
            listObjectInsert(&readyList, waitingThreadObjectPtr);      (13)
            if(waitingThreadObjectPtr->priority < runningThread.priority
            && this function not called from interrupt service routine) (14)
            {
                get the context functionally equivalent to the end
                of this function and insert into running threadObject.
                                                                       (15)
                listObjectInsert(&readyList, runningThreadObjectPtr);
                                                                       (16)
                jump to scheduler;                                     (17)
            }
        }
    }
    else
    {
        if(waitFlag)                                                   (18)
        {
            get context which is functionally equivalent to the start
            of this function and insert it into running threadObject.  (19)
```

```
                listObjectInsert(mailboxObjectPtr->waitList,
                                        runningThreadObjectPtr);
                                                                    (20)
                jump to scheduler;                                  (21)
            }
        else
        {
                returnValue = 0;                                    (22)
        }
    }
    interruptsRestore();                                            (23)
    return returnValue;                                             (24)
}
```

Figure 2-33

Statement (1) shows the prototype. This SROS call takes mailboxObject address, the *waitFlag* (to indicate the intention of whether to get blocked when the *mailboxBuffer* is empty) and address *message*, where the received message from mailbox has to be kept. Statement (3) disables interrupts. This RTOS call updates mailboxObject and SROS variables. Disruption of program flow by interrupts will be fatal. So interrupts should be disabled.

Statement (4) checks if there is at least one message in the *mailboxBuffer*.

If there is at least one message, statement (5) copies the oldest message from the *mailboxBuffer* to *message* address. Statements (6) (7) (8) (9) update the *mailboxBuffer* control variables. Note that *mailboxBuffer* is read in first in first out (FIFO) fashion circularly.

Statement (10) notes the *returnValue* as 1 (to indicate success). Statement (11) checks if there are any threadObjects waiting in the mailboxObject *waitList* for space to keep a message in the mailbox. (Note that no threadObject in the mailboxObject *waitList* waits for message consumption when *mailboxBuffer* has at least one message. All the threadObjects in the *waitList* only wait for space to keep a new message when the *mailboxBuffer* is full). If there are any threadObjects in the *waitList*, the highest priority threadObject is moved from *waitList* to *readyList* with statements (12), (13).

Statement (14) checks if the context switch is necessary. If the waiting threadObject has higher priority (i.e. lower priority number) than running threadObject and the current SROS request is not made from interrupt service routine, context switch is necessary. If context switch is necessary, context which is functionally equivalent to the end if the SROS call is kept into the running threadObject in statement (15), and the running threadObject is inserted into the *readyList* in statement (16) and jump to *scheduler()* is made in statement (17). *Scheduler* starts the highest priority ready thread which is the thread previously waiting for space to keep new message in the *mailboxBuffer*.

When there is no message in the *mailboxBuffer*, statement (18) checks for the *waitFlag*.

If the *waitFlag* is 0, the *returnValue* is initialized to 0 (to indicate failure) in statement (22), interrupts are restored in statement (23) and the *returnValue* is returned in statement (24).

If the *waitFlag* is non zero, context which is functionally equivalent to the start of the SROS call is stored into the running threadObject in statement (19) and the running threadObject is inserted into the *waitList* of the mailboxObject in statement (20) and jump to *scheduler* is made in statement (21). The *scheduler* starts the next highest priority ready thread in the system (i.e. in *readyList*) (as the running thread is moved to the waiting state).

This function need to block the requesting thread in some situations, and collection of context is needed in those situations, which should be done at processor register level. So this function can not be implemented in high level languages like C, and is one of HAL functions. The assembly implementation of *mailboxObjectPend()* on ARM platform can be found in appendix-B and in accompanying CDROM.

2.14 Example application using SROS

Now it is time to see an example application using SROS. Let us see how the threads conceived at abstract level for video-ip-phone in chapter 1 can be implemented using SROS.

The network receive thread in Figure 2-34, get the received packet addresses through *networkReceiveMailbox*. An interrupt service routine that is executed when ever a packet is received should post the packet address to the *networkReceiveMailbox*. The packets will be placed either in audio jitter buffer or video jitter buffer if they are media packets. If the packet is call control packet then it is given to call control processing thread by posting it to *callControlMailbox*.

```
void networkReceiveThread(void)
{
  char* packetAddress;
  While(1)
  {
        mailboxObjectPend(&networkReceiveMailbox, -1, &packetAddress);
        If(packet is video packet) then Place packet in video jitter buffer.
        Else if (packet is audio packet) then Place packet in audio jitter buffer.
        Else if (packet is call control packet) then
        mailboxObjectPost(&callControlMailbox, -1, &packetAddress);
  }
}
```

Figure 2-34 Network receive thread

```
void audioDecodeThread(void)
{
  While(1)
  {
        Decode audio packets after removing them from audio jitter buffer and make
        one audio frame.
        semaphoreObjectPend(&audioPlaySemaphore, -1);
        Update audio playout ping pong buffer to play the decoded audio frame.
  }
}
```

Figure 2-35 Audio decode thread

The audio decode thread in Figure 2-35 continuously removes the packets from audio jitter buffer, decodes them and get them played. The audio decode thread waits on the semaphore audioPlaySemaphore. When ever one buffer in a set of ping pong buffers got played out completely, the interrupt service routine executed for the audio playout hardware interrupt, post the *audioPlaySemaphore* signaling the audioDecodeThread to update the playout ping pong buffer.

```
void videoDecodeThread(void)

{

  While(1)

  {

        Decode video packets after removing them from video jitter buffer and make
        one video frame.

        semaphoreObjectPend(&videoPlaySemaphore, -1);

        Update video playout ping pong buffer to render the decoded frame.

  }

}
```

Figure 2-36 Video decode thread

The functionality of video decode thread in Figure 2-36 is on similar lines with the audio decode thread. The vide decode thread continuously removes the packets from video jitter buffer, decodes them and get them rendered. The video decode thread wait on semaphore videoPlaySemaphore. When ever one video buffer in a set of two ping pong buffers got rendered, the interrupt service routine executed for the video playout hardware interrupt, post the *videoPlaySemaphore* signaling the videoDecodeThread to update the playout video ping pong buffer.

The call control processing thread in Figure 2-37 gets the call control packet address through *callControlMailbox*. When it receives the packet, it processes the packet.

```
semaphoreObject_t audioPlaySemaphore, audioCaptureSemaphore,
                videoPlaySemaphore, videoCaptureSemaphore;
threadObject_t        audioPalyThreadObject, audioCaptureThreadObject,
                videoPlayThreadObject, videoCaptureThreadObject;
int32 audioPlayStack[256], audioCaptureStack[256],
        videoPlayStack[256], videoCaptureStack[256];
void callControlProcessingThread(void)
{
  char *packetAddress;
  while(1)
  {
        mailboxObjectPend(&callControlMailbox, -1, &pactetAddress);
        process call control packet available at pactetAddress.
        If(connecton has to be established)
        {
                semaphoreObjectInit(&audioPlaySemaphore, 2);
                threadObjectCreate(&audioPlayThreadObject,
                        audioDecodeThread,
                        0,
                        0,
                        0,
                        0,
                        &audioPlayStack[256],
                        4,
                        INITIAL_CPSR_ARM_FUNCTION,
                        "audio_playout_thread");
                semaphoreObjectInit(&audioCaptureSemaphore, 0);
                threadObjectCreate(&audioCaptureThreadObject,
                        audioEncodeThread,
                        0,
                        0,
                        0,
                        0,
                        &audioCaptureStack[256],
                        6,
                        INITIAL_CPSR_ARM_FUNCTION,
                        "audio_capture_thread");
```

```
            semaphoreObjectInit(&videoPlaySemaphore, 2);
            threadObjectCreate(&videoPlayThreadObject,
                        videoDecodeThread,
                        0,
                        0,
                        0,
                        0,
                        &videoPlayStack[256],
                        5,
                        INITIAL_CPSR_ARM_FUNCTION,
                        "video_playout_thread");
            semaphoreObjectInit(&videoCaptureSemaphore, 0);
            threadObjectCreate(&videoCaptureThreadObject,
                        videoEncodeThread,
                        0,
                        0,
                        0,
                        0,
                        &videoCaptureStack[256],
                        7,
                        INITIAL_CPSR_ARM_FUNCTION,
                        "video_capture_thread");
        enable audio capture interrupt.

        enable audio playout interrupt.

        enable video capture interrupt.

        enable video playout interrupt.

    }

    if(call has to be teared down)

    {

        disable audio capture interrupt.

        disable audio playout interrupt.

        disable video capture interrupt.

        disable video playout interrupt.

        threadObjectDestroy(&audioPlayThreadObject);

        threadObjectDestroy(&audioCaptureThreadObject);
```

```
                threadObjectDestroy(&videoPlayThreadObject);
                threadObjectDestroy(&videoCaptureThreadObject);
          }
      }
  }
```

Figure 2-37 call control processing thread

If call control processing thread decides to establish the call, it does the following steps to establish the audio and video functionality.

1. Starts the audio playout by initializing the *audioPlaySemaphore* to 2 (as there are two empty buffers in ping pong buffer set), creating the audio_playout_thread.

2. Starts the audio capture by initializing the *audioCaptureSemaphore* to 0 (as there are no filled buffers in ping pong buffer set) and creating the audio_capture_thread.

3. Starts the video playout by initializing the *videoPlaySemaphore* to 2 (as there are two empty buffers in ping pong buffer set), creating the video_playout_thread.

4. Starts the video capture by initializing the *videoCaptureSemaphore* to 0 (as there are no filled buffers in ping pong buffer set) and creating the video_capture_thread.

5. Enable audio capture, audio playout, video capture, video playout interrupts. The audio capture interrupt service routine posts the *audioCaptureSemaphore* when ever one buffer of audio samples is captured in audio capture ping pong buffers. The audio playout interrupt service routine post the *audioPlaySemaphore* when ever one buffer got played in audio playout ping pong buffers. The video capture interrupt service routine posts *videoCaptureSemaphore* when ever the camera captured one video frame into the video capture ping pong buffers. The video playout interrupt service routine posts the *videoPlaySemaphore* when video rendering is finished for one buffer of video playout ping pong buffers.

Note that audio_decode_thread was given priority 4 (highest), video_decode_thread was given priority 5, audio_encode_thread was given priority 6, video encode thread was given priority 7.

If call control processing thread decides to teardown the call it does the following steps to remove audio, video functions.

1. Disables audio capture, audio playout, video capture, video playout interrupts.

2. Destroys the audio_playout_thread, audio_capture_thread, video_capture_thread, video_playout threads.

Destroying the thread means removing the thread from the SROS system. More about destroying the thread, the implementation aspects and implementation in SROS are presented in the next chapter.

```
void userInputProcessingThread (void)
{
  int userInput;
  while(1)
  {
        mailboxObjectPend(&userInputMailbox, -1, &userInput);
        process user input.
  }
}
```

Figure 2-38 User input processing thread

The user input processing thread is shown in Figure 2-38. The user input is collected through the *userInputMailbox*. User input is posted to the *userInputMailbox* in user input interrupt service routine. (i.e. keypad interrupt service routine, touch screen interrupt service routine etc...).

```
void audioEncodeThread(void)
{
  while(1)
  {
        semaphoreObjectPend(&audioCaptureSemaphore, -1);
        Encode the captured audio frame and keep the encoded audio packet(s) in the
        network output packets queue
  }
}
```

Figure 2-39 Audio encode thread

The audio capture thread is shown in Figure 2-39. The audio capture thread waits till a bufferfull of data is captured by pending on the *audioCaptureSemaphore*. The *audioCaptureSemaphore* is posted in the audio capture interrupt service routine when ever a buffer of audio is captured in to one of the audio capture ping pong buffers.

```
void videoEncodeThread(void)
{
  while(1)
  {

      semaphoreObjectPend(&videoCaptureSemaphore, -1);
      Encode the captured video frame in the ping pong buffer and keep the
      packets in network output packets queue.

  }
}
```

Figure 2-40 video encode thread

The video encode thread is shown in Figure 2-40. The video capture thread waits on the *videoCaptureSemaphore*. When ever a video frame is captured in one of the ping pong buffers, the video capture interrupt service routine posts the *videoCaptureSemaphore*. The video capture semaphore encodes the video frame captured and keeps the packets in the network output packets queue.

```
threadObject_t userInputThreadObject, callControlThreadObject,
               networkThreadObject;
mailboxObject_t userInputMailbox, callControlMailbox,
               networkReceiveMailbox;
int8    userInputMailboxBuffer[USER_INPUT_MAILBOX_BUFFER_SIZE],
  callControlMailboxBuffer[CALL_CONTROL_MAILBOX_BUFFER_SIZE],
 networkReceiveMailbox[NETWORK_RECEIVE_MAILBOX_BUFFER_SIZE];
void main(void)
{
        //initialize SROS.
        rtotInit(void)
        //Initialize the synchronization objects and create the threads.
        threadObjectCreate(&userInputThreadObject,
                        userInputProcessingThread,
                        0,
                        0,
                        0,
                        0,
        &userInputStack[USER_INPUT_THREAD_STACK_SIZE],
                        10,
                        INITIAL_CPSR_ARM_FUNCTION,
                        "user_input_processing_thread");

        threadObjectCreate(&callControlThreadObject,
                        callControlProcessingThread,
                        0,
                        0,
                        0,
                        0,
        &callControlStack[CALL_CONTROL_THREAD_STACK_SIZE],
                        11,
                        INITIAL_CPSR_ARM_FUNCTION,
                        "call_control_processing_thread");

        threadObjectCreate(&networkThreadObject,
                        networkReceiveThread,
                        0,
                        0,
                        0,
                        0,
        &networkThreadStack[NETWORK_THREAD_STACK_SIZE],
                        9,
                        INITIAL_CPSR_ARM_FUNCTION,
                        "network_receive_thread");
```

```
mailboxObjectInit(&userInputMailbox,
                userInputMailboxBuffer,
                USER_INPUT_MAILBOX_BUFFER_SIZE,
                USER_INPUT_MAILBOX_MESSAGE_SIZE
                );
mailboxObjectInit(&callControlMailbox,
                callControlMailboxBuffer,
                CALL_CONTROL_MAILBOX_BUFFER_SIZE,
                CALL_CONTROL_MAILBOX_MESSAGE_SIZE
                );
mailboxObjectInit(&networkReceiveMailbox,
                networkReceiveMailboxBuffer,
                NETWORK_RECEIVE_MAILBOX_BUFFER_SIZE,
                NETWORK_RECEIVE_MAILBOX_MESSAGE_SIZE
                );

//do any hardware initializations here.

//start scheduler.
scheduler();                        //this function call never returns.


}
```

Figure 2-41

The typical code structure for video-ip-phone system initialization is shown in Figure 2-41. The system initialization starts with initializing the SROS by making function call rtosInit(). The system initialization proceed with the initialization of SROS synchronization objects and creation of threads in the system. In Figure 2-41 some definitions of constants related to our example video-ip-phone system were not given as they were intuitive by their long names!. Note that user input processing thread has priority 10, call control thread has priority 11 (lowest) and network receive thread has priority 9 in the system. After required SROS objects are created, hardware initializations are carried out. Once all the initializations (both software and hardware) were completed, scheduler is started at the end of the main function. This function call scheduler() never returns and high priority thread in the system will be started scheduler. (in our example it is network receive thread, as high priority media threads were not yet created in the system).

2.15 Exercises, short term assignments

1. Many RTOSes provide Preemption lock with function calls such as OS_enter_critical_section(), OS_exit_critical_section(). The preemption lock does not disable interrupts but make sure that the running thread will not be preempted by higher priority threads even after they become ready after interrupts. Write pseudo code for these functions. To implement such functions for SROS what modifications need to be done to SROS mutexObject, semaphoreObject, mailboxObject functions, interrupt handlers?

2. Some RTOSes support incrementing/decrementing the semaphore count by more than 1 at a time. This support will be useful to allocate multiple instances of a resource at a time. Write the pseudo code for semaphoreObjectInc(), semaphoreObjectDec() which increase and decrease the semaphore count by the input passed to them. What is the implementation difference between these functions and semaphoreObjectPost() and semaphoreObjectPend() functions?

3. Some RTOSes provide queue object to which an arbitrary length of message (data) can be posted and retrieved. Define the queueObject. Write code/pseudo code for queueObject functions such as queueObjectInit(), queueObjectPost(), queueObjectPend(). What is the difference in the implementation of mailboxObject and queueObject functions?

4. Some RTOSes provide pipeObject. A pipeObject is similar to queueObject but a thread can opt to receive from many pipeObjects simultaneously. If at least one pipeObject has data among the group of pipeObjects, it can receive data from that pipeObject. If no pipeObject has the data of required size, the thread will go to wait state. Availability of data in any pipeObject will trigger the thread from waiting state to ready state. Think how the pipeObject can be implemented? Define pipe object. Write the pseudo code for pipeObject functions such as pipeObjectInit(), pipeObjectPost(), pipeObjectPend(). The pipeObjectPost() posts some amount of data to pipeObject. pipeObjectPend() should accept a list of pipeObjects and get required amount of data from one of the pipeObjects. (The *pipeObjectPend()* operation is also called *select* operation in some RTOSes).

   Hint: During the pipeObjectPend(), a thread need to wait in many waitLists instead of just one waitList. So a threadObject should hold a list of waitLists. With the list of waitLists the threadObject can be removed from all the waitLists when it is moved to ready state from waiting state.

3 Timer Support

The timer support is an important and integral part in almost all commercially available RTOSes. In this chapter first we observe the need for timer support with a simple application scenario. We discuss how timer support is usually implemented in RTOSes. We discuss how the SROS calls have to be modified for timer support. Next we see the implementation details of SROS calls with timer support.

3.1 Need for timer support

In most embedded applications many threads usually do some action and wait for response. The response usually is not immediate and may come after some time. The response to the action by a thread is not guaranteed in some situations when uncertain external environment is involved, which is outside the control of the program. When the thread do not get the response expected with in the stipulated time, it may need to take further action.

For example a thread may send a packet across the network and wait for the reply packet to proceed further. The pseudo code to implement this functionality is shown in Figure 3-1 using SROS calls.

```
Create packet                                                          (1)
mailboxObjectPost(&networkTransmitMailbox, -1, &packetAddress);        (2)
mailboxObjectPend(&networkReceiveMailbox, -1, &packetAddress);         (3)
process the reply packet                                               (4)
```

Figure 3-1

The problem with the above code is that this thread will wait indefinitely when the transmit or reply packet got lost in the network.

So we should not wait for the reply packet more than a stipulated time. After the timeout, we need to take further action like retransmit the transmitted packet etc... So SROS call in statement (3) in Figure 3-1 should support a stipulated wait time (not just indefinite wait time). If SROS support a stipulated wait time, the code might be modified as shown in Figure 3-2.

```
Create packet that has to be transmitted.                                    (1)
While(1)                                                                      (2)
{
        mailboxObjectPost(&networkTransmitMailbox, -1, &packetAddress);       (3)
        if(mailboxObjectPend(&networkReceiveMailbox, WAIT_TIME,
                                            &packetAddress))                  (4)
        {
                break;                                                        (5)
        }
}
process the reply packet at packetAddress                                     (6)
```

Figure 3-2

Note that *mailboxObjectPend(networkReceiveMailbox, WAIT_TIME, &packetAddress)* SROS call return TRUE if a packet is received with in the stipulated time. (i.e. *WAIT_TIME*) other wise return FALSE in Figure 3-2.

In some scenarios we need to stop processing for a stipulated time, and resume processing after that time. For example we display some image/message on LCD, we should wait for some time before showing the next image/message. In such a case the image/message displaying thread has to wait for some time. So all commercial RTOSes provide a kind of RTOS call *"sleep(waitTime)"* that makes the thread to wait for *waitTime* timer ticks or *waitTime* absolute time units.

3.2 Timer support implementation in RTOS

Nowadays many embedded micro processors and digital signal processors (DSPs) usually have inbuilt timers. Timer hardware generates timer interrupt periodically, with a period corresponding to configured number of cycles. The period is called tick time. After each tick time, a timer interrupt is generated. To implement the timer support, RTOSes (including SROS) use the hardware timer interrupt. RTOSes count the time after each timer tick and implement the timer support needed for any number of threads with one hardware timer.

3.3 Timer support implementation in SROS

SROS introduces another list called *timerList*. *timerList* is a linked list that keeps all threadObjects which want to wait for a stipulated amount of time. The threadObjects which are waiting for time may also wait for some other synchronization event simultaneously. If the synchronization event happens before timeout, they do not want to wait for timeout anymore. For example In the Figure 3-2 , the statement

mailboxObjectPend(&networkReceiveMailbox, WAIT_TIME , &packetAddress)

makes the thread wait for a message from networkReceiveMailbox at most WAIT_TIME timer ticks. i.e. thread waits simultaneously for reply packet and timeout, and come to ready state which ever happens first. The thread goes to running state when it has chance to run after it go to ready state. The action taken by the thread when it is in running state depends on whether it was awakened by a packet arrival or timeout.

In the previous version of SROS, we are waiting for only one synchronization event atmost. (Time is not considered at all as time out event does not exist). So all the threadObjects will be waiting in one of the waitlists when they are in waiting state. The waitlists belong to mutexObject, semaphoreObject or mailboxObject. So any threadObject can be in one linked list at most. If it is in waiting state, it will be in one of the waitlists. If it is in ready state (i.e. waiting for CPU time) then it is in *readyList*. When it is in running state, the threadObject will not be in any linked list at all.

Now with the introduction of time out event, a thread can be waiting for a synchronization event and also a timeout event. So obviously it has to be kept into two lists i.e. in a waitList, and also in *timerList*. If the synchronization event or timeout event happens in the system, the threadObject has to be moved to ready state, and the threadObject in both the waitList and *timerList* has to be removed. It is like this: Assume you and your friend are sharing some resource. You ask your friend to wake you up after he completes his work by making a phone call so that you can proceed using the resource after his work, and you also keep alarm when you go to sleep. So there are two possibilities exits. Either your friend makes a phone call, or alarm rings. When your friend wake you up with phone call, you remove the alarm and start using the resource he had left. If the alarm rings, you inform your friend and decide what to do.

The waitlist for a resource has to be checked and updated when there is an event with its associated resource. In the same lines *timerList* should be checked and updated every time when there is timer tick (timer interrupt).

3.3.1 mutexObjectLock()

The pseudo code implementation of mutexObject functions with timer support is shown in Figure 3-3.

mutexObjectLock() locks the mutex if no other thread has already locked the mutex. If any other thread already locked the mutex, then *mutexObjectLock()* function checks for *waitTime*. Negative *waitTime* indicates, requesting thread will get blocked indefinitely till the mutex got released. Positive *waitTime* indicates thread will be blocked till *waitTime* timer ticks or till mutex release which ever is earlier. Zero *waitTime* denotes no waiting at all.

When the *mutexObjectLock()* successfully locked the mutex, it return 1 (denoting success) else return 0 (denoting failure).

Statement (1) shows the prototype. This SROS request takes address of the mutexObject and *waitTime*. The return value indicates the success or failure flag. Statement (2) locks the mutex atomically. If the mutex is not locked by any other thread previously, the mutex lock will be successful and 1 is returned (to indicate success) in statement (3).

When mutex is not available, Statement (4) checks the *waitTime*.

If the *waitTime* is 0, 0 is returned in statement (11) to indicate failure in locking the mutex.

```
int32 mutexObjectLock(mutexObject_t *mutexObjectPtr, int32 waitTime)        (1)
{
        if(swap(0, mutexObjectPtr->mutex))                                  (2)
        {
                return 1;                                                   (3)
        }
        else
        {
                if(waitTime)                                                (4)
                {
                        interruptDisable();                                 (5)
                        get the context which is functionally equivalent to
                        thestarting of this function.                       (6)
                        listObjectInsert(&mutexObjectPtr->waitList,
                                                &runningThread);            (7)
                        if(waitTime > 0)                                    (8)
                        {
                                insertIntoTimerList(&runningThreadObject,
                                        mutexObjectPtr->waitList);          (9)
                        }
                        jump to scheduler();                                (10)
                }
                else
                {
                        return 0;                                           (11)
                }
        }
}
```

Figure 3-3

If the *waitTime* is non zero, context switch has to takes place. Statement (5) disables interrupts as allowing interrupts is fatal during context switch. Statement (6) gets the context which is functionally equivalent to the starting of this SROS function, and statement (7) keep that into running threadObject.

Statement (8) checks for *waitTime*. Positive *waitTime* indicates only stipulated amount of waiting. So when *waitTime* is positive, statement(9) inserts the running threadObject into the *timerList*. Negative *waitTime* indicates indefinite waiting till mutex is available. So when *waitTime* is negative, running threadObject is not inserted into *timerList*.

Statement(10) makes a jump to *scheduler()* to start next higher priority thread.

This function need to be blocked in some situations, and collection of context is needed in those situations, which should be done at processor register level. So this function can not be implemented in high level languages like C, and qualifies as one of HAL functions.

The assembly implementation of mutexObjectLock() with timer support is on same lines as the mutexObjectLock() with out timer support. The assembly implementation of this function on ARM platform with timer support is available in the SROS version 2.0 in appendix-B and in the accompanying CDROM.

3.3.2 Timer management in SROS

The threadObjects which are waiting for a stipulated time are kept in the *timerList*. The threadObjects are kept into the *timerList* with out considering their priority. i.e. the priority is not the key field that orders the threadObjects in the *timerList* unlike the *readyList* and other *waitlists* where priority is the key field. When ever timeout occur for a threadObject in the *timerList*, the threadObject has to be removed from the *waitList* where it is waiting for a resource along with timeout event. The *auxInfo* field in each node of the timerList (See the listNode definition in Figure 2-19), holds the address of the *waitList* where the threadObject is waiting for a resource event to happen. If the threadObject is only waiting for the timeout event and not for any other event (as in the case of sleep() SROS call, the threadObject only waits in the *timerList* and not in any other *waitList*) then *auxInfo* field of the *timeList* node is initialized with NULL. The usage of *auxInfo* field in timer list nodes is different from the *readyList* and other *waitlists*. The *readyList*, other *waitlist* nodes hold the replica of priority of threadObject in their *auxInfo* field. But in the *timerList* each node as mentioned earlier holds the address of the *waitList* where the threadObject is simultaneously waiting for an event. The usage of integer field to hold the address is not a good programming practice but this practice is used in SROS to simplify the implementation. (To make the *timerList* node with exactly the same size as the *readyList*, *waitList* nodes to simplify allocation, deallocation of list nodes).

For all threadObjects in the *timerList*, the timer-ticks remaining for the threadObjects to timeout are maintained in the threadObjects themselves. The timeout value of a threadObject is maintained relative to preceding threadObject timeout value in the *timerList*. Usually one of the registers holds the timeout value in the threadObject. (The register that is used to pass the second function argument in SROS). All the threadObjects, waiting through any type of synchronization object or sleeping hold the number of timer ticks to time out in the same register. (For SROS on ARM platform, R1 is the register that is used to pass the second argument so it holds the timeout value). First threadObject in the *timerList*, holds the absolute number of timer ticks needed for it to timeout. The second threadObject in the *timerList* holds the number of timer ticks needed for it to timeout after the first threadObject's timeout. (i.e. for SROS on ARM platform R1 register of the second threadObject holds the timerticks needed for the second threadObject to timeout after the first threadObject timeout). Similarly the third threadObject in the *timerList* holds the number of timer ticks needed for it to timeout after the second threadObject timeout. The Nth threadObject in the *timerList* holds the number of timer ticks needed for it to timeout after the $(N-1)^{th}$ threadObject timeout. So the absolute number of timer ticks needed for N^{th} threadObject to timeout is the sum of all timeout register values from the 1st threadObject to N^{th} threadObject in the *timerList*. This mechanism is needed to avoid updating the timer ticks needed for each waiting threadObject after each timer tick. In this method only the timer ticks needed for timeout for first threadObject in the *timerList* is decremented by 1 after each timer tick (i.e. timer interrupt). So by definition the timer ticks needed for timeout for all the threadObjects will be updated in just one integer decrement operation.

After each timer interrupt, RTOS gets the control. RTOS knows that the interrupt is from timer and call timer interrupt service routine.

In the timer interrupt service routine, timeout of the first threadObject (which is stored in R1 register in SROS ported to ARM platform) in the *timerList* is decremented by 1. By the way we are storing the timeout values of all the threadObjects in the *timerList*, the timeout values of all threadObjects get updated with this operation. If the timeout reaches 0 after the decrement, then that threadObject with timeout 0 which is in the beginning of the *timerList* is moved from *timerList* to *readyList*. If that threadObject is also waiting for an event in some other synchronization object *waitList* (mutexObject, semaphoreObject or mailboxObject etc.), then the threadObject is also removed from that *waitList*. The type of synchronization object (mutex, semaphore or mailbox) is immaterial, as *waitList* is after all a listObject in all the synchronization objects. The interrupt handler continues to repeat moving all waiting threadObjects with timeout 0, to *readyList*, and removing them from any waitlists till it encounter a threadObject with timeout greater than 0. After this operation the timer interrupt service routine return the control back to the timer interrupt handler.

As some threadObjects move to *readyList* from *timerList* in the timer interrupt service routine, timer interrupt handler checks if context switch is needed. If any higher priority thread than the running thread (i.e. interrupted thread) moved to ready state, context switch is needed. To make context switch, the context of the running thread is saved to running threadObject and a jump to scheduler() is made to start the higher priority ready thread (which just got timed out and moved to ready state).

If no context switch is necessary, the thread which is interrupted is given back the control.

Essentially the behavior of timer interrupt handler is similar to normal interrupt handler. The only difference is that in normal interrupt handling the actual interrupt service routine is implemented by the application but in case of timer interrupt both the timer interrupt handler, timer interrupt service routine (i.e. both the layers in interrupt handling. see sections 2.2, 2.3) were implemented by SROS. Interrupt service routine is the actual service (other than context switch) for the interrupt. Calling interrupt service routine and context switch (if necessary) is done by interrupt handler. In case of timer interrupt handler, the actual work need to be done for the interrupt is done by SROS itself.

If there is only one interrupt in the system and timer interrupt is multiplexed to that system interrupt, timer interrupt service routine should be implemented (similar to implementing any other interrupt service routine multiplexed to system interrupt). (On ARM core usually timer interrupt is multiplexed with other interrupts). The timer interrupt service routine in SROS is shown in Figure 3-4. The common interrupt handler checks for the interrupt type and invoke the appropriate interrupt service routine. If the interrupt is from timer, timer interrupt service routine is invoked. The common interrupt handler takes care of context switch if higher priority threads become ready (due to timeout) in the timer interrupt service routine.

The *timerTick()* shown in Figure 3-4 is the timer interrupt service routine in SROS. *timerTick()* is invoked by interrupt handler when the interrupt is caused by the timer.

Statement (1) shows the prototype. *timerTick()* does not take any argument and does not return anything.

Statement (2) increments the global system time. The *"time"* is a global variable that counts the number of ticks from the system startup. *"time"* is initialized to 0 during system startup.

```
void timerTick(void)   //timer interrupt service routine.                    (1)
{
      listObject_t *freedListNodePtr;
      time++;                                                                 (2)
      if(timerList.auxInfo > 0))                                              (3)
      {
            timerList.nextListNode->element->R[1]--;                         (4)
            while(timerList.auxInfo > 0))                                     (5)
            {
                  if(timerList.nextListNode->element->R[1] == 0)             (6)
                  {
                        freedListNodePtr = timerList.nextListNode;           (7)
                        timerList.nextListNode =
                              freedListNodePtr->nextListNode;               (8)
                        if(freedListNodePtr->auxInfo != 0)                   (9)
                        {
                              listObjectDeleteMiddle((listObject_t *)
                              (freedListNodePtr->auxInfo),
                              freedListNodePtr->element);                    (10)
                        }
                        listObjectInsert(&readyList,
                                    freedListNodePtr->element);
                                                                             (11)
                        listNodeFree(freedListNodePtr);                      (12)
                        timerList.auxInfo--;                                 (13)
                  }
                  else
                  {
                        break;                                               (14)
                  }
            }
      }

      return;                                                                (15)
}
```

Figure 3-4

Statement (3) checks if the *timerList* has any threadObjects. (Note that *timerList* also has dummy head at the beginning like *readyList* and other *waitLists*.

The *auxInfo* field in the dummy head of *timerList* counts the number of elements in the *timerList*).

If there are no threadObjects in the *timerList,* no processing is needed. Statement (15) just transfers the control back to the caller. (Either common interrupt handler in case of multiplexed interrupts or timer interrupt handler in case of unmultiplexed interrupts).

If *timerList* is not empty (i.e. at least one threadObject is waiting for timeout event) Statement (4) decrements the timeout ticks of the first threadObject by 1. As mentioned earlier decrementing the timeout ticks of the first threadObject by 1, is equivalent to decrementing the timeout ticks of all threadObjects after it by 1. (Note that R[1] denotes the register R1 in SROS on ARM platform. For SROS on other platforms the corresponding register where timeout value is stored has to be decremented).

Statement (5) succeeds for the first time (as the same condition succeeded in statement (3)) and at all other times when there is at least one thread in the *timerList* with timeout ticks as 0, at the beginning of the list.

Statement (6) checks if the first thread in the *timerList* has 0 timeout ticks.

If the timeout ticks reaches 0 for the first threadObject, then it will be removed from *timerList* in statements (7) (8) (12) (13). The removed thread object is inserted into the *readyList* in statement (11).

Statement (9) checks if the threadObject is also waiting for an event in some synchronization object *waitList*. If it is waiting in any synchronization object *waitList*, it is removed from that list in statement (10).

Statements (7) to (13) are repeated to remove all the waiting threadObjects whose timeout occurred. When there is no threadObject with timeout ticks 0 at the beginning of the *timerList*, statement (14) exit the while loop and statement (15) return the control back to the caller. (Either common interrupt handler or timer interrupt handler).

This function does not need to be blocked at any point of time. So this function does not need to be written in assembly even though the threadObject itself depends on the processor architecture. Even though this function depends on the threadObject definition in SROS, the dependencies can be easily removed with simple function calls that are interface to the threadObject where ever they exists. So this function is not categorized as a HAL function.

3.3.3 Inserting a threadObject into timerList

In *readyList, waitlists* of synchronization objects the priority decides the place of the threadObject in the linked list. But in *timerList* the timeout time determine the position of the threadObject in the linked list. Each threadObject when it is in *timerList* holds a value related to its timeout time in one of its general purpose registers. Let us denote that value as waitTime. The Nth threadObject timeout is given by the sum of the all 1 to N threadObjects waitTimes. We can view waitTime of a threadObject in the *timerList* as the timeout ticks needed after the preceding threadObject timeout. For example in SROS on ARM, R1 register holds the waitTime variable. The Nth threadObject timeout is given by the sum of the all 1st to N^{th} threadObjects R1 registers. The threadObjects are arranged such that no R1 register have negative value. So threadObjects are arranged in the ascending order of their timeout time.

The function that inserts a threadObject into the *timerList* is shown in Figure 3-5.

Statement (1) shows the prototype of the *insertIntoTimerList()* function. It takes the threadObject address, and address of *waitList* of synchronization object in which the threadObject is also waiting simultaneously. This function returns nothing.

If this function is called from *sleep()* system call, the threadObject waits for timeout only and does not wait in the *waitList* of any synchronization object. In such a case NULL is passed as *waitList* address. (See *sleep()* in Section 3.3.9)

Statement (2) notes the waitTime of the threadObject. This function is developed for SROS on ARM platform. So the waitTime of the input threadObject is taken from the R1 register in the context. For other platforms (i.e. for different threadObject definition) the register in which second argument is passed in C calling convention should be taken in place of R1. Except this change this function will be same on all platforms.

Statement (3) continuously parses the *timerList* and come to a listNode such that all threadObjects with lower timeout value than the new threadObject is before that position. (including the listNode at that position).

Statement (4) calculates the timer ticks needed after timeout of the preceding threadObject in the *timerList*. This is updated when parsing each threadObject.

Statement (5) moves the working node to the next list node. (next threadObject).

When the while loop ended we will come to a correct position to insert the new threadObject.

```
void insertIntoTimerList(threadObject_t *newThreadObject,
                        listObject_t *waitList)                                    (1)
{
        int32 waitTime;
        listNode_t *listNodePtr, *newListNodePtr;

        //always the waitTime is in R1 register.
        waitTime = newThreadObject->R[1];                                         (2)

        listNodePtr = &timerList;

        //parse the list past the lower timeout threadObjects.
        while(listNodePtr->nextListNode != 0 &&
                listNodePtr->nextListNode->element->R[1] < waitTime)              (3)
        {
                waitTime = waitTime -
                                listNodePtr->nextListNode->element->R[1];         (4)
                listNodePtr = listNodePtr->nextListNode;                          (5)
        }

        //allocate and initialize the new node.
        newListNodePtr = listNodeAlloc();                                         (6)
        newThreadObject->R[1] = waitTime;                                         (7)
        newListNodePtr->element = newThreadObject;                                (8)

        //In the timer list each node auxInfo field hold the waitList
        //of mutexObject or semaphoreObject or mailboxObject.
        newListNodePtr->auxInfo = (int32)(waitList);                              (9)

        //insert into list
        newListNodePtr->nextListNode = listNodePtr->nextListNode;                (10)
        listNodePtr->nextListNode = newListNodePtr;                              (11)

        //subtract the waiting time for the following list nodes
        //after newListNodePtr
        if(newListNodePtr->nextListNode != 0)                                    (12)
        {
                newListNodePtr->nextListNode->element->R[1] -=
                                newListNodePtr->element->R[1];                    (13)
        }
        //listObject first element is dummy node. Its auxInfo field
        //holds the no of nodes in the list. So increment the auxInfo
        //field of dummy node by 1.
        timerList.auxInfo++;                                                     (14)
}
```

Figure 3-5

Statement (6) allocates the new list node. Statement(7) initializes the R1 register which holds the number of ticks for timeout after its preceding threadObject timeout in the *timerList*.

Statement (8) keeps the threadObject into the newly allocated list node. Statement (9) notes the *waitlist* address into the *auxInfo* field of the newly allocated list node. Keeping an address into an integer is not a good programming practice but it is done for optimum use of list node memory while keeping all the listNodes with same size. (Note that identical listNode is used for *timerList, readyList, waitlists* of synchronization objects).

Statement (10) (11) update the links such that newly allocated node is linked into the *timerList* at the correct position.

Statement (12) checks if there are any threadObjects past the newly inserted threadObject in the *timerList*. If any threadObject exists, the waitTime of those threadObejcts has to be updated to reflect insertion of a new threadObejct (and hence some extra timeout ticks). Statement(13) deduct the extra timer ticks introduced for all the threadObjects past the newly inserted threadObject, by reducing the timer ticks needed for timeout for the immediate next threadObject of the newly inserted threadObject.

As noted earlier the dummy head's *auxInfo* field holds the number of list nodes inside a list. Statement (14) updates the count of the list nodes in the *timerList* by incrementing the *auxInfo* field of the dummy head.

A simple example of inserting threadObjects into the *timeList* is shown in Figure 3-6.

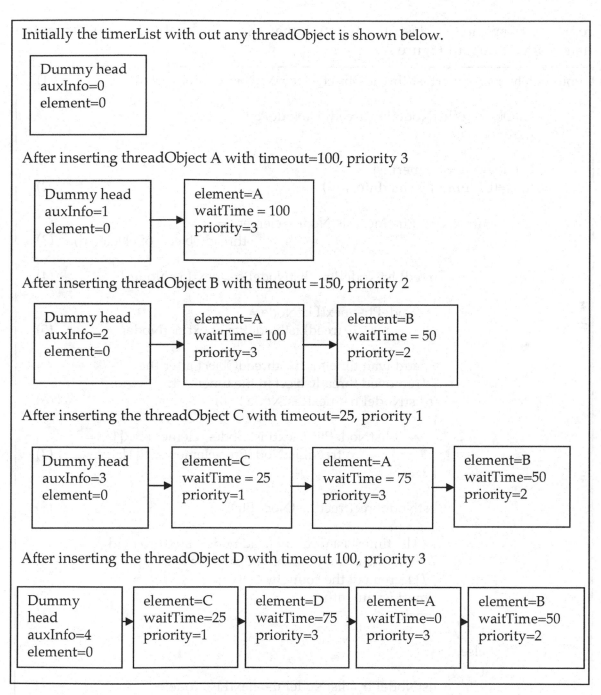

Initially the timerList with out any threadObject is shown below.

After inserting threadObject A with timeout=100, priority 3

After inserting threadObject B with timeout =150, priority 2

After inserting the threadObject C with timeout=25, priority 1

After inserting the threadObject D with timeout 100, priority 3

Figure 3-6

3.3.4 Deleting a threadObject from the timerList

If the synchronization event for which a threadObject is waiting happens before timeout then the threadObject will be moved to *readyList*. In such a case if the threadObject that is also waiting simultaneously for the timeout should be removed from the *timerList*. The function that removes the threadObject from the *timerList* is shown in Figure 3-7.

```
void deleteFromTimerList(threadObject_t *threadObjectToBeDeleted)        (1)
{
        listObject_t *listNodePtr, *freedListNodePtr;
        int i;

        listNodePtr = &timerList;
        for(i=0; i<timerList.auxInfo; i++)                              (2)
        {
                if(listNodePtr->nextListNode->element ==
                                                threadObjectToBeDeleted)    (3)
                {
                        freedListNodePtr = listNodePtr->nextListNode;       (4)

                        listNodePtr->nextListNode =
                                freedListNodePtr->nextListNode;             (5)

                        //add wait time for the threadObject after the
                        //removed threadObject in the timerList.
                        if(listNodePtr->nextListNode != 0)                  (6)
                        {
                                listNodePtr->nextListNode->element->R[1] +=
                                        freedListNodePtr->element->R[1];     (7)
                        }

                        listNodeFree(freedListNodePtr);                     (8)

                        //The timerList dummy head node's auxInfo field
                        //hold the count of no of nodes in the list.
                        //Decrement the count by 1.
                        timerList.auxInfo--;                                (9)
                        break;                                              (10)
                }
                else
                {
                        listNodePtr = listNodePtr->nextListNode;            (11)
                }
        }

        return;                                                         (12)
}
```

Figure 3-7

Statement (1) shows the prototype. This function takes the theradObject address that has to be deleted from the *timerList* and returns nothing.

Statement (2) is the for loop to parse all the listNodes in the *timerList*.

Statement (3) checks if the listNode under consideration holds the threadObject to be deleted. If the check fails, the listNode under consideration is moved to next listNode in statement (11).

If the listNode under consideration holds the threadObject to be deleted, statement (4) notes the listNode to be freed. Statement (5) delinks the listNode from the *timerList*. Statement (6) checks if there is any threadObjects after the threadObject that was deleted. Statement(7) corrects the timeout ticks that were lost for all the threadObjects after removing threadObject in the *timerList* by adding lost timeout ticks to the immediate next threadObject of the deleted threadObject. Statement (8) frees the listNode that hold the threadObject. Statement (9) updates the counter that counts the number of listNodes in the dummy head of the *timerList*. As the objective of deleting the threadObject is complete, statement (10) end the for loop, and the control is transferred back to the calling function.

Example in Figure 3-8 shows how *deleteFromTimerList()* works.

Note that all the timer functions are called from the context where the interrupts are disabled. Enabling interrupts in any of the timer routines we have discussed will be fatal.

All the functions involving timer are implemented in C in SROS on ARM platform. Even though these functions depend on the threadObject definition, the dependency can be easily removed by having some interface to interact with the threadObject. So these functions are not categorized as HAL functions.

100

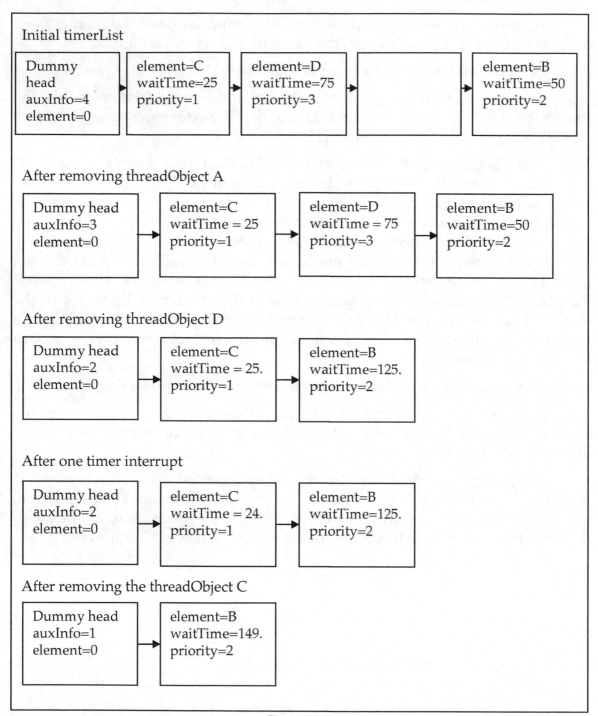

Figure 3-8

3.3.5 mutexObjectRelease()

The *mutexObjectRelease()* with timer support is functionally similar to its previous version (i.e. without timer support) except it will remove the waiting threadObject from *timerList* if the waiting threadObject is also waiting for a timeout.

    mutexObjectRelease() function releases the mutex. If any threadObject is waiting for the release of the mutex, the highest priority thread Object among them has to be moved from the mutexObject *waitList* to *readyList*. If the threadObject moved to *readyList* is also waiting in the *timerList*, then that threadObject has to be removed from the *timerList*.

    If the new thread that became ready to run (if any) has higher priority than running threadObject, and the SROS request is not made from interrupt service routine, context switch has to take place.

    The pseudo code in Figure 3-9 shows the *mutexObjectRelease()* function.

```
void mutexObjectRelease(mutexObject_t *mutexObjectPtr)                    (1)
{
        threadObject_t *waitingThreadObjectPtr;
        interruptDisable();                                              (2)
        mutexObjectPtr->mutex = 1;                                       (3)
        if(listObjectCount(&mutexObjectPtr->waitList))                   (4)
        {
                waitingThreadObjectPtr =
                        listObjectDelete(&mutexObjectPtr->waitList);     (5)
                listObjectInsert(&readyList, waitingThreadObjectPtr);    (6)
                if(waitingThreadObjectPtr->waitTime >= 0)                (7)
                {
                        deleteFromTimerList(waitingThreadObjectPtr);     (8)
                }
                if(waitingThreadObjectPtr->priority < runningThread.priority &&
                This request is not made from interrupt service routine) (9)
                {
                        get the context which is functionally equivalent to
                        the end of this function into runningThreadObject. (10)
                        listObjectInsert(&readyList, runningThreadObjectPtr); (11)
                        Jump to scheduler();                             (12)
                }
        }
        interruptRestore();                                             (13)
        return;                                                        (14)
}
```

Figure 3-9

The statement (1) shows the prototype of *mutexObjectRelease()*. This SROS call takes mutexObject address as input and returns nothing.

Statement (2) disables interrupts. As this function access and update some SROS data, interrupts should be disabled.

Statement (3) unlocks the mutex.

Statement (4) checks if there are any threads waiting in the mutexObject *waitList* for the mutex to be released. If there are threads (one or more) in the *waitList*, statement (5), (6) move the highest priority threadObject among them from *waitList* to *readyList*.

Statement (7) checks if the threadObject is also waiting for a timeout in *timerList*. All the threadObjects when they are waiting for timeout always holds the remaining time left for timeout to happen in their context. See the timer management in the section 3.3.2. The waitTime in the threadObject (R1 register for SROS on ARM platform) denotes the timer ticks that are remaining for the threadObject to timeout, after timeout of its immediate preceding threadObject in the *timerList*. When waitTime is greater than or equal to 0, the threadObject is waiting for a stipulated timeout and can be found in the *timerList*. If the threadObject waitTime is negative, the threadObject is waiting for indefinite time till its desired resource is available, and can not be found in the *timerList*. Statement (8) removes the waiting threadObject, which was previously moved to *readyList* from the *waitList*.

Statement(9) checks if the threadObject which was ready to run has higher priority (lower priority number) than running threadObject and the current SROS request is not made from interrupt service routine. If both the conditions are satisfied then statement (10) saves the context which is functionally equivalent to the end of the function into the running threadObject. Statement (11) inserts the running threadObject into the *readyList*. Statement (12) makes a jump to *scheduler* to start the higher priority ready thread (the higher priority threadObject is the threadObject which was ready to run after the releasing of the mutex). Note that interrupts will be automatically enabled after loading the context of a thread in to processor by the *scheduler*.

Statement (13) restores the interrupts when context switch does not take place due to mutexObject release. Statement (14) returns the control back to the caller.

This function can not be implemented in C as it may block the requesting thread. The assembly implementation of this function is on similar lines to the earlier version of *mutexObjectRelease()* and can be found the in appendix-B and in the accompanying CDROM.

3.3.6 semaphoreObjectPend()

The semaphoreObjectPend() function should be changed on similar lines to the *mutexObjectLock()* for the timer support. The changed *semaphoreObjectPend()* is shown in Figure 3-10.

```
int32 semaphoreObjectPend(semaphoreObject_t *semaphoreObjectPtr,
                          int32 waitTime)                              (1)
{
    interruptsDisable();                                              (2)

    if(semaphoreObjectPtr->count > 0)                                (3)
    {
        semaphoreObjectPtr->count--;                                 (4)
        returnValue = 1;                                             (5)
    }
    else
    {
        if(waitTime)                                                 (6)
        {
            get the context functionally equivalent to start of
            this function and keep it in the running threadObject.   (7)
            listObjectInsert(&semaphoreObjectPtr->waitList,
                             runningThreadObjectPtr);                 (8)
            if(waitTime > 0)                                         (9)
            {
                insertIntoTimerList (runningThreadObjectPtr,
                             &semaphoreObjectPtr->waitList);          (10)
            }
            jump to scheduler();                                     (11)
        }
        else
        {
            returnValue = 0;                                         (12)
        }
    }
    interruptsRestore();                                             (13)
    return returnValue;                                             (14)
}
```

Figure 3-10

The *semaphoreObjectPend()* tries to decrement the semaphore *count*.

If the semaphore *count* is greater than 0, the semaphore *count* is decremented immediately and the control is returned to the calling thread with the success flag (i.e. with return value of 1).

When the semaphore *count* is 0, the *waitTime* is considered. If the *waitTime* is 0, control is immediately returned to the calling thread with failure flag (i.e. with return value of 0).

When the semaphore *count* is 0, nonzero *waitTime* denotes that the calling thread want to get blocked. If the *waitTime* is negative, the blocking is indefinite i.e. till the semaphore *count* is incremented in the system. If the *waitTime* is positive, *waitTime* timer ticks time will be waited before returning the calling thread to ready state. For indefinite wait, (i.e. negative *waitTime*) the running threadObject is kept only into semaphoreObject *waitList*. For stipulated amount of *waitTime*, the running threadObject is kept both into semaphoreObject *waitList* and the *timerList*.

The only modification done for the *semaphoreObjectPend()* without timer support to add timer support is to add the running threadObject to *timerList* when bounded *waitTime* is requested.

Statement (1) shows the prototype of the *semaphoreObejctPend()* function. This SROS request takes address of semaphoreObject, and *waitTime* as inputs. This SROS request returns Success (1) or failure (0) in decrementing the semaphore count.

Statement (2) disables the interrupts as allowing interrupts is fatal when updating RTOS variables.

Statement (3) checks the semaphore count. If the count is greater than 0, the count is decremented by 1 in statement (4), *returnValue* is initialized to 1 in statement (5). Interrupts are restored in statements (13) and Success (i.e.1) is returned in statement (14).

When the semaphore count is not greater than 0, *waitTime* is checked in statement (6).

For zero *waitTime*, the failure flag (i.e.0) is initialized in statement (12) and returned in statement (14). The interrupts are restored in statement (13).

When *waitTime* is not zero, the thread has to be blocked. Statement (7) collects the context which is functionally equivalent to the starting of the function into running threadObject. Statement (8) keeps running threadObject in to semaphoreObject *waitList*. Statement (9) checks if the waiting needed is indefinite or definite. For positive *waitTime* (i.e. waiting time is definite) the running threadObject is also inserted into the *timerList* in statement (10). Statement (11) makes a jump to *scheduler()* to start running the next high priority ready thread.

This function can not be implemented in C as the requesting thread may get blocked. The assembly implementation of this function is on similar lines to the *semaphoreObjectPend()* of the earlier version and can be found in appendix-B and in the accompanying CDROM.

3.3.7 semaphoreObjectPost()

The *semaphoreObjectPost()* function has to be modified on similar lines with the *mutexObjectRelease()* for timer support.

The *semaphoreObjectPost()* increments the semaphore count. If there is any threadObject(s) waiting for semaphore count to be greater than 0, then the highest priority waiting threadObject is moved to *readyList*. If the highest priority waiting threadObject is also waiting in the *timerList*, then it is removed from the *timerList*. If the waiting threadObject priority is higher than the running threadObject priority and context switch is allowed (i.e. the SROS call is not made from the interrupt service routine) then the context which is functionally equivalent to the end of *semaphoreObjectPost()* is collected and kept into the running threadObject, the running threadObject is moved to *readyList*, and a jump is made to *scheduler()* to start the higher priority thread that became ready to run.

The only modification done to the *semaphoreObjectPost()* with out timer support of the earlier version of SROS is checking if the waiting threadObject is also waiting in the *timerList* and removing it from the *timerList* if it do.

The *samaphoreObjectPost()* with timer support is shown in Figure 3-11.

Statement (1) shows the prototype of the function. The prototype is not changed from the earlier version. This function just takes the semaphoreObject address and returns nothing.

Statement (2) disables the interrupts as allowing them during this function is dangerous.

Statement (3) increments the semaphore count.

Statement (4) checks if any threadObject is waiting for the semaphore count to be greater than 0.

If any threadObject is waiting for the semaphore, statements (5),(6) move the highest priority waiting threadObject from *waitList* of semaphoreObejct to *readyList*.

106

```
void semaphoreObjectPost(semaphoreObject_t *semaphoreObjectPtr)                (1)
{
        threadObject_t *waitingThreadObjectPtr;

        interruptsDisable();                                                   (2)
        semaphoreObjectPtr->count++;                                           (3)
        if(listObjectCount(&semaphoreObjectPtr->waitList) > 0)                 (4)
        {
                waitingThreadObjectPtr =
                        listObjectDelete(&semaphoreObjectPtr->waitList);       (5)
                listObjectInsert(&readyList, waitingThreadObjectPtr);          (6)
                if(waitingThreadObjectPtr->waitTime >= 0)                      (7)
                {
                        deleteFromTimerList(waitingThreadObjectPtr);           (8)
                }
                if(waitingThreadObjectPtr->priority < runningThread.priority
                && context switch is allowed)                                 (9)
                {
                        Collect the context which should be functionally
                        equivalent to the end of this function into running
                        threadObject.                                        (10)
                        listObjectInsert(&readyList, runningThreadObjectPtr);(11)
                        Jump to scheduler();                                 (12)
                }
        }
        interruptsRestore();                                                 (13)
}
```

Figure 3-11

Statement (7) checks if the waiting threadObject can also be found in the *timerList*. If it can be found in the *timerList*, the waiting threadObject is removed from the *timerList* in statement (8).

Statement (9) checks if the waiting thread priority is higher than the running thread priority and this SROS call is not made from interrupt service routine (i.e. whether context switch is allowed). If so, the context which is functionally equivalent to the end of the function is saved into the running threadObject in statement (10), running threadObject is inserted into *readyList* in statement (11), and a jump is made to *scheduler()* in statement (12) to start the higher priority threadObject that has just become ready to run.

Statement (13) restores the interrupts if there is no context switch.

This function can not be implemented in C as it may block the caller in which case the collection of the context has to be done at processor register level. The assembly implementation of this function is on similar lines to the *semaphoreObjectPost()* of the earlier version and implementation for ARM platform can be found in appendix-B and in the accompanying CDROM.

3.3.8 mailboxObject functions with timer support

The mailboxObjectPend() function with timer support need similar modifications we have done for the *mutexObjectLock()*, *semaphoreObjectPend()* when the *mailboxBuffer* is empty. The *mailboxObjectPend()* function also need similar modifications we have done for *mutexObjectRelease()*, *semaphoreObjectPost()* when mailboxBuffer is full. After these two modifications, the *mailboxObjectPend()* with timer support is shown in Figure 3-12.

```
int32 mailboxObjectPend(mailboxObject_t *mailboxObjectPtr,
                        int32 waitTime,
                        void *message)
{
      int32 returnValue;
      interruptsDisable();
      //check is the mailbox has atleast one message.
      if(mailboxObjectPtr->emptyBufferSize <=
          mailboxObjectPtr->mailboxBufferSize - mailboxObjectPtr->messageSize)
      {
            //message is available in the mailbox. Copy the message and update
            //control variables of FIFO.
            memcpy(message, &mailboxObjectPtr->mailboxBuffer[readIndex],
                                    mailboxObjectPtr->messageSize);
            mailboxObjectPtr->readIndex += mailboxObjectPtr->messageSize;
            mailboxObjectPtr->emptyBufferSize +=
                                    mailboxObjectPtr->messageSize;
            if(mailboxObjectPtr->readIndex ==
                            mailboxObjectPtr->mailboxBufferSize)
            {
                  mailboxObjectPtr->readIndex = 0;
            }
            returnValue = 1;                  //success flag.
            //check if any thread is waiting for space in the mailbox.
            if(listObjectCount(&mailboxObjectPtr->waitList) > 0)
            {
                  //move the waiting thread from waitList to readyList.
                  waitingThreadObjectPtr =
                            listObjectDelete(&mailboxObjectPtr->waitList);
                  listObjectInsert(&readyList, waitingThreadObjectPtr);
                  //remove waiting thread from timer list if it can be found in it.
                  if(waitingThreadObjectPtr->waitTime >= 0)
                  {
                        deleteFromTimerList(waitingThreadObjectPtr);
                  }
                  //if the waiting thread has higher priority, do context switch.
                  if(waitingThreadObjectPtr->priority < runningThread.priority)
                  {
                        get the context equivalent to the end of this function.
                        listObjectInsert(&readyList, runningThreadObjectPtr);
                        jump to scheduler();
                  }
            }
      }
```

```
        else
        {
                //mailbox is empty.
                if(waitTime)
                {
                        //contex switch is needed. Save context.
                        get the context functionally equal to starting of the function
                        into the runningThread Object.
                        listObjectInsert(&mailboxObjectPtr->waitList,
                                            runningThreadObjectPtr);

                        //for a bounded wait time insert the threadObject into
                        //timerList.
                        if(waitTime > 0)
                        {
                                insertIntoTimerList(runningThreadObjectPtr,
                                                &mailboxObjectPtr->waitList);
                        }
                        //start next highest priority ready thread.
                        Jump to scheduler();
                }
                else
                {
                        //for non blocking call return failure.
                        returnValue = 0;
                }
        }
        interruptsRestore();
        return returnValue;
}
```

Figure 3-12

The *mailboxObjectPost()* function with timer support need similar modifications we have done for the *mutexObjectRelease()*, *semaphoreObjectPost()* when the *mailboxBuffer* is empty. The *mailboxObjecPost()* function also need similar modifications we have done for *mutexObjectLock()*, *semaphoreObjectPend()* when *mailboxBuffer* is full. After these two modifications, the *mailboxObjectPost()* with timer support is shown in Figure 3-13.

```
int32 mailboxObjectPost(mailboxObject_t *mailboxObjectPtr,
                        int32 waitTime,
                        void *message)
{
        int32 returnValue;
        interruptsDisable();

        //check if space for one message is available.
        if(mailboxObjectPtr->emptyBufferSize >= mailboxObjectPtr->messageSize)
        {
                //keep the message in mailboxBuffer and update FIFO control
variables
                memcpy(&mailboxObjectPtr->mailboxBuffer[writeIndex],
                                message, mailboxObjectPtr->messageSize);
                mailboxObjectPtr->writeIndex += mailboxObjectPtr->messageSize;
                mailboxObjectPtr->emptyBufferSize -=
                                        mailboxObjectPtr->messageSize;
                if(mailboxObjectPtr->writeIndex ==
                                mailboxObjectPtr->mailboxBufferSize)
                {
                        mailboxObjectPtr->writeIndex = 0;
                }
                returnValue = 1;                //success flag to be returned.

                //check if any thread waiting for a message.
                if(listObjectCount(&mailboxObjectPtr->waitList) > 0)
                {
                        //move the waiting theadObject from waitList to readyList.
                        waitingThreadObjectPtr =
                                listObjectDelete(&mailboxObjectPtr->waitList);
                        listObjectInsert(&readyList, waitingThreadObjectPtr);

                        //If the waiting threadObject can be found in the timerList
                        //remove it form the timerList.
                        if(waitingThreadObjectPtr->waitTime >= 0)
                        {
                                deleteFromTimerList(waitingThreadObjectPtr);
                        }

                        //If the waiting threadObject has higher priority and context
                        //switch is allowed, do the context switch.
                        if(waitingThreadObjectPtr->priority < runningThread.priority
                        && context switch is allowed)
                        {
```

```
                                    get the context functionally equal to the end of this
                                    function into running threadObject
                                    listObjectInsert(&readyList, runningThreadObjectPtr);
                                    Jump to scheduler();
                            }
                    }
            }
            else
            {
                    //if non zero waitTime block the thread.
                    if(waitTime)
                    {
                            get the context functionally equivalent to the starting of this
                            function into running threadObject.
                            listObjectInsert(&mailboxObjectPtr->waitList,
                                                    runningThreadObjectPtr);

                            //For bounded waitTime insert the running threadObject into
                            //timerList.
                            if(waitTime > 0)
                            {
                                    insertIntoTimerList(runningThreadObjectPtr,
                                                            &mailboxObjectPtr->waitList);
                            }

                            //start next highest priority ready thread.
                            Jump to scheduler();
                    }
                    else
                    {
                            //for non blocking call return failure flag.
                            returnValue = 0;
                    }
            }
            interruptsRestore();                        //restore interrupts.
            return returnValue;
}
```

Figure 3-13

Both the mailboxObject functions shown above will get blocked in some situations and has to be implemented in assembly as in earlier version. The assembly implementations for ARM platform can be found in appendix-B and in the accompanying CDROM.

3.3.9 sleep()

The purpose of the sleep() as mentioned earlier at the beginning of this chapter is to make the running thread wait for some time with out wasting the CPU time. The *sleep()* function implementation is simple. When ever a thread make the sleep request, we need to keep the running threadObject into the *timerList* and jump to the *scheduler()* to start next high priority thread in the *readyList*. The pseudo code of the *sleep()* function is shown in Figure 3-14.

```
void sleep(int waitTime)

{

        interruptsDisable();

        Collect context equivalent to end of the function into the

        running threadObject and keep it into the timerList;

        Jump to Scheduler();

}
```

Figure 3-14

After the required amount of timer ticks were elapsed, timer interrupt service routine moves the waiting threadObject from *timerList* to the *readyList*, and the thread will compete for the CPU time along with other threads in the *readyList*. As this function can not be implemented in C language, this function is implemented in assembly for SROS on ARM platform. The ARM assembly implementation can be found in appendix-B and in the accompanying CDROM.

3.3.10   Destroying a thread in RTOS

Destroying a thread is removing the threadObject from the RTOS system. After removing the threadObject, the threadObject should not be found in *readyList*, any synchronization object *waitlist*, *timerList*. And also obviously the thread should not be in running state.

A running thread can terminate itself by just executing the "return". When a return statement is executed in a running thread, the control is transferred to a module in RTOS that will deallocate all the memory allocated to the running thread and a jump is made to *scheduler*. The return address given to the function when the thread is created is the address of that module. So when a return is executed by the running thread (like executing return when going back to the parent function), then RTOS gets the control. Once the clean up for the running thread is done *scheduler* start running the next high priority thread. After executing the return statement, the running thread is no longer in the system. (As it will not be in *readyList, waitlists, timerList* and also not in running state).

A running thread may request RTOS to remove another thread in the system. Before a thread make a request to kill another thread, the requesting thread should make sure that the victim thread does not hold any resources (mutexes, semaphores etc..) otherwise those resources will be permanently lost from the system. For this kind of request, RTOS has to remove the threadObject where ever it is in the system. If the thread is ready, the threadObject will be in the *readyList*. If the thread is waiting indefinitely till a synchronizing event, the threadObject will be in the *waitlist* of a synchronization object. If the thread is waiting for bounded time for a synchronizing event, then the threadObject will be in both the *waitlist* of the synchronization Object and also in the *timerList*. If the threadObejct is just sleeping, the threadObject will be in the *timerList* only. So when a request to kill a thread is made, RTOS has to first find the status of the threadObject and has to remove it from the appropriate lists.

Some one may suggest checking all the lists in the system and removing the threadObject where ever it is found! This brute force approach is difficult to implement and poor in performance. A simple method is to note all the lists in the threadObject itself in which it resides. When ever the threadObject is moving from one list to another, a corresponding update should be done to the threadObject.

3.3.11   threadObjectDestroy()

In SROS, the threadObject will be in at most in two lists. One is *readyList* or a synchronization object *waitlist* (mutually exclusively. i.e. if the threadObject is in *readyList* it can not be found in any *waitlist*) and the other is the *timerList*. We can consider *readyList* is also one kind of *waitlist*. It is list to wait for CPU resource. So SROS threadObject is augmented with space for two listObject addresses. The new threadObject definition for SROS on ARM platform is shown in Figure 3-15. The new variables are *listObjectResource, listObjectTimer*. Each threadObject holds the address of *waitlist* (or *readyList*) in listObjectResource if it is waiting for a resource. Similarly listObjectTimer holds the address of the *timerList* if it is waiting for timeout. If the threadObject is not waiting for any resource (i.e. just sleeping) then the *listObjectResource* will be NULL. When the threadObject is not waiting for timeout, then *listObjectTimer* should hold NULL.

```
typedef struct _threadObject_
{
        int32 R[16];

        uint32 cpsr;

        uint32 priority;

        listObject_t *waitListResource;

        listObject_t *waitListTimer;

        char   *threadObjectName;
}threadObject_t;
```

Figure 3-15

The threadObjectDestroy() function is shown in Figure 3-16.

```
void threadObjectDestroy(threadObject_t *threadObjectPtr)                  (1)
{
        interruptDisable();                                                (2)

        assert(threadObjectPtr->waitListResource != 0 ||
                              threadObjectPtr->waitListTimer != 0);        (3)
        if(threadObjectPtr->waitListResource != 0)                        (4)
        {
                assert(threadObjectPtr->waitListResource->auxInfo > 0);   (5)
                listObjectDeleteMiddle(threadObjectPtr->waitListResource,
                                              threadObjectPtr);            (6)
        }

        if(threadObjectPtr->waitListTimer != 0)                           (7)
        {
                assert(timerList.auxInfo > 0);                            (8)
                deleteFromTimerList(threadObjectPtr);                     (9)
        }

        interruptRestore();                                               (10)
}
```

Figure 3-16

Statement (1) shows the prototype. This RTOS request takes the threadObject address to be deleted and does not return anything.

Statement (2) disables the interrupts as allowing interrupts is dangerous when updating RTOS data structures.

Statement (3) is an assert statement to check that threadObject to be deleted is active in the system. i.e. it should be found in a *waitList* of a synchronization object (or *readyList)* or *timerList* or in both.

Statements (4) to (6) remove the threadObject if the threadObject is waiting in *readyList* or *waitList* of a synchronization object. Statement (5) is debug statement to catch errors in the debug version. It asserts that the list has at least one element. (Note that the dummy head of any list has number of its nodes in *auxInfo* field).

Statements (7) to (9) remove the threadObject from *timerList* if the threadObject is waiting in *timerList*. Statement (8) is debug statement to catch errors in debug version. This debug statement asserts that the *timerList* has at least one threadObject in it when the threadObject to be deleted is waiting in the *timerList*.

Statement (10) restores the interrupts and returns the control to the caller.

116

4 Priority Inversions

In this chapter we will discuss the anomalies caused by scheduling criteria of RTOSes: always run highest priority ready thread in the system. We will discuss the scenario of higher priority thread waiting for lower priority threads to finish their execution when the higher priority threads share a non sharable resource with a low priority threads. We discuss the methods for preventing this anomaly and system malfunctions when higher priority threads have stringent deadlines. Finally we discuss a simple solution for SROS.

4.1 Bounded priority inversion

Consider the scenario in which a higher priority thread share a non-sharable resource with a lower priority thread. (Non sharable mean the resource can not be used by two or more threads simultaneously). Suppose that the lower priority thread locked the resource and using the resource. Meanwhile if the higher priority thread become ready to run, the scheduler start running the higher priority thread. If the higher priority thread request the same resource that it is sharing with the lower priority thread (which was already locked by lower priority thread), the higher priority thread will be moved to waiting state, and the scheduler start running the lower priority thread. When the lower priority thread voluntarily unlock the resource after its usage, the scheduler gives the resource to the higher priority thread and the higher priority thread start running again. This execution profile of higher priority thread (HPT), lower priority thread (LPT) is shown in Figure 4-1.

The thick line denotes the CPU occupation of the thread (i.e. thread is in running state). Initially LPT is running in the system. No other higher priority thread is ready in the system. At time instant t1, the LPT needed the resource hence locked it and started using it. At t2, the HPT became ready to run (an interrupt or LPT itself triggered HPT to ready state). At time instant t2, the HPT is scheduled to run in the system. At time t3 the HPT needed the resource (which is already locked by LPT) and tried to lock it. As the resource is not available, RTOS keep the higher priority thread into the waiting state and schedule the lower priority thread into running state at time t3. From t3 to t4 LPT continuously occupy the CPU. The HPT is in the waiting state, waiting for the unlocking of resource by LPT. LPT voluntarily unlock the resource at time t4 after its usage. When the resource is unlocked, the HPT will come to ready state. Then RTOS immediately makes context switch and start running the HPT. The HPT lock the resource at time t4 and continue its execution.

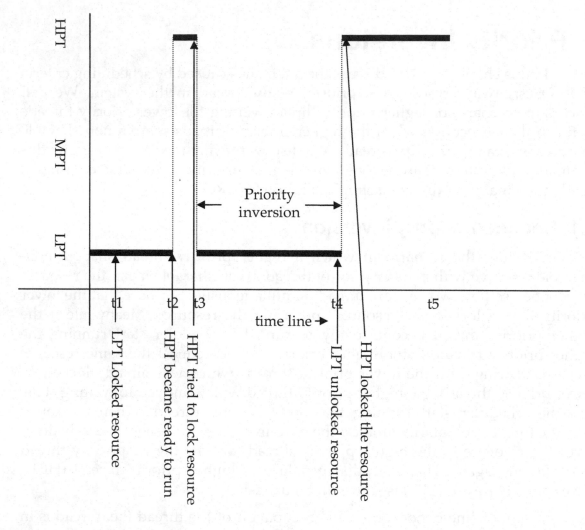

Figure 4-1

During the time between the time instants t3 and t4, the HPT is waiting for the LPT to finish its usage of shared resource. The time period of priority is bounded in this scenario by the execution time of the LPT. When calculating the schedulability and meeting the deadlines of the HPT, we have to consider the execution time of LPT with which it is sharing a resource due to the bounded priority inversion.

4.2 Unbounded priority inversion

Let us consider the bounded priority inversion scenario shown in figure 4-1. If any middle level priority thread (MPT) becomes ready to run between time instants t3 and t4, the MPT is scheduled to run by the scheduler and LPT will be waiting for MPT to finish its execution. Any number of MPTs can keep the LPT to wait for CPU time. The LPT in turn makes the HPT to wait for it. This scenario is shown in figure 4-2.

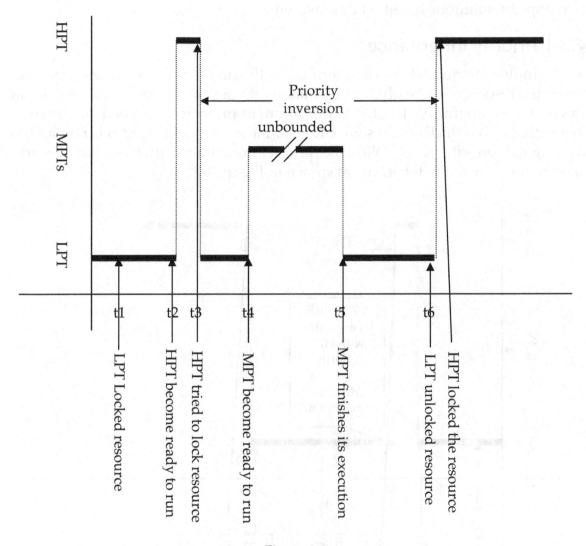

Figure 4-2

This scenario is called unbounded priority inversion. The HPT will wait till all the threads with priority higher than LPT finishes their execution. The time can be bounded or unbounded depending on the threads in the system. Anyway this problem is called unbounded priority inversion problem. Due to this, HPT may miss its stringent deadlines.

4.3 Solution to the unbounded priority inversion

The priority inversion can be solved by increasing the priority of LPT for a short duration, which share a resource with HPT at appropriate time. There are two popular solutions based on this method.

4.3.1 Priority inheritance

In this method whenever a thread say thread A try to lock a resource, and when the resource is already held by another thread say thread B, the priority of thread B is temporarily elevated to maximum of priorities of thread A, thread B. When thread B unlocks the resource it held, the priority of thread B is restored to its original priority level. With the priority inheritance method the scenario shown in Figure 4-2 will become as shown in Figure 4-3.

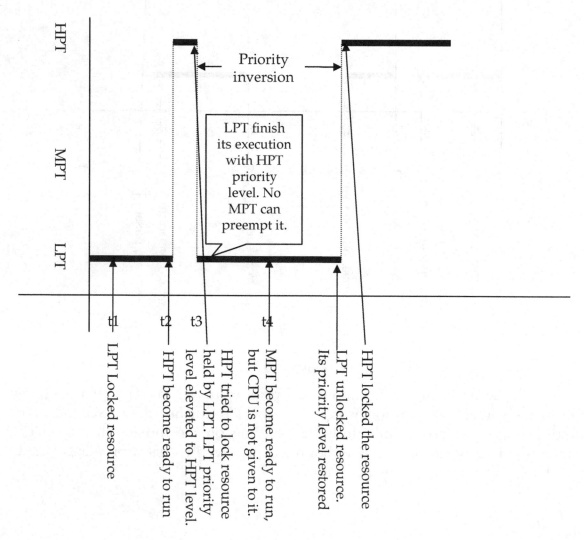

Figure 4-3

4.3.2 Priority ceiling

In priority ceiling method, each resource is also associated with a priority level. The priority level of the resource is determined before hand. The priority level of the resource is set to the priority level of the highest priority thread that can use the resource. The priority level of any thread in the system at any point of time is the maximum of its original priority level and priority levels of all the resources it held.

With the priority ceiling method, the scenario in Figure 4-2 will become as shown in Figure 4-4.

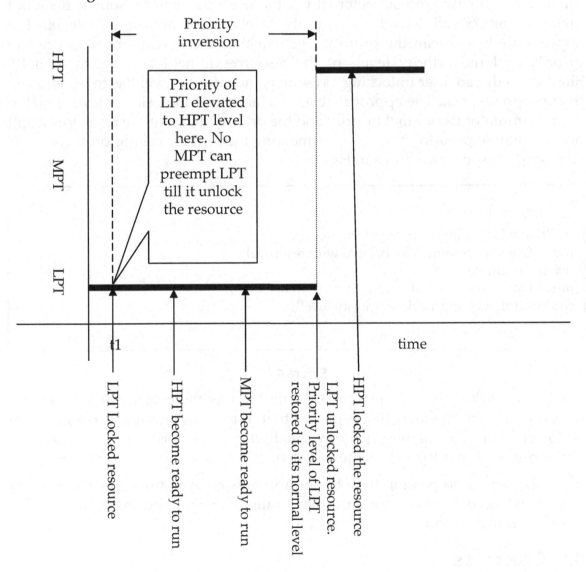

Figure 4-4

4.4 SROS solution to priority inversion

The priority inheritance is more complex than priority ceiling protocol to implement. So the priority ceiling method is chosen for SROS. The priority ceiling solution is simple to implement at application layer rather than at SROS layer. Implementing the priority ceiling protocol at application level limits SROS complexity and overhead when priority ceiling protocol is unnecessary. The application developer can determine the priority level that can be given to each resource according to the priority ceiling method. Each resource is given a priority level equal to the priority level of the highest priority thread that can use the resource. So each thread, before it want to use a particular resource, it should make an SROS call to set the priority level to the appropriate level. The appropriate level mean the priority level equal to the maximum of its original priority and the priority levels of the resources it held and trying to hold. Similarly a thread after unlocking a resource, the priority level has to be adjusted to appropriate level. The appropriate level again mean the priority level equal to the maximum of its original priority and the priority levels of the resources it still hold. A simple pseudo code for implementing the priority ceiling protocol when accessing a resource is shown in Figure 4-5

```
----
----
setPriorityLevel(appropriate priority level);
mutexObjectLock(mutex associated with resource);
use the resource
mutexObjectRelease(mutex associated with resource);
setPriorityLevel(appropriate priority level);
----
----
```

Figure 4-5

The *setPriorityLevel()* is an SROS call that sets the priority of the running thread to the priority level that is passed to it. If the new running thread priority is lower than the highest priority ready thread priority in the *readyList*, *setPriorityLevel()* has to make context switch.

If there is no possibility of the priority inversion in the system, obviously there is no need to assign the priorities to the resources and implementing the priority ceiling protocol.

4.5 Exercises

1. Write pseudo code for the *setPriorityLevel()* SROS request.

2. Show that in a system with priority ceiling protocol, a request for locking the resource never block the requesting thread.

5 Deadlocks

This chapter discusses an important but never the less overlooked problem by many embedded engineers: Deadlocks.

In a multi threading environment, several threads may compete for limited number of resources. The resources mostly non sharable or shared only by finite number of threads at one time. If a thread requests a resource, and the resource is not available, the thread goes into waiting state. The waiting threads may never come out of waiting state, when the resources they have requested are already held among the waiting threads them selves! This situation is called deadlock.

There are many solutions to the problem of deadlocks. This chapter discusses the necessary conditions for deadlocks, and the remedies. The problem of deadlocks in embedded systems is not as severe as in general purpose computers due to their predictable operation, single or limited number of applications they run at one point of time.

5.1 Simple examples of deadlock scenarios

Consider the scenario of two non sharable resources R1, R2. These two resources are shared by the threads T1, T2. Accessing any resource is done as follows.

1. Make RTOS call to lock the resource.

2. Use the resource.

3. Make RTOS call to unlock the resource.

Each shared resource is associated with a mutex. The locking and unlocking of the resource are done with *mutxObjectLock(&mutexAssociatedWithResource, -1)*, *mutexObjectRelease(&mutexAssociatedWithResource)* RTOS calls respectively. It is very common that the threads wait indefinitely for the resource. i.e. without acquiring the resource, the threads can not continue their execution further. The code in threads T1, T2 might look as shown in Figure 5-1.

Assume initially both resources are free. Assume initially T1 is running in the system. Thread T1 needs Resource R1 and it locks the resource at statement (3) in Figure 5-1. -1 in the mutexObjectLock() function argument denotes that the thread wait indefinitely for R1 if R1 is not available. Assume after T1 locked the resource and before T1 acquire the resource R2 (i.e. at statement (4) or statement (5)), it got preempted by thread T2. Thread T2 lock the resource R2 (at statement (3)) and go into waiting state at statement (6) as resource R1 is already held by T1.

Now scheduler starts thread T1, and the thread T1 tries to lock the resource R2 at statement (6). The thread T1 also goes into the waiting state as R2 is already held by T2.

Now the summary is thread T1 held resource R1 and waiting for resource R2. Thread T2 held resource R2 and waiting for resource R1.

-----	(1)		-----	(1)
-----	(2)		-----	(2)
mutexObjectLock(R1, -1);	(3)		mutexObjectLock(R2, -1);	(3)
-----	(4)		-----	(4)
-----	(5)		-----	(5)
mutexObjectLock(R2, -1);	(6)		mutexObjectLock(R1, -1);	(6)
-----	(7)		-----	(7)
-----	(8)		-----	(8)
-----	(9)		-----	(9)
mutexObjectRelease(R1);	(10)		mutexObjectRelease(R2);	(10)
mutexObjectRelease(R2);	(11)		mutexObjectRelease(R1);	(11)
-----	(12)		-----	(12)
-----	(13)		-----	(13)

thread T1   thread T2

Figure 5-1

From this scenario both the threads T1, T2 never come out from the waiting state, because T1 is waiting for the release of R2 which is held by T2 without releasing R1, and at the same time T2 is waiting for the resource R1 held by T1 without releasing R2. Both T1 and T2 wait indefinitely! This situation is called deadlock.

The above scenario shows a simple situation of deadlock involving two threads and two resources only. A deadlock can involve any number of threads and resources. Consider a situation involving 3 different resources R1, R2, R3 and three threads T1, T2, T3. Assume R1, R2, and R3 resources allocated to T1, T2, and T3 threads respectively. If these threads T1, T2, T3 make a request for R2, R3, R1 devices respectively a deadlock will occur. Consider another situation involving three threads T1, T2, T3 and 3 identical resources. Assume each thread is allocated with one resource from the pool of 3 resources. If every thread requests another resource again a deadlock will occur in the system. We can cite many more intricate examples like these involving any number of threads and resources.

Deadlocks may also involve resources that can be sharable by only a finite number of threads at one point of time.

5.2 Resource allocation graph

Resource allocation graph is a convenient way to visualize resource allocations and requests in the system. In the resource allocation graph, threads are shown with circles and the resources are shown with rectangles as shown in Figure 5-2. The number of dots in the rectangle indicates the maximum number of threads that can share the resource at one point of time. A resource which can be used by only one thread at one point of time is indicated by a rectangle with one dot in it.

An arrow from a thread to a resource indicates the request made by the thread for that resource. An arrow from a resource to a thread indicates the allocation of the resource to that thread.

The resource allocation graph for the deadlock scenario explained in Figure 5-1 is shown in Figure 5-2.

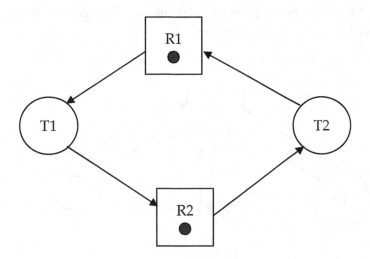

Figure 5-2

The resource allocation graph for the deadlock scenario with three threads T1, T2, T3 and three resources R1, R2, R3 explained at the end of the section 5-1 is shown in Figure 5-3.

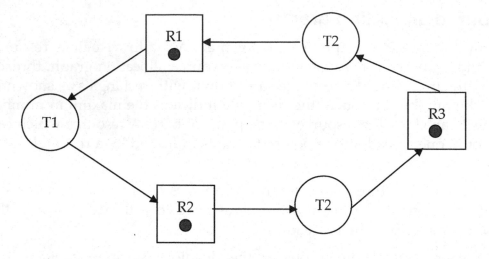

Figure 5-3

The resource allocation graph for the deadlock scenario with three threads T1, T2, T3 and 3 identical resources (which has unified access mechanism) at the end of the section 5-1 is shown in Figure 5-3.

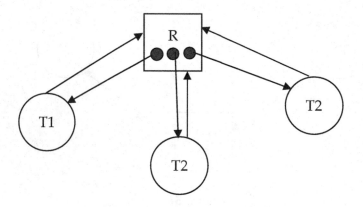

Figure 5-4

From the resource allocation graphs shown in Figures 5-2, 5-3, 5-4, it can be observed that during deadlock, the threads that are in deadlock wait in circular loops. This observation may not be apparent immediately in Figure 5-4.

5.3 Necessary conditions for deadlocks

As we have seen, deadlock only involves resources which can be simultaneously accessed by one or limited number of threads. For deadlock to happen each thread should get the resources one by one (or few at a time, but not all at a time) it needs during the life of its execution. A thread should wait for extra resources which it need to proceed with out releasing the resources it own. The necessary conditions for deadlock to happen are listed below.

1. **Mutual exclusion**: The system should involve at least one device which can be accessed by only one thread or by only limited number of threads simultaneously.

2. **Hold and wait**: All the threads wait for more resources which they need to proceed, without releasing the resources they own. i.e. for example a thread needs two resources R1, R2. If it got resource R1 and resource R2 is not available, it waits for R2 without releasing R1.

3. **No preemption of resources**: When a resource is allocated to a thread, the allocation can not be cancelled by force. The thread only can voluntarily release the resource after its usage. i.e. even when threads are in waiting state the resources can not be deallocated by RTOS.

4. **Circular wait**: The resource allocation graph should show a circular wait.

The conditions mentioned are necessary but not sufficient. In a system if all resources are of one instance only, then a circular wait for resources is necessary and sufficient condition for the deadlock. In a system with multiple instances of resources a circular wait may not necessarily lead to a deadlock. For example consider a simple resource allocation graph shown in Figure 5-5

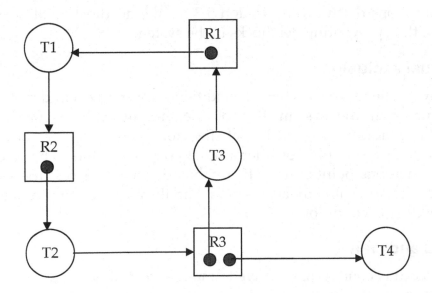

Figure 5-5

We can observe a circular wait T1→R2→T2→R3→T3→R1→T1. But this may not cause deadlock. The resource allocated to T4 may be released by T4 after its usage is over. Then the instance of resource R3 released by T4 will be allocated to T2 and the circular waiting loop will break.

5.4 Dealing with deadlocks

In a small to medium complexity embedded system, where one thread access one hardware device (i.e. no sharing) or a thread at any point of time need only one resource to continue its execution. Deadlocks will never occur in the system. If many threads in the system use the shared resources and the threads in the system need more than one resource at one point of time, deadlocks can happen in the system. Obviously deadlocks are undesirable in the system and have to be taken care of. Deadlocks can be handled in one of the 4 following ways.

1. Deadlock prevention

2. Deadlock avoidance.

3. Deadlock detection and recovery.

4. Manual reset of the system if the system is frozen by deadlock.

5.4.1 Deadlock prevention

We can follow one of several protocols that make sure one of the four necessary conditions discussed in Section 5-3 for the deadlock, will never occur in the system, thus preventing deadlocks in the system.

5.4.1.1 Mutual exclusion

Removing the mutual exclusion condition from the system denote making all the resources in the system sharable i.e. no mutually exclusive access. Obviously this condition can not be satisfied for many hardware devices and shared memory. For example Consider a serial port, which has to be accessed by only one thread at one point of time. If any thread wants to access the serial port when another thread is already accessing, it should wait. So we can not remove the mutual exclusion condition.

5.4.1.2 Hold and wait

To avoid this condition, we have to make sure that no thread should hold the resources in waiting state. We can have a protocol that all threads should request all the resources it need at the beginning of processing in one single RTOS call. To implement this solution obviously RTOS calls should support request for multiple resources in one single RTOS call.

We can alleviate the strict constraint of requesting all the resources at the beginning, by allowing a thread to request for resources only when it had none. This provision has the advantage that if a resource needed only a fraction of time during the thread processing, it can be released for other devices. For example assume a thread need Resources R1, R2, R3. Assume the thread need only R3 for only 0.1% of its processing time at the end. For the initial protocol R3 has to be allocated 100% of thread processing time. With the modified protocol the thread can initially request R1, R2. When ever it need R3 it can release R1, R2 and request R1, R2, and R3 together.

5.4.1.3 No preemption of resources

Avoiding this condition mean, preemption (deallocation) of resources from a waiting thread. When a thread is in wait state, its resources can be deallocated and can be allocated to other waiting threads to avoid deadlock. But saving the status of the resources and restoring the status can be very difficult or impossible for some devices. So deadlock prevention by breaking this condition is not possible.

5.4.1.4 Circular wait

One way to avoid circular wait is by forcing all the threads to request the devices only in an increasing order of enumeration. In this method all the resources are enumerated with a unique integer. Let us assume that there is an enumeration function F() such that F(R1)=N1, F(R2)=N2, F(R3)=N3 and so on, where N1, N2, N3 are unique integers.

With the enumerated numbers fixed and known a priori, all the threads request resources in an increasing order of enumeration. A thread can request a resource only if the enumeration value of new resource is higher than the enumeration value of all the resources it already own. If a thread need a new resource of lower enumeration number during its course of execution, first it has to release all the resources owned by it which have higher enumeration number than the new resource it need. The thread can later rerequest for the resources of higher enumeration number which were released to request the lower enumeration resource.

This method ensures that there is no possibility of circular wait. Let us show the proof using contradiction. Let us assume that there is a circular loop. T1 is waiting for R1 which is held by T2, T2 is waiting for R2 with is held by T3, T3 is waiting for R3 which is held by T4 and so on…. and TN is waiting for RN which is held by T1.

i.e. the resource allocation graph should show the circular loop as shown.

$$T1 \rightarrow R1 \rightarrow T2 \rightarrow R2 \rightarrow T3 \rightarrow R3 \rightarrow \ldots \ldots \ldots \rightarrow TN \rightarrow RN \rightarrow T1 \rightarrow R1$$

Then

$$F(R1) < F(R2) < F(R3) < \ldots \ldots F(RN) < F(R1).$$

So from the above relation $F(R1) < F(R1)$ which is impossible. So a circular wait is impossible when threads request resources in increased order of enumeration.

With this method the resources should be enumerated with natural order of access. For example reading from the network or file system should happen first before displaying on the screen. So F(net work resource) < F(display resource).

5.4.2 Deadlock avoidance

If we allow all four necessary conditions for deadlock in the system, deadlock can happen in the system. The deadlock can be avoided by allocating resources so that there is always a sequence of threads which can be satisfied with the resource requirements one after another with the unallocated and released resources in the system. This sequence is called safe sequence. To make sure that resource requirements of a thread are going to be satisfied, the maximum resource requirements for all the threads should be know a priori. For example the maximum, allocated instances of resources R1, R2, R3 for threads T1, T2, T3 are shown below.

Assume available resources are 5 instances of R1, 5 instances of R2, 5 instances of R3.

Threads	Maximum need (R1, R2, R3)	Currently Allocated(R1, R2, R3)
T1	4, 5, 5	1, 1, 2
T2	1, 2, 2	1, 1, 1
T3	1, 2, 1	1, 1, 1

The table shows T1 has a maximum requirement of 4 instances of R1, 5 instances of R2, 5 instances of R3. But currently it is allocated with and using 1 instance of R1, one instance of R2, 2 instances of R3.

Similarly T2 has a maximum requirement of 1 instance of R1, 2 instances of R2, 2 instances of R3. But currently it is using 1 instance of R1, one instance of R2, 1 instance of R3.

In the same way T3 has a maximum requirement of 1 instance of R1, 2 instances of R2, 1 instance of R3. But currently it is using 1 instance of R1, one instance of R2, 1 instance of R3.

After these allocations 2 instances of R1, 2 instances of R2, 1 instance of R3 are free.

In this scenario we can find a sequence {T3, T2, T1} such that resource requirements can be satisfied sequentially. (Even when the threads make request for maximum resources it need). With the state of current allocation, T3 can only request for 1 instance of R2 at most. This can be satisfied with the free resources in the system. After T3 finishes its execution, there are 3 instances of R1, 3 instances of R2, 2 instances of R3 will be free in the system (i.e. the resources already available + the resources T3 release after its execution). These resources are enough to satisfy the maximum resource requirement of T2 as it can only request for 1 more instance of R2, 1 more instance or R3. After T2 finishes its execution, 4 instances of R1, 4 instances of R2, 3 instances of R3 will be free in the system. These resources are enough to satisfy the maximum resources requirement of T1 too. In this way the resource requirement of all the threads can be satisfied sequentially and all the threads can finish their execution. This sequence is called safe sequence. When we can find a safe sequence in the system the system is said to be in safe state. As long as the system is in safe state, deadlocks are not possible in the system. If we can not find a safe sequence in the system, the system is said to be in unsafe state. An unsafe state may lead to deadlock.

When a resource request is made, OS has to find whether there exist a safe sequence after allocation? If no safe sequence can be found, the allocation can not be made and the requesting thread should wait. If a safe sequence can be found then OS can proceed with allocation of the resources. This way OS can be conservative when allocating the resources to avoid taking the system to unsafe state and probably into deadlock. The disadvantage of this conservativeness is resource under utilization i.e. resources are not utilized to their full extent.

The implementation algorithms and much rigorous discussion of conservative allocation schemes to avoid deadlock are beyond the scope of this book. An excellent discussion on deadlock avoidance techniques and algorithms can be found in Reference-1.

5.4.3 Deadlock detection and recovery

If deadlocks are neither prevented nor avoided, then deadlocks can happen in the system. OS can run a routine periodically or when CPU utilization drops (i.e. when CPU spends significant amount of time in its idle thread) to detect deadlocks. If all the resources are of single instance, a cycle in the resource allocation graph can show the prevalence of deadlock. When there are multiple instances of resources, a cycle is not a sufficient condition for deadlock. (See Section 5.3). So a different algorithm should be used other than cycle detection algorithm to determine if the system is in deadlock when there are resources of multiple instances in the system. Not able to find a resource allocation sequence (a sequence in which resource requirements of all the threads can be satisfied one after another) for all the waiting threads even after considering "all the resources allocated to ready state threads are free resources in the system and ready state threads finished their execution", shows the prevalence of deadlock in the system. Even though these deadlock detection algorithms are part of the kernel, for a simple and medium complex embedded systems, these algorithms in the RTOS can be an over kill. So the implementation of these deadlock detection algorithms are kept out of the scope of this book and can be found in Reference-1.

After detecting the deadlock, the recovery algorithm has to be invoked to recover from the deadlock. A simple and efficient recovery method for embedded systems is to reset the system! A more sophisticated solutions in the general purpose OS are to preempt the resources that are preemptable and cost based termination of processes till the system come out of deadlock or alerting the user for manual intervention.

5.4.4 Manual reset of the system if the system is frozen by deadlock

Another simple solution for deadlocks is to ignore them altogether! When the deadlocks rarely occur (say once in a year) and are acceptable at such low rate, instead of running costly deadlock algorithms it might be better to ignore them altogether. When a deadlock happens in the system, the whole system or some functionality of the system will be frozen and eventually will be restarted manually.

5.5 SROS solution for deadlock avoidance

Implementing deadlock avoidance, recovery algorithms make the SROS more complicated (the complications bring their associated nuisance of bugs and maintenance problems). The best solution for dealing with deadlocks in embedded systems using SROS is to avoid the circular wait condition.

Avoiding circular wait condition can be implemented at application layer similar to priority inversions thus making SROS lean and efficient.

To implement the circular wait avoidance, all the resources in the system should be enumerated with a unique integer. The resources should be requested only in the increasing order of enumeration.

If a thread need a resource with lower enumeration number than any of the resources it own, the thread has to release all the resources with higher enumeration number first before making a request for resource with lower enumeration number. By carefully enumerating the resources with their natural order of access this kind of situations (i.e. need for a resource with lower enumeration number than the maximum enumeration number of the resource the thread own) can be minimized. See section 5.4.1.4 for discussion on avoiding circular wait.

Following this simple enumeration method will straight away avoid the simple and subtle problems of deadlocks that plague the system (which are very difficult to track considering their infrequency) as in the code shown in Figure 5-1.

Reference:

1. Operating System Concepts 6th edition. – By Abraham Silberschatz, Peater Baer Galvin, Greg Gagne. Published by John Wiley & Sons Inc.

Exercise:

1. Show that using the priority ceiling protocol prevent the possibility of deadlock in the system!. Which of the 4 necessary conditions presented in section 5.3 are removed in the system with priority ceiling protocol?.

6 Schedulability of a real-time application

This chapter focuses on the issues of schedulability of a real-time application. In this chapter we discuss the difference between real-time and non real-time application, characterize the soft real-time and hard real-time systems, and develop a formal procedure to determine the schedulability of the threads in a real-time application. (Schedulability means certainty that all the real-time threads can always meet their deadlines)

A real-time application differs from the non real-time application by the definite deadlines it has to meet. A web browsing or email viewing application is an example of non real-time application. In non real-time application, the correct working of the application is governed only by functional correctness, and not by the amount of time it takes to finish its jobs. i.e. as long as it do its job functionally correct the application can work. (Considering the average amount of time it takes most of the times is with in tolerable limits of the user). But in the real-time application the correct operation of the system is not only governed by the functional correctness but also correctness on the time scale. (i.e. all real-time threads should do their job not only functionally correct but also with in the stipulated time). The existence stipulated time limits characterize the application as either real-time or non real-time application.

Again there are two flavors in the real-time systems, Soft real-time and hard-real-time systems. Both soft real-time and hard real-time systems have deadlines to meet. But the penalty to pay for missing a deadline characterizes them as soft real-time or hard real-time systems. If the penalty is too high, a complete catastrophe, or complete system failure for a missed deadline then the system is characterized as the hard real-time system. For example a missile defense system where tracking and destroying an incoming missile has to be done with in the stipulated time otherwise complete catastrophe can occur. Similarly a health care system that continuously makes the patient's heart to beat rhythmically is an example of a hard real-time system. The penalty to pay for the failure to meet deadlines for every heartbeat is huge, and involves human life. In these systems dead lines may have ample time to meet them, but the severity of the deadline (i.e. penalty for the missed deadline) characterizes the system as hard real-time.

The other flavor of real-time systems is soft real-time systems. These types of systems are characterized by the deadlines which are not severe. Not severe does not mean short deadlines on time scale but mean the penalty for missing the deadlines. For example the video-ip-phone application we have seen in chapter 1 is an example of soft real-time application. Failure to display the next frame with in the deadline does not cause the total system failure. The system design that can miss the dead lines is satisfactory if the cost of the system is less for such a design and dead line miss frequency is with in the tolerable limits.

Given the deadlines for the jobs a real-time system has to finish, the priorities assignment of the threads, and the analysis of their execution profile is more complicated in real-time application than non real-time application.

A formal procedure for assigning the priorities and checking whether the system can meet the deadlines is developed by Liu and Laylond in 1973. Their scheduling method is called Rate Monotonic Scheduling (RMS) and their analysis is called Rate Monotonic Analysis (RMA).

The initial RMA by Liu and Laylond (We call it as basic RMA) does not consider the interactions between the threads and priority inversions. Basic RMA is extended to consider interactions between the threads, priority inversions by later researchers. We call it as extended RMA. The extended RMA removes most of the idealized assumptions the basic RMA makes and can be applied to the real-time systems.

6.1 Basic Rate Monotonic Analysis

Before starting discussion let us see the assumptions of rate monotonic analysis.

* All the threads are periodic.

* There is no interaction, blocking due to unavailability resources, priority inversions among the threads.

* Thread switching in the system is instantaneous.

* Each thread has a constant execution time and the execution time does not change with time.

* The deadline for a thread is starting of next period of the thread.

* The thread's priorities are determined by its period. The shorter the execution period of a thread, the higher the priority.

* All the threads in the system are equally critical.

* Aperiodic threads are limited to system initialization and failure recovery and do not have hard deadlines.

Basic Rate monotonic analysis formally proves whether a given set of real-time threads can be schedulable to meet their deadlines if the threads were scheduled using rate monotonic scheduling. Rate Monotonic Scheduling is a priority based preemptive scheduling, in which the threads with the lower periods should be given higher priorities and vice versa. In the Rate Monotonic Scheduling, the priority of the thread is solely determined by its period only with the rule "lower the period higher the priority and vice versa".

If the rate monotonic analysis of the system shows that the threads in the system are schedulable, we can design the system that can meet its deadlines.

When the threads in the system satisfy all the above assumptions stated at the beginning of section 6.1, Liu and Laylond proved that all the threads always meet their deadlines if the following condition for the system is satisfied. (The proof is out of the scope of this book).

$$U = \sum_{i=1}^{i=n} \frac{C_i}{T_i} \le n(2^{1/n} - 1) \dots\dots\dots(1)$$

In the above equation U is called CPU utilization factor. Ui is called CPU utilization factor for ith thread in the system. The Ui is defined as Ci/Ti. Where Ci is the execution time of the thread. Ti is the period of the thread. Ci/Ti denotes the CPU utilization factor for the ith thread(i.e. Ui). n is the total number of threads in the system.

In essence, equation (1) denotes that the threads in a real-time system will always meet their deadlines when the sum of CPU utilization factors of all the threads is less than or equal to $n(2^{1/n} - 1)$ where n is the number of threads in the system.

For a system with only one thread, CPU utilization factor can be 100% to meet its deadlines. For a system with 2 threads the maximum allowed CPU utilization factor is 82.8% and for a system with 3 threads the maximum allowed CPU utilization factor is 77.9%. As n tends to infinite, the maximum allowed CPU utilization factor reaches a limit. As n tends to infinite the maximum limit for the CPU utilization reaches to 69.3% (see equation 2).

$$Lt_{n->\infty} n(2^{1/n} - 1) = \log_e(2) = 0.693147 \dots\dots\dots(2)$$

Rate monotonic analysis does not say that if a system with more CPU utilization factor than the RMA bound can not meet its dead lines. It only state that if a real-time system with CPU utilization factor less than RMA bound will meet its deadlines. A system with CPU utilization factor more than RMA bound may also meet the dead lines depending on the execution times and periods of its threads.

First let us see the importance of giving the threads of lower period with higher priority. Consider a simple real-time system with two threads, thread1 and thread2. Let us assume that C1=100, T1=200, C2=10, T2=50. The CPU utilization factor U=U1+U2=0.5+0.2=0.7. If we give thread1 higher priority than thread2, thread1 will hog the CPU for long time and thread2 will miss the deadlines during the period when CPU is given to thread1. If we give thread 2 higher priority (i.e. following rate monotonic scheduling) both the threads can meet the deadlines.

Now consider a system with two threads with C1=25, T1=50, C2=30, T2=75. The CPU utilization factor U=U1+U2=0.5+0.4=0.9. CPU utilization is greater than RMA CPU utilization bound. RMA can not guarantee whether the system can meet its deadlines. One may at first naively think that the system has CPU utilization factor less than 100% so it can meet the deadlines. But indeed this system can not meet its deadlines. Let us see with the execution profile whether the system can meet its deadlines. Assume that the period of both the threads start at 0. The time periods 0-50, 51-100, 101-150 are periods for thread1. The time periods 0-75, 76-150 are periods for thread2. Thread1 has higher priority than thread2 because it has smaller period.

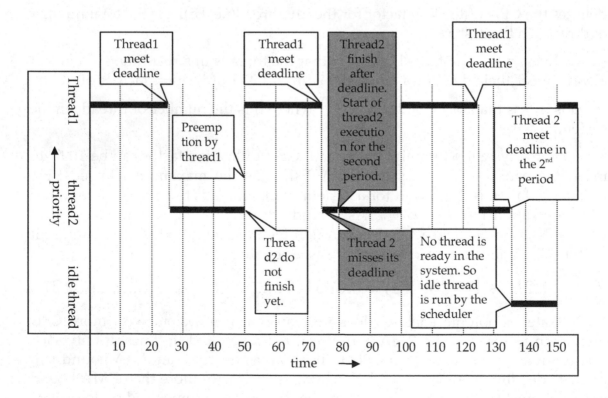

Figure 6-1

In Figure 6-1, thread1, thread2 both are ready from the time instant 0. As thread1 has higher priority than thread2, CPU is given to thread1. When thread1 finishes its execution at time instant 25, scheduler gives the CPU to thread2. Thread2 execute for 25 time units, and at time instant 50, it is preempted by thread1 as thread 1 become ready for its second period. Thread1 execute for 25 time units. After thread1 finishes its execution during its second period, CPU is allocated back to thread2 at time instant 75. Thread2 finishes remaining processing in its first period by time instant 80. Thread2 has to finish its execution by time instant 75 but it missed its deadline. At time instant 80 thread2 is again active for its 2nd round of execution. At time instant 100, it is again preempted by thread1 which is ready for its 3rd period. After thread1 finishes its execution for its 3rd period CPU is given back to thread2. Thread2 meet its deadline during its 2nd period. When no thread is ready at time instant 135, scheduler runs the idle thread to keep the CPU busy. From time instant 150 to 300 the execution profile is same as the execution profile from 0 to 150. The execution profile repeat endlessly with out any modification. From this execution profile it is clear that thread2 will miss half of its deadlines! If the CPU utilization factor kept below are equal to the RMA CPU utilization bound, the problem of missing deadlines shown in Figure 6-1 will never occur.

Actually it should be theoretically possible to meet deadlines when the sum of CPU utilization factors of the threads is below 100%. This is indeed possible if RTOS can assign priorities dynamically and schedule them accordingly instead of scheduling based on static priorities. With dynamic priority allocation, RTOS can assign higher priority to thread2 at the time instant 50 in the Figure 6-1 thus preventing the preemption of thread2. Preemption of thread2 at time instant 50 is the cause of the deadline miss for thread2. If thread 2 is allowed to execute continuously, both thread1, thread2 would have met their deadlines comfortably in the scenario in Figure 6-1.

Obviously the dynamic priority assignment is more complex than static assignment of priorities. So all commercial RTOSes (and also SROS) support only static assignment of priorities. This means the priorities will not be changed by RTOS during the course of execution to meet the deadlines.

If a system can not be schedulable by Rate Monotonic Scheduling, the system obviously can not be schedulable with any other static priority assignment.

If the period of the thread2 in Figure 6-1 is integer multiple of thread1, both thread1 and thread2 can meet the deadlines. If there are more than 2 real-time threads in the system, their periods should be such that when all the threads are arranged in ascending order of their periods, the period of a thread should be integer multiple of its immediate preceding thread to meet the deadlines when the CPU utilization factor is more than the RMA CPU utilization bound.

In a real-time system the CPU processing power left after the RMA CPU utilization bound can be used by non real-time threads safely. For example in a system with 10 real-time threads the RMA CPU utilization bound of the real-time threads is 71.7%. So the rest i.e. at least 28.3% of the CPU time can be used by non real-time threads in the system (assuming CPU is fully utilized after real-time threads finish their execution).

A simple example system with 4 real-time threads with their execution times and period is shown in Figure 6-2. Their Rate Monotonic priority assignment and analysis is shown below.

Thread name	Execution time(m.sec)	Period(m.sec)
Thread 1	20	100
Thread 2	2	26
Thread 3	15	107
Thread 4	30	240

Figure 6-2

Rate monotonic analysis:

Rate monotonic priority assignment: Thread 2, Tread 1, Thread 3, Thread 4 from highest priority to lowest priority. (Using the rule lower the period higher the priority).

The CPU utilization factor = $U = U_1+U_2+U_3+U_4 = (20/100) + (2/26) + (15/107) + (30/240) = 0.2 + 0.077 + 0.140 + 0.125 = 0.542$.

The CPU utilization factor U (i.e. 0.542) is less than RMA bound for 4 threads (i.e. 0.756). So the given system is schedulable using the Rate Monotonic Scheduling.

We should note that according to the Rate monotonic analysis whatever be the number of real-time threads, if the CPU utilization bound is less than 0.693 (which is CPU utilization bound when the number of real-time threads is infinite) the system is schedulable.

6.2 Extended Rate Monotonic Analysis

The basic Rate Monotonic Analysis makes many idealized assumptions. The assumption that the threads do not interact, do not get blocked due to unavailability of resources, do not experience priority inversions is far from true in many real-time systems. So the basic rate monotonic analysis has to be extended to remove these assumptions.

This section assumes priority ceiling protocol is implemented in RTOS to avoid extended priority inversion. (See chapter 4). When priority ceiling protocol is implemented no resource request can take the thread into waiting state due to the unavailability of resource. The resource request by any thread is always successful. But a thread can experience priority inversion when it or any higher priority thread(s) than it share resource(s) with thread(s) of lower priority than it. Due to the priority inversion CPU may not be immediately available to a thread when it becomes ready to run.

This section also assumes that there is no possibility of deadlock in the system. If the deadlocks are possible in the system, it is not possible to schedule the system to meet the real-time deadlines. Using the priority ceiling protocol effectively eliminate the possibility of deadlocks in the system.(See exercises of chapter 5).

When the resources are shared by different priority threads (which is the prime reason for priority inversion) we can not deal with all the threads aggregately. Instead extended rate monotonic analysis deal with one thread at a time to know whether it can meet its deadlines.

Let us first consider the highest priority thread in the system to analyze whether it can meet its deadlines. It can be observed that the highest priority thread can always preempt the lower priority threads and occupy the CPU as long as it do not share any resources with lower priority threads. When there are no constraints to preempt other threads, we can calculate whether the highest priority thread can meet its deadlines by giving 100% CPU time to it. When it share some resource(s) with lower priority threads, the lower priority threads can get the same priority as the highest priority thread when they lock the shared resource because of priority ceiling protocol. In such a case the highest priority thread in the system can not preempt the lower priority threads (infact the lower priority thread's priority also elevated to the same level of highest priority thread when it locked the resource that it share with highest priority thread). The maximum amount of time the highest priority thread can not preempt a lower priority thread is the CPU time not available to the highest priority thread. If the highest priority thread can finish its execution before the deadline even after allowing the time lost to lower priority thread due to priority inversion, then we can conclude that the highest priority thread can meet the deadlines in the system.

The similar analysis can be extended from the perspective of middle, lower priority threads to conclude whether they can meet their deadlines. For middle, lower priority threads in the system we have to consider not only the time lost by them due to priority inversion but also the CPU time they have conceded to threads of higher priority than them.

Let *thread1, thread2,.. threadn* have priority ranks 1, 2,..n respectively in the system. (Priority rank means the position it occupies when the threads are sorted from highest priority to lowest priority with priorities assigned according to rate monotonic scheduling). Let priority inversion time for *threadn* (b_n) is defined as the maximum amount of time any lower priority thread than *threadn*, elevated to equal or higher priority level compared to *threadn*. Even though a thread will never get blocked (go to waiting state due to the unavailability of resource) with priority ceiling protocol, we call the priority inversion time as blocking time. The blocking factor for threadn is defined as the ratio of maximum blocking time (i.e. b_n) to its period (T_n).

After removing the blocking time (b_n) as unavailable CPU time to *threadn*, during its period, we can apply the basic rate monotonic analysis to conclude whether the threadn can meet its deadlines with all other higher priority threads than *threadn* present in the system. i.e. We can conclude that, if

$$(\sum_{i=1}^{i=n} \frac{C_i}{T_i} + \frac{b_n}{T_n}) \leq n(2^{1/n} - 1)\dots\dots\dots\dots\dots\dots\dots(3)$$

Then the threadn will always meet its dead lines. In equation (3) the term $\frac{b_n}{T_n}$ denote the fraction of time (in one period) lost due to priority inversion. The equation (3) can be applied to all the threads in the system to see whether all the threads can meet their deadlines.

For example consider a simple real-time system with 3 real-time threads and 2 resources as shown in Figure 6-3.

In Figure 6-3, rectangles denote the threads, and ovals denote the resources. The arrows denote the resources needed for the threads during their execution. Thread1 has an execution time of 25 units and has a period of 100 units. Thread1 share Resource2 with thread2, thread3. Thread1, Thread2, Thread3 use the resource2 for 20, 25, 30 time units respectively. The maximum amount of time thread1 can be waiting for CPU is 30 time units. (When the resource2 is locked by thread3 and thread3 elevated to the same priority level as thread1). Thread2 has a period of 25 units, and a period of 150 units. Thread2 uses both resource1 and resource2.

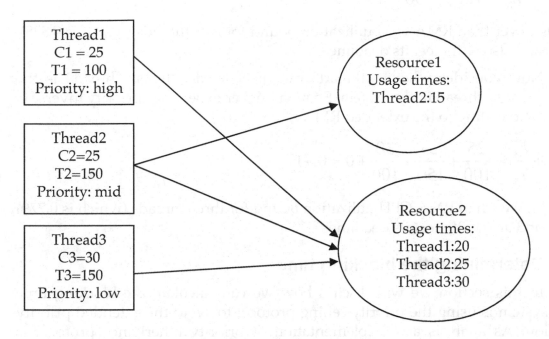

Figure 6-3

Thread2 can wait for CPU by a maximum amount of 30 time units. (When thread3 lock the resource and elevated to higher priority level than thread2). Thread3 has execution time of 30 units, and a period of 150 units. Thread3 use resource 2 for 30 time units during its execution time. Note that thread3 will never experience priority inversion. (As thread3 is the lowest priority thread in the system).

Note that the priorities for the threads are assigned such that the system follow Rate monotonic scheduling (lower the period, higher the priority).

Now consider whether thread1 can meet its deadlines. Thread1 has CPU utilization factor of (25/100) and a blocking factor of (30/100). (Note that $b_1=30$). According to extended RMA

$$\sum_{i=1}^{i=1} \frac{C_i}{T_i} + \frac{b_1}{T_1} = \frac{25}{100} + \frac{30}{100} = 0.55$$

0.55 is less than RMA CPU utilization bound for 1 thread. (i.e. 100%). So thread1 will always meet its dead lines.

Now consider whether thread2 can meet its deadlines. Thread1, thread2 have CPU utilization factors of (25/100), (25/150) respectively. Thread2 has a blocking factor of (30/150). (Note that $b_2=30$). According to extended RMA

$$\sum_{i=1}^{i=2} \frac{C_i}{T_i} + \frac{b_2}{T_2} = \frac{25}{100} + \frac{25}{150} + \frac{30}{100} = 0.717$$

0.717 is lower than RMA CPU utilization bound for two threads (which is 0.828). So thread2 also will meet its deadlines.

Now consider whether thread3 can meet its deadlines. Thread3 is the lowest priority thread in the system. So it will never experience priority inversion. So b_3=0. According to the extended RMA

$$\sum_{i=1}^{i=3} \frac{Ci}{Ti} + \frac{b_3}{T_3} = \frac{25}{100} + \frac{25}{150} + \frac{30}{100} + 0 = 0.717$$

0.717 is lower than RMA CPU utilization bound for three threads (which is 0.779). So thread3 also will meet its deadlines.

6.2.1 Determining the blocking time

In this section we will discuss how we can calculate the blocking time when system is using the priority ceiling protocol to avoid the extended priority inversion. As analysis and implementation of priority inheritance protocol is complex, and also SROS does not support priority inheritance protocol, we discuss only priority ceiling protocol.

From the example in Figure 6-3, it looks at the first instant, blocking time of a thread can be computed easily from the resources a thread share with lower priority threads than it. But a middle priority thread which does not share any resources with other threads, may still need to wait for CPU time when two threads one with equal or priority higher than it, and another with priority lower than it share a resource in the system. The waiting for lower priority thread happens when the lower priority thread's priority artificially elevated to avoid extended priority inversion. For example see a sample system with just 3 threads and 1 resource. The higher priority thread, lower priority thread share the resource. The medium priority thread does not share any resources with other threads. Assume the priority ceiling protocol is used in the system. Assume *thread3* acquired the resource. When ever *thread3* acquires the resource, its priority is increased to the priority level of *thread1*. (As the resource is shared by *thread1* too). Assume *thread2* became ready to run after *thread3* is allocated with the resource. Now *thread2* can not preempt *thread3* and will experience a maximum blocking time of 30 time units due to *thread3*.

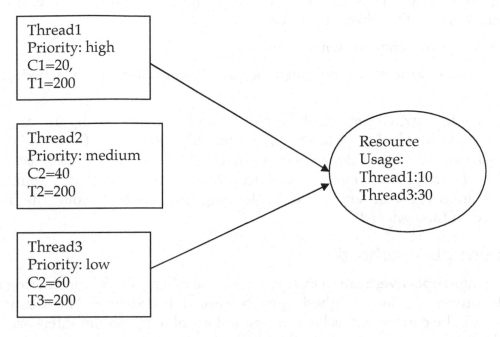

Figure 6-4

The maximum blocking time of *threadi* due to threads of lower priority than it is equal to the maximum of time durations in which any thread of lower priority than *threadi* can hold any resource which makes its priority level equal to or higher priority level than that of *threadi*. The blocking time of a thread *threadi* is given in the equation below.

$$b_i = Max(t_{k,s})$$

Where $t_{k,s}$ is the amount of time *threadk* whose priority is lower than *threadi*, hold a resource lock S which can make its priority equal or higher than *threadi*. In the above equation k in $t_{k,s}$ belongs to set of all the threads of lower priority than *threadi*, and S belongs to set of all resource locks whose acquiring can make a thread's priority equal or higher than the *threadi*.

6.2.2 Consideration for Scheduling overhead

Another assumption of basic RMA which is far from true is "task switching is instantaneous". In real systems, the thread switching time depend on the amount of context(i.e. number of processor registers and status) need to be saved to and retrieved from memory. Each thread causes one context switch for its execution during its one period. Note that following the priority ceiling protocol all the resource requests are always successful. There will not be any context switch when requesting the resources. So all the context switches occur for starting the execution of a thread in its period. So effectively the context switching overhead can be added to the execution time of the thread. So effective C_i after adjusting for the scheduling overhead is

$C_i \bullet = C_i$ + one context switch time.

Where $C_i \bullet$ is the execution time of a thread after adjusting for scheduling overheads.

The context switch time can be divided into two parts. Saving the context to either a *readyList*, *waitList* or *timerList*, and loading the context from *readyList*. Time for saving the context depends on number of threads in *readyList*, *waitList* or *timerList*. Loading the context into the processor takes constant amount of time.(as it involves constant work of loading the context from the first threadObject in the *readyList*).

6.2.3 Interrupts overhead

The interrupts overhead in the system can be taken care by considering all interrupts processing as a highest priority thread processing. The fictitious threads should be considered as having a period equal to minimum inter- arrival time of the interrupts and the execution time equal to the interrupt processing time.

6.2.4 Timer overhead

The timer overhead can also be considered as interrupt overhead. But the problem with timer interrupt handling is that the execution time is not constant. The amount of processing time depends on the number of threads using the timer. In worst case the processing time is equal to moving all the threads using the timer from *timerList* to the *readyList*.

worst case timer interrupt processing time = minimum timer interrupt service routine overhead + execution time for moving one thread from *timeList* to *readyList* * number of threads using the timer.

The timer interrupt processing is considered as fictitious highest priority thread processing with period equal to one tick time, and execution time equal to its worst case execution time.

6.2.5 Consideration for aperiodic events

In the real-time systems the aperiodic real-time events processing should be considered as periodic events processing with the period equal to their minimum inter arrival time, and the execution time as the execution time needed to process one aperiodic event.

7 Other components of RTOS

All RTOSes should have kernels. We have discussed services of kernel to real-time systems in the earlier chapters. Apart from the kernel services, many real-time systems need many common services such as network access, file systems, I/O subsystem etc. In this chapter we discuss few aspects about the network stack (i.e. Internet Protocol stack), file system, I/O subsystem. Many RTOSes implement kernel, network stack, and file system, I/O subsystems as independent units to have scalability, ease of development, configuration and maintenance. The network stack, file system, I/O subsystem and other RTOS modules, all use kernel services like any other application for synchronization and scheduling. All these modules outside the kernel are usually developed with out worrying about the implementation of the kernel like any embedded application that uses the kernel.

7.1 I/O sub system

Embedded systems have a variety of input output devices. The I/O devices vary widely in their operation, and characteristics across the span of embedded systems. Even in a single system there can be many I/O devices which are unique and all need to be handled differently. For example the video-ip-phone system we have seen in chapter 2, has key pad, touch screen, mic, speaker, camera, lcd as I/O devices.

The objective of I/O sub system of RTOSes is to provide a unified access mechanism to these varieties of I/O devices where each kind of device is unique among themselves!.

The unified access mechanism is desirable, as this provides the application developers the same set of application interface to handle any type of I/O device. The application developer need not worry about the physical properties and internal operation of the I/O device. All he needs to do is to use the API's provided by the RTOS to handle the device. This makes the job of developing and maintaining the application easy when compared to handling each I/O device in a different way. Another advantage of using unified I/O access mechanism is to make the application easily portable across different I/O devices. i.e. for example changing the I/O device just need changing the device driver, and there will be minimal or no changes in the application code.

Anyway some body need to understand physical properties of the device and develop the code to configure the device correctly (In case of multiple instances, specific device has to be recognized before configuration), send data to device, receive data from the device, and issue various commands to control the device operation. The code that does these operations is called device driver. From the device driver developer perspective, the I/O operations involve configuring the device, controlling the device, sending and receiving data from the device. On the other hand from the perspective of Application developer, I/O operation involves just set of API's provided by RTOS to control the I/O device operation. RTOS acts as mediator to communicate the unified I/O operations visible to the application developer to the I/O operations of the device driver(which are unique to the device).

The software structure of an embedded application with kernel and I/O subsystem is shown in Figure 7-1.

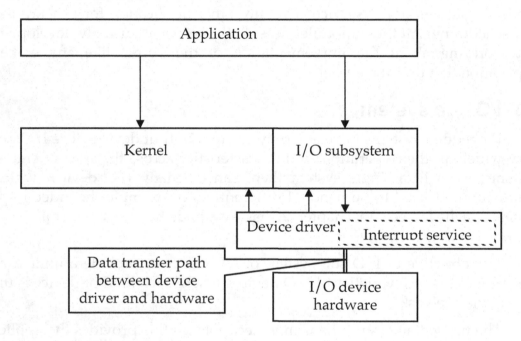

Figure 7-1

For the arrangement shown in Figure 7-1 to work, the responsibilities are divided among the modules as shown below.

- The I/O subsystem defines the I/O access API set.

- The Device driver implements each function defined by the I/O subsystem API set.

- The device driver and the device association (usually the name of the device) are loaded by the application with a standard I/O subsystem API.

Once the application loads the device driver into the I/O subsystem, the device is ready to be operated with the I/O subsystem APIs. The I/O subsystem APIs are usually similar to the file operations in C language. In fact, file operations are one kind of input output operations.

7.1.1 Methods of data transfer between device driver and I/O device

The I/O devices are usually either port mapped or memory mapped.

Port mapping also called IO mapped I/O. Port mapping means, the I/O devices are kept in a separate address space than processor memory space. For some embedded processors with system on chip designs, they may not even share the address and data busses with processor memory. When the I/O devices are external to the processor, they usually share the address and data busses with memory but will be in different address space (usually called I/O space) anyway. The devices are accessed(i.e. data transmitted to and received from devices) with special instructions like IN, OUT on Intel processors. The advantage of this kind of I/O device access is, memory space will not be lost because of I/O devices.

For memory mapped I/O devices, the I/O devices share the processor memory space. I/O device share the same buses that processor use for memory access. The communication with I/O device is done in the same way as reading and writing memory. As the I/O device is sharing the memory space, all instructions that access memory can be used to access the I/O device. The disadvantage of memory mapped I/O is, loosing memory space and special care needed such as not caching, not combining consecutive writes into memory space as single write operation etc... that were usually done by "write buffers" if they exist in the system.

Direct memory access(DMA) is another mechanism in which a special hardware module is used to transfer data to from memory to the I/O device directly, without CPU copying each memory word at a time. The DMA unit share busses with memory, I/O device. The DMA unit is configured by the device driver to transfer the data between the I/O device and memory. The I/O device can be either memory mapped or port mapped. As there is no processor intervention in the data transfer, the data transfer is faster than the data transfer that can be done by CPU instructions. Usually DMA is used by I/O devices that need to transfer large chunks of data, like disk drives, or audio, video devices etc.

7.1.2 Typical API's available to application from I/O subsystem

The typical Application interfaces available to application from I/O subsystem are simple and similar to the file operations available in C language. Before using the file, we have to ask the OS that we need to open the file in read, write, or read/write mode. The OS gives the file handle with which one can perform read/write operations. After the file operations are complete, file is closed.

The similar API's are usually available from I/O subsystem of a typical RTOS. In fact, file is one kind of input output device. The typical functions are

Create() – Creates an instance of I/O device in to the I/O subsystem. This function is like installing the device driver into the I/O subsystem, making the I/O subsystem know about the existence of a device. The I/O subsystem will prepare the device for subsequent operations. This function will install interrupt service routine if needed, and configure the device to a known state.

Open() – Opens the device for use. The *open()* function returns the handle with which subsequent read/write/control operations can be performed on the device. This system call also provides another opportunity for the device driver to configure the device to a known state. This system call will call the *device_open()* routine available in the device driver. The caller of the *open()* system call is not needed to know how to configure the device or whether to get the lock for the device. The I/O subsystem and *device_open()* routines will take care of those. If the device open fails, error code will be returned. In case of non sharable device, the device is locked and will not be available for other threads in the system.

Read() – This operation reads data from the device. The caller just specifies the amount of data he wants to read. The device operations are completely isolated from the application. If the read fails, an error code will be returned.

Write() – This operation writes the specified amount of data to the device. Similar to *read()*, the caller is isolated from the device operations. If the write() fails, the error code will be returned.

IO_control() – This system request is used to control the operation of the device. A simple control operation of serial port can be used to change the baud rate. A video display device might have control operation to change the frame rate etc..

Close() – This function closes the device .The handle given by the I/O subsystem will become invalid and no I/O request should be made with that handle. The device can be readily opened and used by other threads.

Destroy() – This function is opposite of the *create()* function. This function removes the instance of I/O device from the I/O subsystem.

7.1.3 Typical device driver responsibilities

The device driver should implement the actual core functionalities that access and control the device say, *device_open()*, *device_read()*, *device_write()*, *device_control()*, *device_close()*. These functions are mapped to API's for the device instance that exists in the I/O subsystem through the *create()* system call. After creating the device instance through the *create()* system, the application can use the I/O subsystem API's to access the device.

7.2 Network stack

The Network stack implements Transmission Control Protocol, Internet Protocol (TCP/IP) which form the core of the internet, and simple protocols like SNMP, FTP etc. and many other user level protocols. The TCP/IP stack usually have Berkeley socket interface to the application. The Berkeley socket interface is just a set of API's to open/close connections and send/receive packets. All the applications that need network access use this interface. The network stack has the interface to attach seamlessly to the underlying kernel for scheduling and synchronization services, and a hardware independent interface to attach to the physical hardware. So the network stack can be used with different types of kernels, and any kind of hardware like an Ethernet, ISDN or ADSL modem. TCP/IP stack vendors usually provide an interface to configure many parameters of TCP/IP stack.

The position of the TCP/IP stack in the system is shown in Figure 7-2.

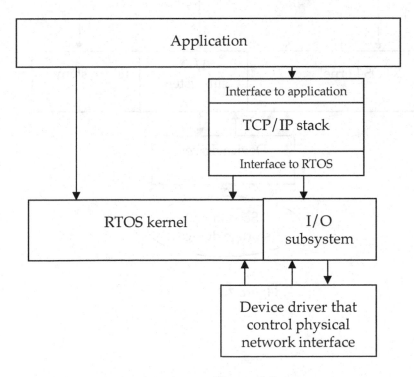

Figure 7-2

154

7.3 File System

The file system is one of the important modules in RTOS. The file system module structures the storage space of secondary storage device according to the supported file system format (for example floppy disks, hard disks, flash memories are usually managed with MS-DOS FAT file system format). The structured storage space is used to store the files in it. Each file is usually divided into chunks of data according to the file system format. The management information of these chunks of data is also stored into the same secondary storage device according to the file system format by the file system module of RTOS. The file system module support creation, deletion, reading, writing of the files, creation and deletion of directories in this structured storage space. The file system modules will in turn use kernel, I/O subsystem services to carryout the file related operations. The typical position file system module with RTOS kernel is shown in Figure 7-3.

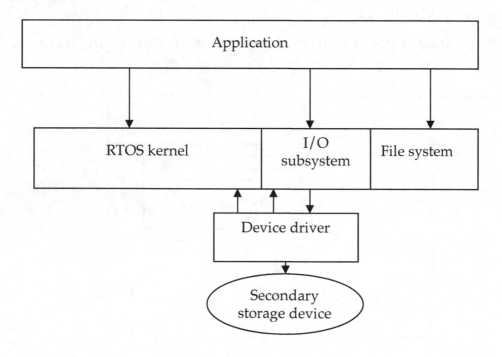

Figure 7-3

8 Appendix-A Brief note on ARM-V5 architecture

ARM-V5 architecture is improved version of ARM-V4 architecture. In this document it is simply referred as ARM architecture. ARM core or ARM processor referred in this appendix to refer to the hardware built using the ARM architecture. This appendix is a brief introduction to the ARM architecture. For comprehensive and authoritative details, refer to the ARM architecture reference manual.

ARM architecture is a typical example of RISC architecture. It has 16 registers (R0-R15) available at any point of time on which all arithmetic and logical instructions operate on. The register R15 is used as program counter and can not be used as a general purpose register. So R15 is also referred as program counter (PC). Nevertheless PC is used in some instructions. Writing the PC causes branch to the written address. Reading the PC gives the address corresponding to the current instruction[1].

R14 register is used as return address register. This register is also called as link register(LR). When ever a function/subroutine is called the return address is passed to the called function in R14 register. R14 or LR register can be used as a general purpose register. To use LR as a general purpose register, the called function should save the LR on the stack and retrieve it at a later point of time to return correctly to the parent function. When ever an interrupt/exception occur, the address of the next instruction will be saved to the banked LR register corresponding to the processor mode of the interrupt/exception (See processor modes in the next section).

R13 register is used as stack pointer. So this register is also called as SP. By software convention, ARM compiler operate stack in "Full Descending" mode. "Full" means, SP always point to a recently pushed content on the stack. "Descending" means, SP should be decremented as the new values are pushed into the stack. In Full descending mode, pushing a register on the stack means, decrementing SP and then storing the register on the stack. Popping the register means loading the register with the content at the memory pointed by SP and then incrementing SP afterwards. (There are 3 other modes possible. "Empty Descending", "Full Ascending", "Empty Ascending").

---

[1] When PC is read in an instruction (for example in an arithmetic instruction) the (instruction address + 8) or (instruction address + 12) is read depending on the version of the ARM core in ARM state. The (instruction address + 4) or (instruction address + 6) is read in Thumb state.

The rest of the registers R0-R12 are used as general purpose registers. They do not have any special purpose.

ARM has a status register called as CPSR (current program status register). This register holds the status of the CPU. The anatomy of the register is shown in Figure 8-1.

31	30	29	28	27	26		8	7	6	5	4	3	2	1	0
N	Z	C	V	Q				I	F	T	M4	M3	M2	M1	M0

Figure 8-1

N – This bit is set to 1 when the result of the arithmetic/logic instruction result is negative value and to 0 otherwise.

Z – This bit is set to 1 when the result of the arithmetic/logic instruction result is zero and to 0 otherwise.

C – This bit is set to 1 when the addition result produce a carry or successful subtraction without a barrow and to 0 otherwise. This bit is also effected by leftshift of a register or rotation through carry operations. This bit usually will not be effected for other operations.

V – This bit is set to 1 when the addition/subtraction resulted in overflow. For non addition/subtraction instructions this bit will be left unchanged.

Q – This bit is a sticky bit used in ARM core with DSP (Digital Signal Processing) extensions. This bit is set to 1 during overflow in DSP extension instructions. This bit can only be manually reset to 0 by writing to CPSR. DSP extension instructions are not necessary for SROS and not used.

I – When this bit is set to 1, the IRQ interrupt (normal interrupt) will be masked.

F – When this bit is set to 1, the FIQ interrupt (fast interrupt) will be masked.

T – This bit indicates the processor state. 0 denote ARM state, 1 denote THUMB state. In the ARM state, all the instructions are executed as ARM instructions(which are 32bits in length). In THUMB state, all the instructions are executed as specialized THUMB instructions(which are 16 bit in length). Changing this bit by changing the CPSR register is not allowed. This bit should be changed automatically with specialized instructions such BX, BLX etc...or by writing the SPSR (Saved Program Status Register) to CPSR. The THUMB instructions are less flexible compared to ARM instructions due to their limited field space for operands. So more number of THUMB instructions are needed compared to ARM instructions to perform the same task. Anyway THUMB state provide higher code density and program space-execution time trade off.

M – This is a 5 bit field and specify the processor mode. There are 7 processor modes defined. See the processor modes in Figure 8-3 for the modes defined depending on the M field value.

The CPSR is divided into 4 fields. Bits 31-24 are referred as Flag bits. Bits 23-16 are referred as status bits. Bits 15-8 are referred as extension bits. Bits 7-0 are referred as control bits. Status and extension bits are empty and reserved for future use. The instructions that change the CPSR or SPSRs (Saved Program Status Registers) (see processor modes) of privileged modes provide the provision to change one or a combination of these 4 fields without effecting other bits in the CPSR or SPSR.

ARM has 5 SPSR registers corresponding to 5 privileged exception modes(See processor modes in next section). When an exception occurs, the CPSR is copied to SPSR of the corresponding exception mode. CPSR control bits are automatically changed to reflect the current processor mode, processor state is changed to ARM state and the I, F bits are affected depending on the type of exception. When the processor return from the exception handler, the SPSR is copied back to CPSR so that original mode, state, interrupt masks of the processor will be restored.

8.1 Processor modes

6 different privileged processor modes other than user mode are defined for convenience and to speed up the execution of interrupt/exception handlers. User mode is non privileged mode and all other modes are privileged modes. When ever a processor is in privileged mode, the banked registers corresponding to that mode will be used by the instructions instead of the registers in the user mode. The banked registers are separate physical registers active only when the processor is in the corresponding mode. See Figure 8-2 for the processor registers available in all the modes. For example in interrupt (IRQ) mode, the R0-R12 registers are same physical registers as user/system mode registers. But R13_irq, R14_irq registers are used in place of R13, R14 available in user/system mode. The R13_irq, R14_irq registers are physically different registers that replace R13, R14 for all instructions executed in IRQ mode. All the banked registers are referred with "register name_<mode>". Figure 8-3 shows the mode bits in CPSR, processor mode name, and the corresponding registers accessible in that processor mode. System mode does not have any banked registers and use the same registers as user mode.

Changing the mode by changing the CPSR is prohibited in User mode. Changing the processor mode, interrupts masks is only allowed from privileged modes. When user mode tries to execute privileged instructions such as changing the processor mode, an exception will be raised. An exception is also raised when ever any errors like memory abort occurs or interrupt request is given to the processor.

When ever an exception occurs, the CPSR is written into the SPSR_<mode> register. The processor mode in CPSR is changed to the corresponding mode for the exception and the processor state is changed to ARM state. R14_<mode> is written corresponding to the address of the next instruction to be executed after handling the interrupt/exception. R13_<mode> is used as the stack pointer during the exception handling. So the user/system mode R13, R14 will not be effected because of the exception. It should be noted that the exception handler will run in a different stack space as R13 is banked for all processor modes which are entered due to interrupt/exception. After handling the interrupt/exception, program return using the address stored in R14_<mode> and restoring the SPSR_<mode> to CPSR thus restoring the previous processor mode and state before exception has occurred.

Modes						
	Privileged modes →					
		Exception modes →				
User	**System**	**Supervisor**	**Abort**	**Undefined**	**Interrupt**	**Fast interrupt**
R0	R0	R0	R0	R0	R0	R0
R1	R1	R1	R1	R1	R1	R1
R2	R2	R2	R2	R2	R2	R2
R3	R3	R3	R3	R3	R3	R3
R4	R4	R4	R4	R4	R4	R4
R5	R5	R5	R5	R5	R5	R5
R6	R6	R6	R6	R6	R6	R6
R7	R7	R7	R7	R7	R7	R7
R8	R8	R8	R8	R8	R8	R8_fiq
R9	R9	R9	R9	R9	R9	R9_fiq
R10	R10	R10	R10	R10	R10	R10_fiq
R11	R11	R11	R11	R11	R11	R11_fiq
R12	R12	R12	R12	R12	R12	R12_fiq
R13	R13	R13_svc	R13_abt	R13_und	R13_irq	R13_fiq
R14	R14	R14_svc	R14_abt	R14_und	R14_irq	R14_fiq
PC	PC	PC	PC	PC	PC	PC

CPSR	CPSR	CPSR	CPSR	CPSR	CPSR	CPSR
		SPSR_svc	SPSR_abt	SPSR_und	SPSR_irq	SPSR_fiq

◺ indicates that the normal register used by User or System mode has been replaced by an alternative register specific to the exception mode

Figure 8-2

M[4:0]	Mode	Accessible registers
0b10000	User	PC, R14 to R0, CPSR
0b10001	FIQ	PC, R14_fiq to R8_fiq, R7 to R0, CPSR, SPSR_fiq
0b10010	IRQ	PC, R14_irq, R13_irq, R12 to R0, CPSR, SPSR_irq
0b10011	Supervisor	PC, R14_svc, R13_svc, R12 to R0, CPSR, SPSR_svc
0b10111	Abort	PC, R14_abt, R13_abt, R12 to R0, CPSR, SPSR_abt
0b11011	Undefined	PC, R14_und, R13_und, R12 to R0, CPSR, SPSR_und
0b11111	System	PC, R14 to R0, CPSR (ARM architecture v4 and above)

Note: 0b prefix denote binary number. (The same way as 0x denote hexadecimal number).

Figure 8-3

8.2 Exceptions

Exceptions are generated by internal and external sources to cause the processor to handle an event, such as externally generated interrupt, an attempt to execute an undefined instruction or a memory abort etc... The processor state just before handling the exception is preserved so that the original program can be resumed when the exception routine has completed.

ARM supports 7 types of exceptions. Figure 8-4 lists the types of exceptions and the processor mode that is used to process the exception. When the exception occurs, execution is forced from a fixed memory address corresponding to the type of exception. These fixed addresses are called exception vectors. Figure 8-4 shows the exception vector addresses.

Exception type	Mode	Normal address	High vector address
Reset	Supervisor	0x00000000	0xFFFF0000
Undefined instructions	Undefined	0x00000004	0xFFFF0004
Software interrupt (SWI)	Supervisor	0x00000008	0xFFFF0008
Prefetch Abort (instruction fetch memory abort)	Abort	0x0000000C	0xFFFF000C
Data Abort (data access memory abort)	Abort	0x00000010	0xFFFF0010
IRQ (interrupt)	IRQ	0x00000018	0xFFFF0018
FIQ (fast interrupt)	FIQ	0x0000001C	0xFFFF001C

Figure 8-4

The Normal addresses or high vector addresses are configurable input to the ARM core. Once this input to the ARM core during the design process is configured, the address locations will be fixed.

When an exception occurs, the banked versions of R14, SPSR for that exception mode are used to save the state as follows.

R14_<mode> = return address.

SPSR_<mode> = CPSR.

CPSR[4:0] = exception mode number as shown in Figure 8-3.

CPSR[5] = 0   /*execution start in ARM mode after exception*/

If (exception mode = = RESET or FIQ) then

CPSR[6] = 1 /*disable the fast interrupts*/

CPSR[7] = 1 /*disable the normal interrupts*/

PC = exception vector address.

To return after handling the exception, the SPSR is moved to CPSR, and R14 is moved to the PC thus restoring the original state of the processor. This can be done in two ways.

- Using the data processing instruction with the S bit set, and the PC as the destination. (see ARM Instruction set).

- Using the Load Multiple with Restore CPSR instruction, as described in LDM(3) instruction. (See ARM Instruction set).

8.3 ARM Instruction set

As all of the SROS, HAL is presented in this book in ARM assembly, only ARM state instructions are enough and THUMB state instructions are not necessary to understand the SROS HAL for ARM platform. So only ARM state instructions are presented in this appendix. As the coprocessor instructions, DSP extension instructions are not used in SROS HAL, they were not presented in this appendix.

8.3.1 The condition field

Most of the instructions of ARM core can be conditionally executed. Conditional execution means, the instruction will have effect on state of the processor, memory etc only if the condition specified (i.e. the state of N, Z, C, V flags) in the instruction is satisfied. If the condition is not satisfied, the instruction is treated as NOP (no operation instruction).

Every instruction contains 4 bit condition field in bits 31-28 as shown in Figure 8-5.

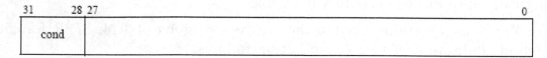

| 31 | 28 | 27 | 0 |

Figure 8-5

The 4 bit cond field specify 16 possible conditions as shown in the figure 8-6.

Opcode [31:28]	Mnemonic extension	Meaning	Condition flag state
0000	EQ	Equal	Z set
0001	NE	Not equal	Z clear
0010	CS/HS	Carry set/unsigned higher or same	C set
0011	CC/LO	Carry clear/unsigned lower	C clear
0100	MI	Minus/negative	N set
0101	PL	Plus/positive or zero	N clear
0110	VS	Overflow	V set
0111	VC	No overflow	V clear
1000	HI	Unsigned higher	C set and Z clear
1001	LS	Unsigned lower or same	C clear or Z set
1010	GE	Signed greater than or equal	N set and V set, or N clear and V clear (N == V)
1011	LT	Signed less than	N set and V clear, or N clear and V set (N != V)
1100	GT	Signed greater than	Z clear, and either N set and V set, or N clear and V clear (Z == 0,N == V)
1101	LE	Signed less than or equal	Z set, or N set and V clear, or N clear and V set (Z == 1 or N != V)
1110	AL	Always (unconditional)	-
1111	(NV)		

Figure 8-6

When no condition is specified in the instruction, the AL (Always) condition is used. The "1111" condition in Figure 8-6 is not a valid condition. Most instructions can be appended with a valid condition to make them execute conditionally.

Example:

ADD	R0, R1, R2	;R0=R1+R2
ADDEQ	R0, R1, R2	;R0=R1+R2 only if Z (zero) flag = 1

8.3.2 Affecting the condition flags

The arithmetic and logic instructions can effect the N, Z, C, V condition flags optionally. The option to affect the condition flags is specified in the instruction through one bit in the opcode field. For the arithmetic and logic instructions, "S" is appended to specify that bit. Because the condition flags are effected optionally, ARM instruction set has a flexible feature of any number of arithmetic/logic instructions can be in between the condition setting and condition evaluation with out effecting the condition flags.

Example:

ADD	R1, R2, R3	;R1=R2+R3, flags will not be affected.
ADDS	R1, R2, R3	;R1=R2+R3, flags were set to reflect
		;the result in R1.
ADDEQS	R1, R2, R3	;if Z flag=1 then R1=R2+R3 and affect
		;the flags.

8.3.3 Notation used in the description of syntax of instructions

< >   Any item bracketed by < and > is a short description of a type of value to be supplied by the user in that position.

{ }   Any item bracketed by { and } is optional.

| This indicates an alternative character string. For example LDM|STM is either LDM or STM.

;   Specify the comment during the description of example instructions.

8.3.4 Data processing instructions

The data processing instructions with two sources and a destination has the syntax as shown.

mnemonic{<cond>}{S} <Rd>,   <Rn>, <shifter_operand>

Where:

mnemonic	is the instruction name and is one of "ADD", "SUB", "RSB", "ADC", "SBC", "RSC", "AND", "BIC", "EOR", "ORR". See figure 8-7 for individual instruction description.
<cond>	Is the optional condition under which the instruction is executed. See Figure 8-6 for possible conditions.
S	Is the optional mnemonic extension appended to effect the condition flags based on the current instruction. Note that if the instruction is not executed because if it does not satisfy the condition given in the instruction then it will not effect any flags even if S is appended (as instruction will not be executed).
<Rd>	It is the destination. It is one of general purpose register. If Rd is R15, the instruction acts as a branch instruction. If Rd is R15 and S is set, then the SPSR is also copied to CPSR. (Using S mnemonic extension with PC as destination is useful when returning from exception/interrupt handlers).
<Rn>	It is one of the source. It is one of the general purpose registers.
<Shifter_operand>	
	It is one of the source. It can be either a general purpose register, an immediate value or a general purpose register shifted(or rotated) with shift amount specified by an immediate value or other register. See shifter operand in the next section.

Examples:

AND	R0,	R1,	R2	;R0=R1&R2 (bit wise AND).
ANDEQ	R0,	R1,	R2	;if Z flag is 1, then R0=R1&R2
ANDS	R0,	R1,	R2	;R0=R1&R2 and affect the flags based ;on the result R1&R2.
SUB	R4,	R5,	R6	;R4=R5-R6
RSB	R4,	R5,	#6	;R4=6-R5
SUB	PC,	R14,	#4	;branch to address R14-4
SUBS	PC,	R14,	#4	;branch to address R14-4 and copy SPSR ;to CPSR
SUBEQS	PC,	R14,	#4	;if Z flag is 1, then branch to address ;R14-4 and copy SPSR to CPSR

For instructions meant for affecting only flags, for example compare instructions the S option is not necessary. The syntax of this kind of instructions is

mnemonic{<cond>}   <Rn>, <shifter_operand>

mnemonic   Is one of "CMP", "CMN", "TST", "TEQ" See figure 8-7 for individual instruction description.

<cond>   Is the optional condition under which the instruction is executed. See Figure 8-6 for possible conditions.

<Rn>   It is one of the source. It should be one of the general purpose register.

<Shifter_operand>

It is one of the source. It can be either a general purpose register, an immediate value or a general purpose register shifted(or rotated) with shift amount specified by an immediate value or other register. See shifter operand in the next section.

Examples:

CMP   R0,   R2   ;affect the flags based on the result R0-R2

CMPEQ   R0,   #100   ;if Z flag is set then affect the flags based on
                             ;the result R0-100

The data processing instruction with only one source and destination (like negating, complementing etc.) has the following syntax.

mnemonic{<cond>}{S} <Rd>, <shifter_operand>

mnemonic   Is one of "MOV" or "MVN" instructions. See figure 8-7 for individual instruction description.

<cond>   Is the optional condition under which the instruction is executed. See Figure 8-6 for possible conditions.

S   Is the optional mnemonic extension appended when Rd is PC to indicate that SPSR has to be copied to CPSR.

<Rd>   It is the destination. It should be one of general purpose register. If Rd is R15 then the instruction acts as a branch instruction. If Rd is R15 and S is set, then the SPSR is also copied to CPSR. (Using S mnemonic extension with PC as destination is useful when returning from exception/interrupt handlers).

<Shifter_operand>

It is one of the source. It can be either a general purpose register, an immediate value or a general purpose register shifted(or rotated) with shift amount specified by an immediate value or other register. See shifter operand in the next section.

Examples:

MOV	R0,	#100	;R0=100
MOVEQ	R0,	R1	;if Z flag is set then R0=R1
MOV	PC,	R14	;branch to address in R14
MOVS	PC,	R14	;branch to address in R14 and CPSR=SPSR
			;This instruction can be used to return from
			;exception handler.
MOVEQS	PC,	R14	;If Z flag is set then branch to address in R14
			;and CPSR=SPSR.

Mnemonic	Operation	Action
AND	Logical AND	Rd := Rn AND shifter_operand
EOR	Logical Exclusive OR	Rd := Rn EOR shifter_operand
SUB	Subtract	Rd := Rn - shifter_operand
RSB	Reverse Subtract	Rd := shifter_operand - Rn
ADD	Add	Rd := Rn + shifter_operand
ADC	Add with Carry	Rd := Rn + shifter_operand + Carry Flag
SBC	Subtract with Carry	Rd := Rn - shifter_operand - NOT(Carry Flag)
RSC	Reverse Subtract with Carry	Rd := shifter_operand - Rn - NOT(Carry Flag)
TST	Test	Update flags after Rn AND shifter_operand
TEQ	Test Equivalence	Update flags after Rn EOR shifter_operand
CMP	Compare	Update flags after Rn - shifter_operand
CMN	Compare Negated	Update flags after Rn + shifter_operand
ORR	Logical (inclusive) OR	Rd := Rn OR shifter_operand
MOV	Move	Rd := shifter_operand (no first operand)
BIC	Bit Clear	Rd := Rn AND NOT(shifter_operand)
MVN	Move Not	Rd := NOT shifter_operand (no first operand)

Figure 8-7

8.3.4.1 Shifter_operand

The shifter_operand is produced by the shifter in side the ARM processor. The shifter produces a carry-out which some instructions write into the carry flag.

The shifter_operand has one of the following 3 basic forms.

1. Immediate operand value

An immediate operand value is formed by rotating an 8 bit constant (in a 32-bit word) by an even number of bits (0, 2, 4, ...26, 28, 30). Therefore, each instruction contains an 8-bit constant and 4 bit rotate to be applied to that constant.

Some valid constants are:

0xFF, 0x104, 0xFF0, 0xFF00, 0xFF000, 0xFF000000, 0xF000000F

Some invalid constants are:

0x101, 0x102, 0xFF1, 0xFF04, 0xFF003, 0xFFFFFFFF, 0xF000001F

Examples:

MOV	R0, #0	;R0=0
ADD	R3, R3, #1	;R3=R3+1
CMP	R7, #0x1000	;affect the flags based on the result R7-0x1000
BIC	R9, R9, #0xFF00	;R9 = R9 & ~(0xFF00). ~denote bitwise not ;operation.

2. Register operand value

A register operand value is simply the value of a register. The value of the register is used directly as the operand to the data-processing instruction.

Examples:

MOV	R2, R0	;R2=R0
ADD	R4, R3, R2	;R4=R3+R2
CMP	R7, R9	;affect the flags based on the result R7-R9

3. Shifted register operand value

A shifted register operand value is the value of a register, shifted (or rotated) before it is used as the data processing operand. The number of shifts (or rotation) can be provided through a short 5 bit immediate value or through another register. There are 5 types of shift operation.

ASR – Arithmetic Shift Right.

LSL – Logical Shift Left.

LSR – Logical Shift Right.

ROR – Rotate Right.

RRX – Rotate Right with extend. (Rotation right through carry by 1 bit. i.e. 33 bit rotation by 1 bit considering carry as MSB)

Examples:

MOV	R2, R0, LSL #2	;R2=R0<<2.
ADD	R9, R5, R5, LSL #3	;R9=R5+(R5<<3).
RSB	R9, R5, R5, LSL #3	;R9=(R5<<3)-R5
SUB	R9, R9, R8, LSR #4	;R9=R9-(R8>>4)
MOV	R12, R4, ROR #3	;R12=R4 rotated right by 3 times.

MOV	R2, R0, LSL R3	;R2=R0<<R3
ADD	R9, R5, R5, LSL R4	;R9=R5+(R5<<R4).
RSB	R9, R5, R5, LSL R6	;R9=(R5<<R6)-R5
SUB	R9, R9, R8, LSR R0	;R9=R9-(R8>>R0)
MOV	R12, R4, ROR #R0	;R12=R4 rotated right by R0 times.

Note that only LSB 5 bits are effective when number of shifts (or rotation) specified through a register.

RRX operation does not take the number of rotations through immediate value or register. The number of rotations is always one.

Example.

| MOV | R0, R0, RRX | ;perform 33 bit rotation right through carry. |
| | | ;C(one bit) concatenated with R0(32bits). |

8.3.5 Multiply Instructions

ARM has two classes of Multiply instructions.

One that produces normal, 32-bit result.

Other that produce long, 64-bit result.

All multiply instructions take two register operands as the input to the multiplier.

8.3.5.1 Normal Multiplies

There are two multiply instructions that produce 32 bit result.

MUL – Multiplies the values of two registers together, truncates the result to 32 bits, and stores the result in a third register.

MLA – Multiplies the values of two registers together, adds the value of a third register, truncates the result to 32 bits, and stores the result in a fourth register. This can be used to perform multiply-accumulate operations.

Both multiply instructions can optionally set the N(negative) and Z(zero) condition flags. No distinction is made between signed and unsigned variants. Only the least significant 32 bits of the result are stored in the destination register, and the sign of the operands does not affect the least significant 32 bits.

Syntax of MUL

MUL{<cond>}{S} <Rd>, <Rm>, <Rs>

Where

<cond>   Is the condition under which instruction is executed. See the possible conditions in Figure 8-6.

S   Option to affect the CPSR N, Z flags based on the result of multiplication. If S is omitted, CPSR is unaffected.

<Rd>   Specifies the destination register of instruction.

<Rm>   Specifies the register that contains the first value to be multiplied.

<Rs>   Holds the value to be multiplied with the value of <Rm>

Example:

MUL   R4, R2, R1   ; R4=R2*R1

MULS   R1, R2, R1   ; R1=R2*R1, affect N and Z flags.

Syntax of MLA

MLA{<cond>}{S} <Rd>, <Rm>, <Rs>, <Rn>

Where

<cond>   Is the condition under which instruction is executed. See the possible conditions in Figure 8-6.

S   Option to affect the CPSR N, Z flags based on the result of multiply accumulate. If S is omitted, CPSR is unaffected.

<Rd>   Specifies the destination register of instruction.

<Rm>	Specifies the register that contains the first value to be multiplied.
<Rs>	Holds the value to be multiplied with the value of <Rm>
<Rn>	Contains the value that is added to the product of <Rs> and <Rm>

Example:

MLA   R7, R8, R9, R3   ; R7=R8*R9+R3

8.3.5.2 Long multiplies

There are 4 multiply instructions that produce 64-bit results.

Two of the variants multiply the values of two registers together and store the 64-bit result in third and fourth registers. These are SMULL (signed multiply) and UMULL (unsigned multiply) instructions.

The remaining two variants multiply the values of two registers together, add the 64-bit value from the third and fourth registers and store the 64-bit result back into the third and fourth registers. These are SMAL (signed multiply accumulate) and UMLAL (unsigned multiply accumulate) variants.

Syntax of SMULL:

SMULL{<cond>}{S} <RdLo>,   <RdHi>, <Rm>, <Rs>

Where:

<cond>	Is the condition under which instruction is executed. See the possible conditions in Figure 8-6.
S	Option to affect to the CPSR N, Z flags based on the result of multiplication. If S is omitted, CPSR is unaffected.
<RdLo>	Register that stores the lower 32 bits of the result.
<RdHi>	Register that stores the upper 32 bits of the result.
<Rm>	Register that holds the signed value to be multiplied to <Rs>
<Rs>	Register that holds the signed value to be multiplied to <Rm>

Example:

SMULL   R4, R8, R2, R3   ; R4 = bits 0 to 31 of R2*R3

                                  ; R8 = bits 32 to 63 of R2*R3

Syntax of SMLAL:

SMLAL{<cond>}{S} <RdLo>, <RdHi>, <Rm>, <Rs>

Where:

\<cond\>	Is the condition under which instruction is executed. See the possible conditions in Figure 8-6.
S	Option to affect the CPSR N, Z flags based on the result of multiply accumulate. If S is omitted, CPSR is unaffected.
\<RdLo\>	Supplies the lower 32 bits of the value to be added to the product of \<Rm\>, \<Rs\> and is the destination register for the lower 32 bits of the result.
\<RdHi\>	Supplies the upper 32 bits of the value to be added to the product of \<Rm\>, \<Rs\> and is the destination register for the upper 32 bits of the result.
\<Rm\>	Register that holds the signed value to be multiplied to \<Rs\>
\<Rs\>	Register that holds the signed value to be multiplied to \<Rm\>

Example:

SMLAL   R4, R8, R2, R3   ; R8, R4 = R2*R3 + R8, R4

Syntax of UMULL

UMULL{\<cond\>}{S} \<RdLo\>, \<RdHi\>, \<Rm\>, \<Rs\>

\<cond\>	Is the condition under which instruction is executed. See the possible conditions in Figure 8-6.
S	Option to affect the CPSR N, Z flags based on the result of multiplication. If S is omitted, CPSR is unaffected.
\<RdLo\>	Register that stores the lower 32 bits of the result.
\<RdHi\>	Register that stores the upper 32 bits of the result.
\<Rm\>	Register that holds the unsigned value to be multiplied to \<Rs\>
\<Rs\>	Register that holds the unsigned value to be multiplied to \<Rm\>

Example:

UMULL   R6, R8, R0, R1   ; R8, R6 = R0*R1

Syntax of UMLAL

UMLAL {\<cond\>}{S} \<RdLo\>, \<RdHi\>, \<Rm\>, \<Rs\>

Where:

\<cond\>	Is the condition under which instruction is executed. See the possible conditions in Figure 8-6.

S	Option to affect the CPSR N, Z flags based on the result of multiply accumulate. If S is omitted, CPSR is unaffected.
<RdLo>	Supplies the lower 32 bits of the value to be added to the product of <Rm>, <Rs> and is the destination register for the lower 32 bits of the result.
<RdHi>	Supplies the upper 32 bits of the value to be added to the product of <Rm>, <Rs> and is the destination register for the upper 32 bits of the result.
<Rm>	Register that holds the unsigned value to be multiplied to <Rs>
<Rs>	Register that holds the unsigned value to be multiplied to <Rm>

Example:

UMLAL   R5, R8, R0, R1   ; R8, R5 = R0*R1 + R8, R5

8.3.6 Miscellaneous Arithmetic instructions

In addition to the normal data processing and multiply instruction, ARM architecture V5 and above include a Count Leading Zeros (CLZ) instruction. This instruction returns the number of 0 bits at the most significant end of its operand before the first 1 bit is encountered (or 32 if the operand is 0).

Syntax:

CLZ{<cond>} <Rd>, <Rm>

Where:

<cond>	Is the optional condition under which the instruction is executed. See Figure 8-6 for possible conditions.
<Rd>	Destination register. It is one of the general purpose registers.
<Rm>	Source register. It is one of the general purpose registers.

Example:

Assume before instruction execution R0=0x0FE00FE1

CLZ   R1, R0

After execution of instruction R0=0x0FE00FE1, R1=0x4. (as there are 4 leading zeros in R0).

8.3.7 Status Register access instructions

There are two instructions for moving the contents of a program status register to or from a general-purpose register. Both CPSR and SPSR can be accessed.

Each status register is split into four 8-bit fields that can be individually written.

Bits[31:24]   The flags field.

Bits[23:16]   The status field.

Bits[15:8]   The extension field.

Bits[7:0]   The control field.

ARM architecture does not use status and extension fields and they are reserved for future use. Altering the CPSR is needed to enable/disable the interrupts, and to change the processor mode, for instance to initialize the stack pointers. Note that T bit must not be changed directly by writing CPSR, but only via the BX, BLX instructions and in the implicit SPSR to CPSR moves in instructions designated for exception return. Attempts to enter or leave THUMB state by directly altering the T bit can have unpredictable consequences.

Syntax of MRS instruction

MRS{<cond>} <Rd>, CPSR

MRS{<cond>} <Rd>, SPSR

<cond>   Is the optional condition under which the instruction is executed. See Figure 8-6 for possible conditions.

<Rd>   Destination register. It is one of the general purpose registers.

Example:

MRS   R0, CPSR   ;Read CPSR into R0 register.

Syntax of MSR instruction

MSR{<cond>} CPSR_<fields>, #<immediate>

MSR{<cond>} CPSR_<fields>, <Rm>

MSR{<cond>} SPSR_<fields>, #<immediate>

MSR{<cond>} SPSR_<fields>, <Rm>

Where:

<cond>   Is the optional condition under which the instruction is executed. See Figure 8-6 for possible conditions.

174

\<fields\>	Is a sequence of one of more of the following.

     c   sets the control field mask bit (i.e. write to control field)

     x   sets the extension field mask bit.(i.e. write to extension field)

     s   sets the status field mask bit. (i.e. write to status field)

     f   sets the flags field mask bit (i.e. write to flags field)

\<immediate\> Is the immediate value to be transferred to CPSR or SPSR. Allowed immediate value are 8-bit immediate (in the range of 0x00 to 0xFF) and values that can be obtained by rotating them right by an even amount in the range of 0-30. These immediate values are same as those allowed in immediate form allowed as shifter_operand. (See shifter operand in Section 8.3.4.1).

\<Rm\> Is the general-purpose register to be transferred to CPSR or SPSR.

Examples:

MSR	CPSR_f, R0	;Move R0 into CPSR. Affect only flags field.
MSR	CPSR_c, R0	;Move R0 into CPSR. Affect only control field.
MSR	CPSR_fc, R0	;Move R0 into CPSR. Affect flags, control ;fields
MRS	R1, SPSR	;Move SPSR into R1
MSR	SPSR, R1	;Move R1 into SPSR.

8.3.8 Load and Store instructions

The ARM architecture supports two broad types of instructions which load or store the value of single register from or to memory.

- The first type can load or store 32-bit word or an 8-bit unsigned value.

- The second type can load or store a 16-bit unsigned halfword, and can load and sign extend a 16-bit halfword or an 8-bit byte.

Addressing modes:

In both types of instruction, the addressing of the memory is done with two parts of the instruction. They are the base register and the offset.

The base register can be any one of the general purpose registers (including the PC, which allows PC-relative addressing for position-independent code).

The offset takes one of three formats.

Immediate   The offset is an unsigned number that can be added to or subtracted from the base register.

Register   The offset is a general-purpose register (not the PC), that can be added to or subtracted from the base register.

Scaled Register

The offset is a general purpose register(not the PC), shifted by an immediate value, then added to or subtracted from the base register. Scaled register offsets are available only for word and unsigned byte instructions.

As well as the three types of offset, the offset and base register are used in three different ways to form the memory address. The addressing modes are described as follows.

Offset   The base register and offset are added or subtracted to form the memory address.

Pre-indexed   The base register and offset are added or subtracted to form the memory address. The base register is then updated with this new address, to allow for automatic indexing through an array or memory block.

Post-indexed: The value of the base register alone is used as the memory address. The base register and offset are added or subtracted and resultant value is stored back in the base register, to allow automatic indexing through an array or memory block.

8.3.8.1 Loading/storing a word or unsigned byte

General form for loading and storing 32bit word and unsigned byte.

LDR|STR{<cond>}{B}{T} <Rd>, <addressing_mode>

Where:

<cond>   Is the optional condition under which the instruction is executed. See Figure 8-6 for possible conditions.

B   This mnemonic extension specify whether an unsigned byte has to be loaded into the destination register. If this extension is omitted, 32-bit word is loaded into the destination register.

T   This option specifies the memory management unit to load/store with user mode privileges. The memory management unit is outside the scope of this book. The memory management is not needed for RTOS with single embedded application for which SROS is designed.

<Rd>   Destination register into which data is loaded. If byte is loaded, 24 most significant bits will be set to 0.

<Addressing_mode>

The addressing mode takes one of the 9 forms shown below.

1. [Rn, # ± offset_12]

The address is computed as Rn ± offset_12. Where Rn is a general purpose register. Offset_12 is a 12 bit offset. The value of Rn is not changed.

Example instructions:

LDR R0, [R1, #20]   ;Load R0 with the 32-bit memory content

    ;available at address (R1+20)

STRB R0, [R2, #-30] ;Store least significant byte of R0 into memory

    ;at address (R2-30)

2. [Rn, ± Rm]

The address is computed as Rn ± Rm. Where Rn, Rm are general purpose registers. The value of Rn is not changed.

Example instructions:

LDRB R0, [R1, R2]   ;Load R0 with a byte of memory content

    ;available at address (R1+R2)

STR R0, [R1, -R2]   ;Store R0 to the memory at address (R1-R2)

3. [Rn, ± Rm, <shift> #<shift_amount>]

The address is computed by adding/subtracting base register(Rn) with shifted register(Rm) offset. The type of shift, and the shift amount (5 bits) is specified in the instruction. Rn will not be changed after the instruction. The shift type can be one of "LSL", "LSR", "ASR", "ROR", "RRX" as in data processing instructions.

Example instructions:

LDR R0, [R1, R2, LSL #2]   ;Load R0 with 32-bit memory content

    ;available at address (R1+(R2<<2)).

STRB R2, [R0, -R3, ASR #2] ;Store least significant byte of R2 to

;the memory at address (R0-(R3>>2)).

4. [Rn, #± offset_12]!

This form is same as the 1ˢᵗ form of addressing mode except that base register Rn is updated as Rn = Rn ± offset_12.

Example instructions.

LDR R0, [R1, #20]!   ;Load R0 with the 32-bit memory content
;available at address (R1+20)
;R1=R1+20.

STRB R0, [R2, #-30]! ;Store least significant byte of R0 into
;memory at address (R2-30)
;R2=R2-30.

5. [Rn, ± Rm]!

This form is same as the 2ⁿᵈ form except that the base register Rn is updated as Rn = Rn ± Rm

LDRB R0, [R1, R2] ! ;Load R0 with a byte of memory content
;available at address (R1+R2)
;R1=R1+R2.

STR R0, [R1, -R2] !   ;Store R0 to the memory at address (R1-R2)
;R1=R1-R2.

6. [Rn, ± Rm, <shift> #<shift_amount>]!

This form is same as the 3ʳᵈ form except that the base register Rn is updated as Rn = Rn added with shifted version of ± Rm. The shift type and shift amount is specified in the addressing mode.

Example instructions:

LDR R0, [R1, R2, LSL #2]!   ;Load R0 with 32-bit memory content
;available at address (R1+(R2<<2)).
;R1=(R1+(R2<<2)).

STRB R2, [R0, -R3, ASR #2]!
;Store least significant byte of R2
;to the memory at address (R0-(R3>>2)).
;R0=(R0-(R3>>2)).

7. [Rn], # ± offset_12

The address for the memory access is given by the base register Rn itself. The base register is updated as Rn=Rn ± offset_12.

Example instructions:

LDR R0, [R1], #20   ;Load R0 with the 32-bit memory content

;available at address R1

;R1=R1+20

STRB R0, [R2], #-30 ;Store least significant byte of R0 into memory

;at address R2

;R2=R2-30

8. [Rn], ± Rm

The address for the memory access is given by the base register Rn itself. The base register is updated as Rn=Rn ± Rm.

Example Instructions:

LDRB R0, [R1], R2   ;Load R0 with a byte of memory content

;available at address R1.

;R1=R1+R2.

STR R0, [R1], -R2   ;Store R0 to the memory at address R1

;R1=R1-R2.

9. [Rn], ± Rm, <shift> #<shift_amount>

The address for the memory access is given by the base register Rn itself. The base register is updated as Rn= "Rn added with shifted version of Rm" where shift type and shift amount is specified in the addressing mode.

LDR R0, [R1], R2, LSL #2

;Load R0 with 32-bit memory content

;available at address R1.

;R1=(R1+(R2<<2)).

STRB R2, [R0], -R3, ASR #2

;Store least significant byte of R2

;to the memory at address R0.

;R0=(R0-(R3>>2)).

8.3.8.2 Loading/Storing half word or signed byte

LDR|STR{<cond>}H|SH|SB <Rd>, <addressing_mode>

Where:

<cond>   Is the optional condition under which the instruction is executed. See Figure 8-6 for possible conditions.

H   Load or store unsigned half word.

SH   Load or store signed half word.

SB   Load or store signed byte.

<Rd>   Is the destination register. This is one of the general purpose registers.

<addressing_mode>

take one of the 6 forms mentioned below.

1. [Rn, # ± offset_8]

The address is computed as Rn ± offset_8. Where base register Rn is a general purpose register. Offset_8 is 8 bit offset. The value of Rn is not changed.

Example instructions:

LDRH R0, [R1, #20]   ;Load R0 with the 16-bit memory
                        ; content available at address (R1+20).
                        ;The most significant 16 bits will be set
                        ; to 0

LDRSH R0, [R1, #20]   ;Load R0 with the 16-bit memory
                        ;content available at address
                        ;(R1+20). The most significant 16 bits
                        ;will be sign extended.

LDRSB R0, [R2, #-30]   ;Load R0 with the 8-bit memory content
                        ;available at address (R2-30). The most
                        ;significant 24 bits will be sign extended.

STRH R5, [R10, #-100]   ;Store least significant 16-bits of

;R5 into memory at address (R10-100)

2. [Rn, ± Rm]

The address is computed as Rn ± Rm. Where base register Rn, offset Rm are general purpose registers. The value of Rn is not changed.

Example instructions:

LDRH R0, [R1, R2]   ;Load R0 with the 16-bit memory content
                          ;available at address (R1+R2). The most
                          ;significant 16 bits will be set to 0.

LDRSH R0, [R1, R2]   ;Load R0 with the 16-bit memory
                          ;content available at address (R1+R2).
                          ;The most significant 16 bits will be sign
                          ;extended.

LDRSB R0, [R1, R2]   ;Load R0 with a byte of memory content
                          ;available at address (R1+R2). The most
                          ;significant 24 bits of R0 will be sign
                          ;extended.

STRH R0, [R1, -R2]   ;Store least significant 16-bits of R0 to
                          ;the memory at address (R1-R2)

3. [Rn, #± offset_8] !

This form is same as the 1st form of addressing mode except that base register Rn is updated as Rn = Rn ± offset_8.

Example instructions.

LDRH R0, [R1, #20]!   ;Load R0 with the 16-bit memory content
                          ;available at address (R1+20). The most
                          ;significant 16 bits will be set to 0.
                          ;R1=R1+20.

STRH R5, [R10, #-100] ! ;Store least significant 16-bits of
                          ;R5 into memory at address (R10-100)
                          ;R10=R10-100.

4. [Rn, ± Rm] !

This form is same as the 2nd form except that the base register Rn is updated as Rn = Rn ± Rm

Example Instructions:

LDRSH   R0, [R1, R2]   ;Load R0 with the 16-bit memory

    ;content available at address (R1+R2).

    ;The most significant 16 bits will be sign

    ;extended.

    ;R1=R1+R2

STRH   R0, [R1, -R2]   ;Store least significant 16-bits of R0 to

    ;the memory at address (R1-R2)

    ;R1=R1-R2

5. [Rn], #± offset_8

The address for the memory access is given by the base register Rn itself. The base register is updated as Rn=Rn ± offset_8.

Example instructions:

LDRSH   R0, [R1], #20   ;Load R0 with the 16-bit memory

    ;content available at address location

    ;pointed by R1.

    ;The most significant 16 bits will be sign

    ;extended.

    ;R1=R1+20.

STRH   R0, [R2], #-30   ;Store least significant 16bits of R0 into

    ;memory at address R2

    ;R2=R2-30

6. [Rn], ± Rm

The address for the memory access is given by the base register Rn itself. The base register is updated as Rn=Rn ± Rm.

Example Instructions:

LDRSB	R0, [R1], R2	;Load R0 with a byte of memory content
		;available at address R1. The most
		;significant 24 bits will be sign extended.
		;R1=R1+R2.
STRH	R0, [R1], -R2	;Store least significant 16 bits of R0 to
		;the memory at address R1
		;R1=R1-R2.

8.3.9 Load and store multiple instructions

Load multiple instructions (LDM) load a subset, or possibly all, of the general-purpose registers from memory.

Store multiple instructions (STM) store a subset, or possibly all, of the general-purpose registers to memory.

The general form of LDM/STM instruction is

LDM | STM{cond}<addressing_mode> <Rn>{!}, <registers>{^}

There are 3 different forms of load multiple and 2 different forms of store multiple instructions defined.

8.3.9.1 LDM(1)

This form of LDM (Load multiple) instruction is useful for block loads, stack operations and procedure exit sequences. It loads a non-empty subset, or possibly all, of the general-purpose registers from sequential memory locations.

The general-purpose registers loaded can include the PC. If they do, the word loaded for the PC is treated as an address and a branch occurs to that address. In ARM architecture version 5 and above, bit[0] of the loaded value determines whether execution continues after this branch in ARM state or in Thumb state, as though a BX (loaded_value) instruction has been executed. For earlier versions of the architecture, bits[1:0] of the loaded_value are ignored and execution continue in ARM state, as though MOV PC, (loaded_value) has been executed.

Syntax:

LDM{<cond>}<addressing_mode> <Rn>{!}, <registers_list>

Where

<cond>   Is the optional condition under which the instruction is executed. See Figure 8-6 for possible conditions.

one of IA, IB, DA, DB, FD, FA, EA, ED. See section 8.3.9.6

<Rn>   Specifies the base registers used by <addressing_mode>. The base register is one of the general purpose registers other than PC.

!   Specifies the option that base register has to be updated based on the addressing_mode. If ! is omitted, then the instruction do not update the base register. The base register anyway can be updated if the base register is one of the registers in the registers_list.

<registers_list>

Is a list of registers, separated by commas and surrounded by { and }. It specifies the set of registers to be loaded by the LDM instruction.

The registers are loaded in sequence, the lowest-numbered register from the lowest memory address (start_address), through to the highest-numbered register from the highest memory address (end_address). If the PC is specified in the register list, the instruction cause a branch to the address (data) loaded in to the PC.

Examples:

LDMIA   R0, {R1, R2}   ;Load R1, R2 registers from memory pointed
                         ;by R0 register. R0 register is not changed.
                         ;R1=memory(R0)
                         ;R2=memory(R0+4)

LDMIA   R0!, {R1, R2}   ;Load R1, R2 registers from memory pointed
                         ;by R0 register. R0=R0+8 as two registers
                         ;are loaded.
                         ;R1=memory(R0)
                         ;R2=memory(R0+4)

LDMFD   SP!, {R4-R11, PC}   ;Load R4, R5, R6....R11, PC registers
                              ;from stack. Loading the PC causes
                              ;branch to the loaded address.
                              ;PC=memory(SP)
                              ;R11=memory(SP-4)
                              ;R10=memory(SP-8)

		;...
		;R4=memory(SP-32)
		;SP = SP – 36 (as 9 registers are loaded).
LDMEQIA	R0, {R1, R2}	;If Z flag is set then
		;Load R1, R2 registers from memory pointed
		;by R0 register. R0 register is not changed.
		;R1=memory(R0)
		;R2=memory(R0+4)

8.3.9.2 LDM(2)

This form of LDM (load multiple) instruction loads user mode registers when the processor is in a privileged mode (useful when performing process swaps). The instruction loads a subset of user mode general-purpose registers from sequential memory locations.

Syntax:

LDM{<cond>}<addressing_mode> <Rn>, <registers_without_pc>^

Where

<cond>   Is the optional condition under which the instruction is executed. See Figure 8-6 for possible conditions.

<addressing_mode>

      one of IA, IB, DA, DB, FD, FA, EA, ED. See section 8.3.9.6

<Rn>   Specifies the base register used by the addressing_mode. The base register is a general purpose register other than PC.

<Registers_without_pc>

      Is a list of registers, separated by commas and surrounded by { and }. This list must not include the PC, and specifies the set of registers to be loaded by the LDM instruction.

      The registers are loaded in sequence, the lowest-numbered register from the lowest memory address(start_address), through the highest-numbered register from the highest memory address (end_address).

^   For an LDM instruction that does not load the PC, this indicates that User mode registers are to be loaded.

In this type of LDM instruction, the base register can not be updated.

Examples:

```
LDMIA      R0, {R0-R14}^            ;Load user mode registers R0, R1,
                                    ;R2, R3...R14 from memory irrespective
                                    ;of the current processor mode.
                                    ;start_address = R0
                                    ;R0=memory(start_address)
                                    ;R1=memory(start_address +4)
                                    ;R2=memory(start_address +8)
                                    ;R3=memory(start_address +12)
                                    ;....
                                    ;R14=memory(start_address +56)
LDMDB      R0, {R13, R14}^          ;Load user mode registers R13, R14
                                    ;irrespective of the current processor
                                    ;mode.
                                    ;start_address = R0-8
                                    ;R13=memory(start_address)
                                    ;R14=memory(start_address+4)
```

8.3.9.3 LDM(3)

This form of LDM instruction is useful for returning from exceptions. It loads a subset (or possibly all) of the general purpose registers and the PC from sequential memory locations. Also the SPSR of the current mode is copied to the CPSR.

The value loaded for the PC is treated as an address and a branch occurs to that address. In ARM architecture version 5 and above, the value copied from the SPSR T bit to the CPSR T bit determines whether execution continues after the branch in ARM state or in Thumb state.

Syntax:

LDM{<cond>}<addressing_mode> <Rn>{!}, <registers_and_pc>^

Where:

<cond>   Is the optional condition under which the instruction is executed. See Figure 8-6 for possible conditions.

one of IA, IB, DA, DB, FD, FA, EA, ED. See section 8.3.9.6

<Rn> Specifies the base register used by the <addressing_mode>. The base register is one of the general purpose register other than PC.

! This option specifies whether to update the base register or not. If this option is omitted the base register is not updated. If the base register is one of the register in the register list, the register is loaded anyway.

<registers_and_pc>

Is the list of registers, separated by commas and surrounded by { and }. This list must include the PC, and specifies the set of registers to be loaded by the LDM instruction.

The registers are loaded in sequence, the lowest-numbered register from the lowest memory address(start_address), through to the highest-numbered register from the highest memory address(end_address).

^ For an LDM instruction that loads the PC, this indicates that the SPSR of the current mode is copied to the CPSR.

Examples:

LDMEQFD R13, {R0-R3, R12, PC}^   ;If Z flag is set then

                                        ;Load R0, R1, R2, R3, R12, PC

                                        ;from memory location starting at

                                        ;address R13-20. and copy SPSR

                                        ;to CPSR

                                        ;start_address = R13-20.

                                        ;R0=memory(R13-20)

                                        ;R1=memory(R13-16)
                                        ;R2=memory(R13-12)

                                        ;R3=memory(R13-8)

                                        ;R12=memory(R13-4)

                                        ;PC=memory(R13)

                                        ;SPSR=CPSR.

LDMEQFD R13!, {R0-R3, R12, PC}^   ;Same as above instruction except

;R13 is updated as R13=R13-24

;as 6 registers are loaded.

8.3.9.4 STM(1)

This form of STM (store multiple) instruction stores a non-empty subset (or possibly all) of the general purpose registers to sequential memory locations.

Syntax:

STM{<cond>}<addressing_mode> <Rn>{!}, <registers>

Where

<cond>   Is the optional condition under which the instruction is executed. See Figure 8-6 for possible conditions.

<addressing_mode>

               one of IA, IB, DA, DB, FD, FA, EA, ED. See section 8.3.9.6

<Rn>   Specifies the base register used by the <addressing_mode>. The base register is any general purpose register other than PC.

!   This option specifies whether the base register has to be updated or not. If this option is omitted, the base register is not updated.

<registers>   Is a list of registers, separated by commas and surrounded by { and }. It specifies the set of registers to be stored by the STM instruction.

               The registers are stored in sequence, the lowest-numbered register to the lowest memory address(start_address), through to the highest-numbered register to the highest memory address(end_address).

Examples:

STMIA   R0!,   {R2, R3}   ;Save R2, R3 starting from memory location

                                 ;pointed by R0

                                 ;memory(R0)=R2

                                 ;memory(R0+4)=R3

                                 ;R0=R0+8

STMIB   R0!,   {R2, R3}   ;Save R2, R3 starting from memory location

                                 ;pointed by R0+4

                                 ;memory(R0+4)=R2

```
                                ;memory(R0+8)=R3
                                ;R0=R0+8
STMDA     R0!,    {R2, R3}      ;Save R2, R3 starting from memory location
                                ;pointed by R0-4
                                ;memory(R0)=R3
                                ;memory(R0-4)=R2
                                ;R0=R0-8
STMDB     R0!,    {R2, R3}      ;Save R2, R3 starting from memory location
                                ;pointed by R0-8
                                ;memory(R0-4)=R3
                                ;memory(R0-8)=R2
                                ;R0=R0-8
```

8.3.9.5 STM(2)

This form of STM stores a subset (or possibly all) of the User mode general purpose registers to sequential memory locations.

Syntax:

STM{<cond>}<addressing_mode> <Rn>, <registers>^

Where

<cond>   Is the optional condition under which the instruction is executed. See Figure 8-6 for possible conditions.

<addressing_mode>

        one of IA, IB, DA, DB, FD, FA, EA, ED. See section 8.3.9.6

<Rn>   Specifies the base register used by the <addressing_mode>. The base register is one of the general purpose registers other than PC.

<registers>   Is a list of registers, separated by commas and surrounded by { and }. It specifies the set of registers to be stored by the STM instruction.

        The registers are stored in Sequence, the lowest-numbered register to the lowest memory address(starting_address), through to the highest-numbered register to the highest memory address (end_address).

^   For the STM instruction, indicates the User mode registers are to be stored.

Examples:

STMIA   R0, {R2-R14}^   ;Save user mode registers R2-R14

     ;starting from the memory location pointed by

     ;R0 irrespective of the current processor mode.

     ;memory(R0)=R2

     ;memory(R0+4)=R3

     ;memory(R0+8)=R4

     ;...

     ;memory(R0+48)=R14

8.3.9.6 Addressing mode for STM, LDM instructions

Load and Store Multiple addressing modes produce a sequential range of addresses. The lowest-numbered register is stored at the lowest memory address and the highest-numbered register at the highest memory address given by the addressing mode in all addressing modes.

The general instruction syntax is:

LDM | STM{cond}<addressing_mode> <Rn>{!}, <registers>{^}

Where <addressing_mode> is one of the following four addressing modes.

1. IA (Increment After)

In this addressing mode the start_address, end_address of sequential addresses is given as follows.

Start_address = base register Rn

End_address = base register Rn + ((number of registers in <registers> * 4) – 4)

Examples

LDMIA   R0!, {R1}   ;Load R1 from address R0.

     ;R1=memory(R0)

     ;R0=R0+4

LDMIA   R0!, {R1, R2}   ;Load R1, R2 from the address starting

     ;R0

     ;R1=memory(R0)

;R2=memory(R0+4)

;R0=R0+8

2. IB (Increment Before)

In this addressing mode the start_address, end_address of sequential addresses is given as follows.

Start_address = base register Rn+4

End_address = base register Rn + (number of registers in <registers> * 4)
Examples

LDMIB	R0!, {R1}	;Load R1 from address R0+4
		;R1=memory(R0+4)
		;R0=R0+4
LDMIB	R0!, {R1, R2}	;Load R1, R2 from the address starting
		;R0+4
		;R1=memory(R0+4)
		;R2=memory(R0+8)
		;R0=R0+8

3. DA (Decrement After)

In this addressing mode the start_address, end_address of sequential addresses is given as follows.

Start_address = base register Rn – (number of registers in <registers> * 4) + 4

End_address = base register Rn

Examples

LDMDA	R0!, {R1}	;Load R1 from address R0
		;R1=memory(R0)
		;R0=R0-4
LDMDA	R0!, {R1, R2}	;Load R1, R2 from the address starting
		;R0-4.
		;R1=memory(R0-4)
		;R2=memory(R0)
		;R0=R0-8

4. DB (Decrement Before)

In this addressing mode the start_address, end_address of sequential addresses is given as follows.

Start_address = base register Rn – (number of registers in <registers> * 4)

End_address = base register Rn – 4.

Examples

LDMDB	R0!, {R1}	;Load R1 from address R0-4
		;R1=memory(R0-4)
		;R0=R0-4
LDMDA	R0!, {R1, R2}	;Load R1, R2 from the address starting
		;R0-8.
		;R1=memory(R0-8)
		;R2=memory(R0-4)
		;R0=R0-8

Load and Store Multiple addressing modes (alternative names)

The four addressing mode names IA, IB, DA, DB are most useful when a load and store multiple instruction is being used for block data transfer. It is likely that LDM, STM instructions will have same addressing mode, so that data is stored in the same way that was loaded.

However, if LDM, STM are used to access stack, the data is not loaded with the same addressing mode that used to store the data, because the load(pop) and store(push) operations must adjust the stack in opposite directions.

Stack operations:

Load Multiple and Store Multiple addressing modes can be specified with an alternative syntax, which is more applicable to stack operations.

Full Stacks	Have the stack pointer that point to the last used (full) location.
Empty Stacks	Have stack pointers that point to the first unused (empty) location.
Descending Stacks	Grow towards decreasing memory address (towards the bottom of memory)
Ascending stacks	Grow towards increasing memory address.(towards top of memory).

Two attributes allow four types of stack to be defined.

- Full Descending, with the syntax FD.

- Empty Descending, with the syntax ED.

- Full Ascending, with the syntax FA.

- Empty Ascending, with the syntax EA.

The Figures 8-8, 8-9 show the equality of Non-stack addressing mode to the stack addressing mode for LDM, STM instructions respectively. Note that stack addressing modes are just defined for programmer convenience and both Non-stack, Stack addressing modes are encoded in the same way. i.e. the corresponding table entries will be encoded with the same instruction opcode.

Non-stack addressing mode	Stack addressing mode
LDMDA (Decrement After)	LDMFA (Full Ascending)
LDMIA (Increment After)	LDMFD (Full Descending)
LDMDB (Decrement Before)	LDMEA (Empty Ascending)
LDMIB (Increment Before)	LDMED (Empty Descending)

Figure 8-8

Non-stack addressing mode	Stack addressing mode
STMDA (Decrement After)	STMED (Empty Descending)
STMIA (Increment After)	STMEA (Empty Ascending)
STMDB (Decrement Before)	STMFD (Full Descending)
STMIB (Increment Before)	STMFA (Full Ascending)

Figure 8-9

8.3.10   Semaphore instructions

The ARM instruction set has two semaphore instructions.

SWP – swap

SWPB – swap byte.

These instructions are provided for thread synchronization without disabling the interrupts. Both instructions generate an atomic load and store operation, allowing a memory semaphore to be loaded and altered without interruption.

SWP and SWPB have single addressing mode, whose address is the contents of a register. Separate registers are used to specify the value to store and destination of the load. If the same register is specified for the both of these, SWP exchanges the value in the register and the value in the memory.

The semaphore instructions do not provide a compare and conditional write facility. If wanted, this must be done explicitly.

Syntax:

SWP|SWPB{<cond>} <Rd>, <Rm>, [<Rn>]

<cond>   Is the optional condition under which the instruction is executed. See Figure 8-6 for possible conditions.

<Rd>   Specifies the destination register for the instruction.

<Rm>   Register that contains the value to be stored to memory.

<Rn>   Register that contains the memory address to load from.

Examples:

SWP   R12, R10, [R9]   ;Load R12 from address R9 and
                                  ;Store R10 to address R9

SWPB   R3,   R4,   [R8]   ;Load byte(unsigned) to R3 from
                                  ;address
                                  ;R8 and store byte from R4 to address
                                  ;R8.

SWP   R1,   R1,   [R2]   ;Exchange value in R1 and
                                  ;memory content at address in R2.

8.3.11   Exception-generating instructions

The Arm instruction set provides two types of instructions whose purpose is to cause a processor exception to occur:

8.3.11.1   Software Interrupt (SWI)

The Software Interrupt (SWI) instruction is used to cause a SWI exception to occur. When the user mode programs are executed in non-privileged modes, to request a particular privileged operating system function, user mode program can use this instruction. As SROS is designed for one embedded application which always run in privileged mode, this instruction is not necessary and not used in SROS code.

Syntax of SWI instruction:

SWI{<cond>} <immed_24>

Where

<cond>   Is the condition under which the instruction is executed. The conditions are defined in Figure 8-6.

<immed_24> Is the 24-bit immediate value that is put into the instruction. This value is ignored by the ARM processor, but can be used by an operating system SWI exception handler to determine what operating system service is being requested.

Example:

SWI   #0x10   ;raise the SWI exception with 0x10 code in the SWI
                           ;instruction.

When SWI instruction is executed, the processor enters supervisor mode. The operation of the SWI instruction is as shown below.

R14_svc = address of next instruction after the SWI instruction.

SPSR_svc = CPSR

$CPSR[4:0] = 10011_{(2)}$ /*Enter supervisor mode*/

$CPSR[5] = 0$ /*Enter ARM state*/

$CPSR[7] = 1$ /*disable normal interrupts*/

If high vectors configured then

        PC = 0xFFFF0008

Else

        PC = 0x00000008

To return after performing the SWI operation, use the following to restore the PC (from R14_svc) and CPSR (from SPSR_svc) and return to the instruction following SWI

MOVSPC,   R14

8.3.11.2   Breakpoint (BKPT)

The BKPT (Breakpoint) instruction causes a software breakpoint to occur. This breakpoint can be handled by an exception handler installed on the prefetch abort vector. In implementations which include debug hardware (like emulator), the hardware can optionally override this behavior and handle the breakpoint itself. When this occurs, the prefetch abort vector is not entered. The emulator replaces the instruction with BKPT instruction whenever a software breakpoint is placed on it during debugging. When the breakpoint is hit, the effect of replacing the instruction is compensated by restoring the instruction and executing the restored instruction and keeping the breakpoint BKPT instruction again. Keeping the break points in this way is not possible in ROM code. So hardware breakpoints are used to keep the break points in ROM code. Unlike the software breakpoint, hardware break point facility need separate register and comparator to compare the program counter continuously in hardware. So hardware breakpoints are limited in number unlike the software breakpoints.

Syntax:

BKPT   <immediate_16>

Where

<immediate_16>   Is a 16-bit immediate value, the top 12 bits of which are placed in the instruction. This value is ignored by ARM hardware, but can be used by a debugger to store additional information about the breakpoint.

Example:

BKPT   0x0

The operation of the BKPT instruction is, if debug hardware is not overridden the BKPT instruction

R14_abt = address of BKPT instruction + 4

SPSR_abt = CPSR

$CPSR[4:0] = 10111_{(2)}$ /*Enter abort mode*/

CPSR[5] = 0   /*Enter ARM state*/

CPSR[7] = 1   /*Mask IRQ interrupt*/

If high vectors configured then

        PC = 0xFFFF000C

Else

        PC = 0x0000000C

8.3.12   Branch Instructions

All ARM processors support a Branch instruction (B) that allows a conditional branch forwards or backwards up to 32MB. As the PC is one of the general-purpose registers (R15), a branch or jump can also be generated by writing a value to R15.

A subroutine call is performed by a variant of the standard branch instruction. As well as allowing a branch forward or backward up to 32MB, the Branch with Link (BL) instruction preserves the address of the instruction after the branch (the return address) in the LR (R14).

The Branch and Exchange (BX) instruction copies the contents of a general purpose register to the PC (like MOV PC, Rm instruction), with the additional functionality that if bit[0] of the transferred value is 1, the processor shifts to Thumb state. Together with the corresponding Thumb instruction, this allows interworking branches between ARM and Thumb code.

In ARM architecture version 5 and above, there are also two types of Branch with Link and Exchange (BLX) instruction:

One type takes a register operand Rm, like a BX instruction. This instruction behaves like a BX instruction, and additionally writes the address of the next instruction into LR. This provides an efficient interworking subroutine call than a sequence of MOV LR, PC[1] followed by BX Rm.

The other type behaves like a BL instruction, branching backwards or forwards by up to 32MB and writing a return link to the LR, but shifts to Thumb state rather than staying in ARM state as BL does. This provides a more efficient alternative to loading the subroutine address into Rm followed by BLX Rm instruction when it is known that a Thumb subroutine is being called and that the subroutine lies within the 32MB range.

A load instruction that loads into PC provides a way to branch anywhere in the 4GB address space (known as long branch). A long branch can be preceded by MOV LR, PC or another instruction that writes the LR to generate a long subroutine call. The bit[0] of the value loaded by a long branch controls whether the subroutine is executed in ARM state or Thumb state, just like bit[0] of the value moved to the PC by a BX instruction.

In non-T variants of ARM architecture version 5, the instructions described can cause an entry into Thumb state despite the fact that the thumb instruction is not present. This causes the instruction at the branch target to generate the undefined instruction exception. See the CPSR register in figure 8-1.

---

[1] When PC is read in an instruction, the value read is the current instruction address + 8 or current instruction address + 12 depending on the ARM architecture version when the processor is in ARM State.

8.3.12.1   B, BL instructions

The B (Branch) and BL (Branch and Link) instructions cause branch to a target address, and provide conditional and unconditional changes to program flow.

Syntax:

B{L}{<cond>} <target_address>

Where:

L   Causes the LR register to be loaded with the address of the next instruction. This option is useful to make sub-routine calls.

<cond>   Is the condition under which the instruction is executed. The conditions are defined in Figure 8-6

<target_address>

This is the 24-bit signed (two's complement) value. The branch target address is calculated as

1. Sign extending the 24-bit signed (two's complement) immediate to 32 bits.

2. Shifting the result left two bits.

3. Adding this to the contents of the PC, which contains the address of the branch instruction plus 8.

The instruction can therefore specify a branch of approximately ± 32MB.

Note that if the target label in the assembly program is given, the assembler calculates the 24 bit signed constant and form the instruction correctly.

Examples:

B   label   ;Branch unconditionally to "label"

BL   function   ;Branch to the address specified by "function" and save the

                  ;next instruction address in the LR register.

BGT label   ;If GT (greater than) condition is satisfied branch to label

8.3.12.2   BLX(1)

This form of BLX (Branch with Link and Exchange) instruction is used to call a Thumb subroutine from the ARM code at an address specified in the instruction. This instruction is unconditional (always causing a change in program flow) and preserves the address of the instruction following the branch in the link register (R14). Execution of Thumb instruction begins at the target address.

Syntax:

BLX   <target_address>

Where:

<target_addr>

This is the 24-bit signed (two's complement) value to specify the branch target address. The branch target address is calculated as

1. Sign extending the 24-bit signed (two's complement) immediate to 32 bits.

2. Shifting the result left by two bits.

3. Adding this to the contents of the PC, which contains the address of the branch instruction plus 8.

The instruction can therefore specify a branch of approximately ± 32MB.

Note that if the target label in the assembly program is given, the assembler calculates the 24 bit signed constant and form the instruction correctly.

Example:

BLX   thumb_sub_routine ;Branch to the label "thumb_sub_routine"

                              ;change the processor state to Thumb state

                              ;Load the LR register with the instruction

                              ;following the BLX instruction.

8.3.12.3   BLX(2)

This form of BLX is used to call an ARM or Thumb subroutine from the ARM code, at an address specified in a register. The branch target address is the value of register Rm, with its bit[0] forced to zero. The instruction set to be used at the branch target is chosen by setting the CPSR T bit to bit[0] of Rm.

Register R14 is set to a return address. To return from the subroutine, use a BX R14 instruction, or store the R14 on the stack and re-load the stored value into the PC.

Syntax:

BLX{<cond>} <Rm>

Where

<cond>   Is the condition under which the instruction is executed. See the conditions defined in Figure 8-6.

<Rm>   Is the register containing the address of the target instruction. Bit[0] of Rm should be 0 to select a target ARM instruction, or 1 to select a target Thumb instruction.

Example:

BLX   R0   ;target address = R0 & 0xFFFFFFFE.

                   ;PC = target address.

                   ;LR = next instruction.

                   ;CPSR T bit = R0 & 0x1.

8.3.12.4   BX

The BX (Branch and Exchange) instruction branches to an address held in a register Rm, with an optional switch to Thumb execution. The branch target address is the value of Rm, with its bit[0] forced to zero. The instruction set to be used at the branch target is chosen by setting the CPSR T bit to bit[0] of Rm.

Syntax:

BX{<cond>}   <Rm>

Where:

<cond>   Is the condition under which instruction is executed. See Figure 8-6 for possible conditions.

<Rm>   Is the register containing the address of the target instruction. Bit[0] of Rm is 0 to select a target ARM instruction, or 1 to select a target Thumb instruction.

Example:

BX   R0   ;target_address = R0 & 0xFFFFFFFE;

                   ;PC = target address.

                   ;CPSR T bit = R0 & 0x1.

8.3.13   Loading a 32 bit immediate value into a register

One can not initialize a register with an arbitrary 32 bit constant. But one can load an arbitrary 32 bit constant from memory into a register. If the 32 bit value corresponds to an address one can add an 8 bit constant (with appropriate rotation to it) to PC to generate a 32 bit address. So ARM assembler supports two directives to initialize a register with a arbitrary 32 bit constant/address.

8.3.13.1   ADR

The syntax of ADR mnemonic is

ADR   <Rd>,   label

The mnemonic "ADR <Rd>, label" is converted into "ADD|SUB Rd, PC, #constant" such that Rd is initialized correctly with address of the label. If the label is far away from PC or Rd can not be initialized in this way then assembler issue the error message. Refer to your ARM tools for more detailed explanation.

8.3.13.2   LDR

The syntax of LDR mnemonic is

LDR <Rd>, =#constant

The constant can be any arbitrary 32 bit value.

If the constant can be generated by 8 bit value with rotation in a 32 bit register then the instruction is converted by assembler as "MOV|MVN <Rd>, <shifter_operand>" instruction where shifter_operand is a 8 bit immediate value with rotation.

If the constant can not be generated by a 8 bit value with rotation, the assembler places the 32 bit value in the literal pool and convert the instruction as "LDR <Rd>, [PC, #offset]". Where the offset is chosen such that it will load the 32 bit value placed in the literal pool. Please see the documentation of your ARM tools for more detailed explanation.

9 Appendix-B SROS source code

This appendix is divided into two parts. First part i.e. Section 9.1 is the source code for SROS V1.0 on ARM platform. The V1.0 code is the code the materialize all the concepts discussed till chapter 2. i.e. SROS without timer support. The V2.0 code i.e. section 9.2 is the SROS code with timer support that materialize all the concepts discussed till chapter 3.

9.1 SROS V1.0

9.1.1 rtos.h

```
#ifndef __rtos__
#define __rtos__

#include "typeDef.h"

#define   INITIAL_CPSR_ARM_FUNCTION   0x0000001F
#define   INITIAL_CPSR_THUMB_FUNCTION 0x0000003F
```

extern int64 time; //This gloable variable is incremented after every timer tick. At the starting of the system this variable is initialized to 0.

```
//Work around to make sure that threadObject_t have *listObject_t inside it,
//and listObject_t has *threadObject_t inside it.
struct _threadObject_;
struct _listObject_;

typedef struct _listObject_
{
    struct _threadObject_ *element;
    int32 auxInfo;
    struct _listObject_ *nextListNode;

}listNode_t;

typedef listNode_t listObject_t;

typedef struct _threadObject_
{
    int32 R[16];
    uint32 cpsr;
    uint32 priority;
    char   *threadObjectName;
```

```
}threadObject_t;

typedef struct
{
    int32 mutex;
    listObject_t waitList;
}mutexObject_t;

typedef struct
{
    uint32 count;
    listObject_t waitList;
}semaphoreObject_t;

typedef struct
{
    int8 *mailboxBuffer;
    int32 readIndex;
    int32 writeIndex;
    int32 mailboxBufferSize;
    int32 emptyBufferSize;
    int32 messageSize;
    listObject_t waitList;
}mailboxObject_t;


listNode_t *listNodeAlloc(void);

void listNodeFree(listNode_t *listNodePtr);

void listObjectModuleInit(void);

void listObjectInit(listObject_t *listObjectPtr);

void listObjectInsert(listObject_t *listNodePtr, threadObject_t *newThreadObject);

threadObject_t *listObjectDelete(listObject_t *listObjectPtr);

int32 listObjectCount(listObject_t *listObjectPtr);

void threadObjectCreate(threadObject_t *threadObjectPtr,
            void *functionPtr,
            int32 arg1,
            int32 arg2,
```

```
            int32 arg3,
            int32 arg4,
            int32* stackPointer,
            uint32 priority,
            uint32 cpsr,
            char   *threadObjectName);

void mutexObjectInit(mutexObject_t *mutexObjectPtr, int32 initialFlag);

int32 mutexObjectLock(mutexObject_t *mutexObjectPtr, int32 waitFlag);

void mutexObjectRelease(mutexObject_t *mutexObjectPtr);

void semaphoreObjectInit(semaphoreObject_t *semaphoreObjectPtr, uint32
initialCount);

int32 semaphoreObjectPend(semaphoreObject_t *semaphoreObjectPtr, int32 waitFlag);

void semaphoreObjectPost(semaphoreObject_t *semaphoreObjectPtr);

void mailboxObjectInit(mailboxObject_t *mailboxObjectPtr,
            int8 *mailboxBuffer,
            int32 mailboxBufferSize,
            int32 messageSize);

int32 mailboxObjectPend(mailboxObject_t *mailboxObjectPtr,
        int32 waitFlag,
        void *message);

int32 mailboxObjectPost(mailboxObject_t *mailboxObjectPtr,
        int32 waitFlag,
        void *message);

void scheduler(void);     //This function never returns.
void rtosInit(void);
void block(void);


#endif
```

9.1.2 rtos.c

```c
#include "rtos.h"
#include "assert.h"

#define MAX_THREADS_IN_THE_SYSTEM   100
#define MAX_LIST_NODES          MAX_THREADS_IN_THE_SYSTEM
listNode_t listNodes[MAX_LIST_NODES];
uint32    listNodesAvailableCount;
listNode_t *listNodesAvailable[MAX_LIST_NODES];

listObject_t readyList;
threadObject_t *runningThreadObjectPtr;
threadObject_t idleThread;
int32       idleStack[5];

extern void rtosInitAsm(void);
extern void interrupt_disable(void);
extern void interrupt_restore(void);

/*
Description:
This function
initializes the pool unallocated listNodes in the
"listNodesAvailable" global array.
initializes the "listNodesAvailableCount" which count the number of
listNodes in the pool.
*/
void listObjectModuleInit(void)
{
    int32 i;

    assert(MAX_LIST_NODES > 0);

    listNodesAvailableCount = MAX_LIST_NODES;

    for(i=0; i<MAX_LIST_NODES; i++)
    {
        listNodesAvailable[i] = &listNodes[i];
    }
}

/*
Description:
This function just return the last available listNode from the
```

pool (i.e."listNodesAvailable" array) and decrement the counter
(i.e."listNodesAvailableCount")that count the number of listNodes in the pool.
*/

```
listNode_t *listNodeAlloc()
{
    assert(listNodesAvailableCount > 0);

    return listNodesAvailable[--listNodesAvailableCount];
}
```

/*
Description:
This function just add the freed listNode to the pool of available
listNodes and increment the counter(i.e."listNodesAvailableCount") that
count the number of listNodes in the pool.
*/

```
void listNodeFree(listNode_t *listNodePtr)
{
    listNodesAvailable[listNodesAvailableCount++] = listNodePtr;

    assert(listNodesAvailableCount <= MAX_LIST_NODES);
}
```

/*
Description:
This function initilizes the listObject. ListObject is the dummy listNode
in the beginning of list in the linked list data structure. The dummy node
contain number of list nodes in the "auxInfo" field. This function initializes the
listObject. (i.e. initializes the dummy first node in the linked list).
*/

```
void listObjectInit(listObject_t *listObjectPtr)
{
    //The list object is the dummy head at the beginning of the linked list.
    //It is an invalid node.
    //It holds the number of list nodes in auxInfo field.
    assert(listObjectPtr != 0);
    listObjectPtr->element = 0;
    listObjectPtr->auxInfo = 0;
    listObjectPtr->nextListNode = 0;
}
```

/*
Description:
This function insert a new listNode into the linked list. The linked
list hold the threadObjects as its elements. It take "newThreadObject"

206

and insert it at appropriate place in the list according to the priority.
All the threadObjects in the list are stored in the descending order of
priority. (Note lower the priority number, higher the priority).
In each list node, the "priority" field of threadObject is noted into
the auxInfo field of the listNode.
*/
```c
void listObjectInsert(listObject_t *listNodePtr,
          threadObject_t *newThreadObject)
{
   listNode_t *newListNodePtr;
   uint32 newThreadObjectPriority;

   assert(newThreadObject != 0);
   assert(listNodePtr != 0);

   newThreadObjectPriority = newThreadObject->priority;
   //listObject first element is dummy head. Its auxInfo hold
   //the number of list nodes available in the list.
   //So the count is increased when inserting an element.
   listNodePtr->auxInfo++;

   //parse the list till we reach the correct place for the newThreadObject.
   while(listNodePtr->nextListNode != 0 &&
     listNodePtr->nextListNode->auxInfo <= newThreadObjectPriority)
   {
      listNodePtr = listNodePtr->nextListNode;
   }

   //allocate and initialize the new node.
   newListNodePtr = listNodeAlloc();
   newListNodePtr->element = newThreadObject;
   newListNodePtr->auxInfo = newThreadObjectPriority;

   //insert into the list.
   newListNodePtr->nextListNode = listNodePtr->nextListNode;
   listNodePtr->nextListNode = newListNodePtr;
}

/*
Description:
This function delete the first listNode from the linked list
and return the threadObject (i.e. "element") in the listNode.
*/
threadObject_t *listObjectDelete(listObject_t *listObjectPtr)
{
```

```
    threadObject_t *element;

    listNode_t *freedListNodePtr;

    assert(listObjectPtr != 0);
    assert(listObjectPtr->nextListNode != 0);
    assert(listObjectPtr->auxInfo > 0);

    //decrement the number of listNodes counter.
    listObjectPtr->auxInfo--;

    //Note the element to be freed.
    freedListNodePtr = listObjectPtr->nextListNode;
    element = freedListNodePtr->element;

    //adjust the link from dummy head to the second listNode
    //in the list (as first one is removed).
    listObjectPtr->nextListNode = freedListNodePtr->nextListNode;

    //free the removed listNode.
    listNodeFree(freedListNodePtr);

    //return the threadObject (i.e. element) available
    //in the first listNode (which is deleted).
    return element;
}

/*
Description:
This function just return the number of listNodes available in the linked list.
The number of listNodes in the list are maintained in the dummy header "auxInfo"
field. So this function just return the value in the "auxInfo" field of
the dummy head.
*/
int32 listObjectCount(listObject_t *listObjectPtr)
{
    return listObjectPtr->auxInfo;
}

/*
Description:
This function implement the idle loop to execute in the idle thread.
*/
void idleFunction(void)
{
```

208

```c
  while(1)
  {
     ;
  }
}

/*
Description:
This function initializes the SROS.
It initializes the list module to create unallocated pool of listNodes.
Initalizes the "readyList" which hold the threadObjects waiting
for the CPU time.
Initializes the "runningThreadObjectPtr" (which always hold the
running threadObject address) to NULL.
Create the Idle thread in the sytem.
*/
void rtosInit(void)
{
   listObjectModuleInit();

   listObjectInit(&readyList);

   runningThreadObjectPtr = 0;

   rtosInitAsm();

   threadObjectCreate(&idleThread,
            (void *)idleFunction,
            0,
            0,
            0,
            0,
            &idleStack[5],
            127,
            INITIAL_CPSR_ARM_FUNCTION,
            "idleThread"
            );

   return;
}

/*
Description:
This function check whether a context switch is needed.
This function return 1 (denoting context switch is needed) when
```

the currently running thread in the system has lower priority than
highest priority thread available in the readyList. Otherwise this function
return 0. Note that lower the priority number higher the thread priority.
*/
int is_thread_switch_needed(void)
{
    //check if the runningThreadObject has less priority than
    //highest priority thread in the ready list. If so return 1
    //else return 0.

    int returnValue = 0;

    if(readyList.auxInfo > 0)   //if the number of threads in the ready list > 0
    {
        if((readyList.nextListNode)->auxInfo < runningThreadObjectPtr->priority)
        {
            returnValue = 1;
        }
    }

    return returnValue;
}

/*
Description:
This function initializes the mailboxObject.
"mailboxBuffer" is the memory space where messages are stored.
"mailboxBufferSize" is the size of the "mailboxBuffer"
"messageSize" is the size of each message.
*/
void mailboxObjectInit(mailboxObject_t *mailboxObjectPtr,
            int8 *mailboxBuffer,
            int32 mailboxBufferSize,
            int32 messageSize)
{
    mailboxObjectPtr->mailboxBuffer = mailboxBuffer;
    mailboxObjectPtr->readIndex = 0;
    mailboxObjectPtr->writeIndex = 0;
    mailboxObjectPtr->mailboxBufferSize = mailboxBufferSize;
    mailboxObjectPtr->emptyBufferSize = mailboxBufferSize;
    mailboxObjectPtr->messageSize = messageSize;

    listObjectInit(&mailboxObjectPtr->waitList);

    assert(mailboxObjectPtr->mailboxBufferSize % messageSize == 0);

```
}

/*
Description:
This function initializes the mutexObject. The initial status of mutex
is initialized with the "initialFlag" which can be either 0 or 1.
*/
void mutexObjectInit(mutexObject_t *mutexObjectPtr, int32 initialFlag)
{
    assert(initialFlag == 0 || initialFlag == 1);

    mutexObjectPtr->mutex = initialFlag;

    listObjectInit(&mutexObjectPtr->waitList);
}


/*
This funciton initializes the semaphoreObject. The initial count of the
semaphore is initialized with the "initialCount" passed to this function.
*/
void semaphoreObjectInit(semaphoreObject_t *semaphoreObjectPtr,
            uint32 initialCount)
{
    semaphoreObjectPtr->count = initialCount;

    listObjectInit(&(semaphoreObjectPtr->waitList));
}
```

9.1.3 rtosAsm.h

```
                    IF :LNOT::DEF: __rtosAsm_h__

            GBLS    __rtosAsm_h__
__rtosAsm_h__       SETS   "1"

USER_MODE           EQU    2_10000
SYSTEM_MODE          EQU    2_11111
FIQ_MODE           EQU    2_10001
IRQ_MODE           EQU    2_10010
SVC_MODE            EQU    2_10011
ABT_MODE            EQU    2_10111
UND_MODE            EQU    2_11011


        MACRO
$lable    INTERRUPTS_DISABLE $scratchRegister

        MRS    $scratchRegister, CPSR

        ;disable 6th (F), 7th (I)bits. (bit count starts from 0)
        ORR    $scratchRegister, $scratchRegister, #0x000000C0 ;set F, I bits.

        MSR    CPSR_c, $scratchRegister

        MEND

        MACRO
$lable    INTERRUPTS_SAVE_DISABLE $cpsrSaveMemoryAddress, $scratchRegister1,
$scratchRegister2

        MRS    $scratchRegister1, CPSR

        MOV    $scratchRegister2, $scratchRegister1

        ;disable 6th (F), 7th (I)bits. (bit count starts from 0)
        ORR    $scratchRegister1, $scratchRegister1, #0x000000C0   ;clear F, I bits.

        MSR    CPSR_c, $scratchRegister1

        LDR    $scratchRegister1, =$cpsrSaveMemoryAddress

        STR    $scratchRegister2, [$scratchRegister1]

        MEND
```

```
        MACRO
$lable   INTERRUPTS_RESTORE  $cpsrSaveMemoryAddress, $scratchRegister

        LDR     $scratchRegister, =$cpsrSaveMemoryAddress   ;get the oldCPSR address
into register.

        LDR     $scratchRegister, [$scratchRegister] ;load the old CPSR

        MSR     CPSR_c, $scratchRegister    ;restore the old CPSR.

        MEND


        MACRO
$label   MEMCPY $destAddressRegister, $sourceAddressRegister, $noOfBytesRegister,
$scratchRegister

$label.loop
        LDRB    $scratchRegister, [$sourceAddressRegister], #1

        STRB    $scratchRegister, [$destAddressRegister], #1

        SUBS    $noOfBytesRegister, $noOfBytesRegister, #1

        BGT     $label.loop

        MEND


        MACRO
        SET_IRQ_MODE    $scratchRegister

        MRS     $scratchRegister, CPSR

        BIC     $scratchRegister, $scratchRegister, #0x1F   ;keep only mode bits.

        ORR     $scratchRegister, $scratchRegister, #IRQ_MODE

        MSR     CPSR_c, $scratchRegister

        MEND


        MACRO
        SET_STATE_OF_PC_IN_CPSR $pcRegister, $cpsrRegister
```

```
        AND    $pcRegister, $pcRegister, #0x1      ;$pcRegister = the mode of the PC when
the thread starts next time (0-ARM, 1-Thumb)

        ORR    $cpsrRegister, $cpsrRegister, $pcRegister, LSL #5      ;set the appropriate
mode for the next PC.  5 is THUMB bit position in CPSR.

        MEND

listNode_t_element_offset      EQU 0
listNode_t_auxInfo_offset      EQU 4
listNode_t_nextListNode_offset EQU 8
listNode_t_size                EQU 12

listObject_t_element_offset      EQU 0
listObject_t_auxInfo_offset      EQU 4
listObject_t_nextListNode_offset   EQU 8
listObject_t_size                EQU 12


mutexObject_t_mutex_offset      EQU    0
mutexObject_t_waitList_offset   EQU    4
mutexObject_t_size              EQU    (4+listObject_t_size)

threadObject_t_R_offset              EQU    0
threadObject_t_cpsr_offset           EQU    64
threadObject_t_priority_offset       EQU    68
threadObject_t_threadObjectName_offset EQU    72
threadObject_t_size                  EQU    76

mailboxObject_t_mailboxBuffer_offset   EQU    0
mailboxObject_t_readIndex_offset       EQU    4
mailboxObject_t_writeIndex_offset      EQU    8
mailboxObject_t_mailboxBufferSize_offset EQU    12
mailboxObject_t_emptyBufferSize_offset EQU    16
mailboxObject_t_messageSize_offset     EQU    20
mailboxObject_t_waitList_offset        EQU    24
mailboxObject_t_size                   EQU    (24+listObject_t_size)

semaphoreObject_t_count_offset        EQU    0
semaphoreObject_t_waitList_offset     EQU    4
semaphoreObject_t_size                EQU    (4+listObject_t_size)

        ENDIF
        END
```

9.1.4 rtosAsm.s

```
            INCLUDE rtosAsm.h

            IMPORT  runningThreadObjectPtr
            IMPORT  listObjectInsert
            IMPORT  listObjectDelete
            IMPORT  readyList
            IMPORT  irq_interrupt_service_routine
            IMPORT  is_thread_switch_needed
            IMPORT  __main

            EXPORT  scheduler
            EXPORT  rtosInitAsm
            EXPORT  block
            EXPORT  irq_interrupt_handler
            EXPORT  threadObjectCreate
            EXPORT  oldCPSR

            AREA srosData, DATA

oldCPSR DCD 0

            GBLS    R13_irq
            GBLS    R14_irq
            GBLS    SPSR_irq

R13_irq     SETS    "R13"
R14_irq     SETS    "R14"
SPSR_irq    SETS    "SPSR"

;The below section is vector table of ARM processor.
;This code section has to be placed at 0x00000000 for low vectors
;or at 0xFFFF0000 for high vectors.

            AREA    vectorTable, CODE

            B       reset_interrupt_handler
                        ;0x0000 for reset interrupt
            B       reset_interrupt_handler
                        ;0x0004 for Undefined instructions interrupt
            B       reset_interrupt_handler
                        ;0x0008 for SWI interrupts.
            B       reset_interrupt_handler
                        ;0x000c for instruction fetchabort.
```

```
B    reset_interrupt_handler
            ;0x0010 for data abort.
B    reset_interrupt_handler
            ;0x0014 reserved.
B    irq_interrupt_handler
            ;0x0018 for irq interrupts.
B    reset_interrupt_handler
            ;0x001c for fiq interrupts.
```

;The below code section changes the processor mode to IRQ mode
;i.e (kernel mode).
;This code section also initializes the current mode (superviser mode)
;stack pointer to IRQ mode stack pointer. This function copies the
;return address in superviser mode to IRQ mode LR so that it can use
;it for returning.

```
    AREA   rtosInitAsm_code, CODE
rtosInitAsm
    ;This function changes the processor mode to IRQ mode.
    MRS   R0, CPSR       ;get the status.

    BIC   R0, R0, #0x1F   ;remove mode bits.

    ORR   R0, R0, #IRQ_MODE  ;make mode as IRQ mode.

    ;before writing the mode into CPSR, save R13, R14 and keep
    ;the same R13, R14 into IRQ mode.
    MOV   R1, R13        ;get the stack pointerof superviser
                ;mode.

    MOV   R2, R14        ;save the return address to return
                ;later.

    MSR   CPSR_c, R0     ;write the status register to change
                ;the processor mode.

    MOV   R13, R1        ;initialize the stack pointer for IRQ
                ;mode.

    MOV   R14, R2        ;Get the return address into LR.

    BX    LR             ;return using the return address.
```

;This code section is code section for block() function. This block function

216

;keep the runnning threadObject into the readyList and jump to scheduler to
;start the highest priority ready thread. If the running thread is the highest
;priority ready thread then calling block() function does not result in
;context switch and do not have any effect in the system.
;Note: As interrupt service routine is not a thread, this function should
;not be called from interrupt service routine.

```
        AREA    block_code, CODE
block
        INTERRUPTS_SAVE_DISABLE oldCPSR, R2, R3     ;disable interrupts

        ;creating context for the current running thread.
        ;take the context as the end of the block() function.

        LDR     R1, =runningThreadObjectPtr
                        ;R1=&runningThreadObjectPtr

        LDR     R1, [R1]        ;R1=&runningThreadObject

        ASSERT  threadObject_t_R_offset = 0

        STMIA   R1, {R0-R14}
                        ;saved registers R0-R14 in
                        ;the running threadObject.

        STR     R14, [R1, #(15*4)]
                        ;save the return address as the
                        ;starting point (i.e. PC) when the
                        ;thread starts later.

        LDR     R4, =oldCPSR

        LDR     R4, [R4]
                        ;get current status of the thread
                        ;when it enters this function.

        SET_STATE_OF_PC_IN_CPSR R14, R4
                        ;This macro keep the correct state for
                        ;later starting point of the thread
                        ;in R4

        STR     R4, [R1, #threadObject_t_cpsr_offset]
                        ;save the correct status of the
                        ;thread into the threadObject CPSR
```

;insert the running thread into readyList.

LDR   R0, =readyList

BL   listObjectInsert
                ;insert the running threadObject
                ;into the readyList.

;jump to scheduler

B   scheduler

;The below code section is code for scheduler. The scheduler first disables
;interrupts and set the mode to kernel mode (irq mode)
;and loads the context of the highest priority ready thread in the system.
;As starting of the highest priority read thread is also done in the
;interrupt handler code, the below code section just jump to interrupt
;handler code section to reuse the code in interrupt handler.
;The pseudo code of the scheduler is shown below.
;void scheduler(void)
;{
;   threadObject_t *threadObjectPtr;
;
;   disableInterrupts();
;   change the processor mode to kernel mode; (if it is not in kernel mode).
;   threadObjectPtr = listObjectDelete(&readyList);
;
;   load the context in the threadObjectPtr.
;   start running from the PC in the threadObjectPtr.
;}

        AREA   schuduler_code, CODE

scheduler
scheduler INTERRUPTS_DISABLE R0   ;disable interrupts.

        ;change to kernel mode.
        ;This is necessary as we do not have SPSR in system mdoe.
        ;So go to IRQ mode to load SPSR and copy that into CPSR.
        SET_IRQ_MODE   R0

        ;make a jump to the interrupt handler code section which has
        ;the functionality of starting the highest priority thread
        ;from readyList.

218

```
        B      start_high_priority_thread
```

;The below code section is the reset interrupt handler code section.
;The reset interrupt handler just jump to the entry point of the embedded
;application.

```
        AREA   reset_interrupt_handler_code, CODE
```

reset_interrupt_handler

```
        B      __main  ;branch to entry point. If the embedded
                       ;application entry point is not __main
                       ;__main has to be replaced by the entry
                       ;point.
```

;The below code section implement the irq_interrupt_handler.
;The irq interrupt handler just call irq_interrupt_service_routine().
;Note that irq_interrupt_service_routine() should not use interrupt
;key word of C language. The irq_interrupt_service_routine() should
;be developed like normal C function. The saving and restoring of
;callee preserve register in the calling convention i.e.R0-R3, R12
;are done by the interrupt handler.
;The irq_interrupt_handler do context switch if needed after the
;irq_interrupt_service_routine() returns. Note that any SROS call that
;can block should not be called in irq_interrupt_service_routine().
;After the irq_interrupt_service_routine() returns, irq_interrupt_handler
;do context switch if needed. Note that instead of jumping to schuduler()
;irq_interrupt_handler() implemented the code to start the highest priority
;ready thread in the system. (Infact schuduler() function is also using the
;same code that is irq_interrupt_handler_code section.
;The pseudo code of the irq_interrupt_handler() is shown below.
;void irq_interrupt_handler(void)
;{
;   irq_interrupt_service_routine();
;   if (running thread priority higher than highest
;   thread priority in the readyList)
;   {
;   return to the interrupted thread.
;   }
;   else
;   {
;   Get the context exactly equal to the position when
;   interrupt happened in the running thread, Save that
;   context into the running threadObject.
```
```

```
;     Insert the running threadObject into readyList.
;     jump to scheduler tostart the highest priority ready thread.
;   }
;}


      AREA   irq_interrupt_handler_code, CODE

irq_interrupt_handler

      ;R13_irq, R14_irq, spsr_irq are active here. cpsr of the interrupted
      ;thread is stored in spsr_irq.
      ;So we are operating on irq stack here.

      SUB    $R14_irq, $R14_irq, #4
                  ;calculate the actual address to be returned.

      STMFD  $R13_irq!, {R0-R3, R12, $R14_irq}
                  ;save the interrupted thread registers.
                  ;This step is necessary as the
                  ;irq_interrupt_service_routine() may destroy
                  ;those registers.

      BL     irq_interrupt_service_routine
                  ;call the user defined
                  ;irq_interrupt_service_routine().

      BL     is_thread_switch_needed
                  ;check if context switch is necessary.
                  ;If irq_interrupt_service_routine() has
                  ;triggered a higher priority thread than
                  ;running thread to ready state,
                  ;then context switch will become necessary.

      CMP R0, #0           ;if(is_thread_switch_needed()==0)

      LDMEQFD $R13_irq!, {R0-R3, R12, PC}^
                  ;thread switch is not needed. So returning
                  ;to the interrupted (i.e. running) thread.
                  ;SPSR_irq copied to CPSR. This is LDM (3)
                  ;instruction.

      ;context switch is necessary. So
      ;save the current thread context first
      LDR    R0, =runningThreadObjectPtr
```

```
LDR    R0, [R0]      ;R0=&runningThreadObject

MRS    R1, $SPSR_irq   ;interrupted thread CPSR is on SPSR_irq.
                 ;So get that.

ASSERT  threadObject_t_R_offset = 0

STR    R1, [R0, #threadObject_t_cpsr_offset]
                 ;save interrupted thread CPSR.

LDMFD  $R13_irq!, {R2, R3}
                 ;get interrupted thread R0, R1 into R2, R3
                 ;respectively.

STMIA  R0!, {R2, R3}   ;save interrupted thread R0, R1.
                 ;R0=&runningThread+8

LDMFD  $R13_irq!, {R2, R3, R12, $R14_irq}
                 ;load the interrupted thread registers that
                 ;we have saved on the stack.
                 ;(NOTE:R14 loaded is R14_irq as we are in
                 ;IRQ mode).

STR    $R14_irq, [R0, #(15*4-8)]
                 ;save the R14_irq as the starting point of
                 ;execution of the interrupted thread.

STMIA  R0, {R2-R14}^
                 ;Save the interrupted thread registers.
                 ;save user/system mode registers.
                 ;This instruction
                 ;loads always user mode registers even though
                 ; we are in IRQ mode. (STM (2) instruction).
                 ;Note that previously R0=&runningThread.R[2]

;now insert the runningThread into readyList.
;listObjectInsert(listObject_t *listNodePtr, void *newElement)

SUB    R1, R0, #(2*4)
                 ;R1=&runningThread

LDR    R0, =readyList
                 ;R0=&readyList.

BL     listObjectInsert
```

;insert the interrupted threadObject into the
;readyList.

;Now we are ready to load the context of the highest priority
;threadObject from the readyList.

start_high_priority_thread

;get the new thread object to be started.
;threadObject = void *listObjectDelete(listObject_t *listObjectPtr);

```
LDR    R0, =readyList

BL     listObjectDelete
                ;get the high priority thread to be run.
                ;After this function R0 holds the
                ;&threadObject

LDR    R1, =runningThreadObjectPtr

STR    R0, [R1]      ;store runninThreadObject pointer.

LDR    R12, [R0, #threadObject_t_cpsr_offset]
                ;get the cpsr of the threadObject.

MSR    $SPSR_irq._fsxc, R12
                ;save the cpsr into SPSR (SPSR will be copied
                ;into CPSR at exit of this function).

ASSERT  threadObject_t_R_offset = 0

LDR    $R14_irq, [R0, #(15*4)]
                ;get PC value into R14_irq (R14_irq will be
                ;copied into PC at exit of this function).

LDMIA  R0, {R0-R14}^   ;load saved R0-R14 of high priority thread
                ;into user mode R0-R14 registers. (LDM (2)
                ;instruction)

NOP                 ;can not use banked registers after user
                ;mode LDM.


MOVS   PC, $R14_irq   ;PC=R14_irq, CPSR=SPSR_irq
                ;After this instruction the highest priority
```

```
                    ;ready thread in the system will start running

;The below code section create a new thread in the system. The new thread
;creation is done by saving appropriate context for the new thread in to the
;readyList.
;If the new thread created has higher priorty than running thread, context
;switch will happen. (if context switch is allowed).
;The pseudo code of the threadObjectCreate() function is shown below.
;void threadObjectCreate(threadObject_t *threadObjectPtr,
;               void (*functionPtr)(void*, ...),
;               int32 arg1,
;               int32 arg2,
;               int32 arg3,
;               int32 arg4,
;               int32* stackPointer,
;               uint32 priority,
;               uint32 cpsr,
;               int8 *threadObjectName)
;{
;   threadObjectPtr->R[15] = (int32)(functionPtr);
;   threadObjectPtr->R[0] = arg1;
;   threadObjectPtr->R[1] = arg2;
;   threadObjectPtr->R[2] = arg3;
;   threadObjectPtr->R[3] = arg4;
;   threadObjectPtr->R[13] = (int32)(stackPointer);
;   threadObjectPtr->R[14] = scheduler;
;   threadObjectPtr->priority = priority;
;   threadObjectPtr->threadObjectName = threadObjectName;
;   interruptDisable();
;
;   listObjectInsert(&readyList, threadObjectPtr);
;
;   if(priority < runningThreadObjectPtr->priority &&
;        context switch is allowed)
;   {
;     get the context of running thread functionally equivalent to end of
;     this function.
;     listObjectInsert(&readyList,
;             runningThreadObjectPtr);
;     jump to scheduler().
;   }
;
;   interruptsRestore();
;}
```

```
        AREA    threadObjectCreate_code, CODE

threadObjectCreate

        GBLS    threadObjectPtrR0
        GBLS    functionPtrR1
        GBLS    arg1R2
        GBLS    arg2R3

threadObjectPtrR0  SETS   "R0"
functionPtrR1      SETS   "R1"
arg1R2             SETS   "R2"
arg2R3             SETS   "R3"
arg3_offset        EQU    0
arg4_offset        EQU    4
stackPointer_offset EQU    8
priority_offset    EQU    12
cpsr_offset        EQU    16
threadObjectName_offset EQU 20

        ASSERT  threadObject_t_R_offset = 0

        STR    $functionPtrR1, [$threadObjectPtrR0, #(15*4)]
                    ;threadObjectPtr->R[15]=functionPtr

        STR    $arg1R2, [$threadObjectPtrR0, #(0*4)]
                    ;threadObjectPtr->R[0] = arg1

        STR    $arg2R3, [$threadObjectPtrR0, #(1*4)]
                    ;threadObjectPtr->R[1] = arg2

        LDR    R12, [SP, #arg3_offset]
                    ;R12=arg3

        STR    R12, [$threadObjectPtrR0, #(2*4)]
                    ;threadObjectPtr->R[2]=arg3

        LDR    R12, [SP, #arg4_offset]
                    ;R12=arg4

        STR    R12, [$threadObjectPtrR0, #(3*4)]
                    ;threadObjectPtr->r[3]=arg4

        LDR    R12, [SP, #stackPointer_offset]
                    ;R12=stackPointer
```

```
STR    R12, [$threadObjectPtrR0, #(13*4)]
              ;threadObjectPtr->R[13]=stackPointer.

LDR    R12, =scheduler

STR    R12, [$threadObjectPtrR0, #(14*4)]
              ;threadObjectPtr->R[14]=scheduler

LDR    R12, [SP, #priority_offset]
              ;R12=priority.

STR    R12, [$threadObjectPtrR0, #threadObject_t_priority_offset]
              ;threadObjectPtr->priority=priority.

LDR    R1, [SP, #cpsr_offset]
              ;R1=cpsr

STR    R1, [$threadObjectPtrR0, #threadObject_t_cpsr_offset]
              ;save CPSR

LDR    R1, [SP, #threadObjectName_offset]
              ;R1=threadObjectName

STR    R1, [$threadObjectPtrR0, \
          #threadObject_t_threadObjectName_offset]
              ;save name pointer.

INTERRUPTS_SAVE_DISABLE oldCPSR, R1, R2

MOV    R1, R0          ;R1=threadObjectPtr

LDR    R0, =readyList    ;R0=readyList

STMFD  SP!, {LR}

;listObjectInsert(&readyList, threadObject);
BL     listObjectInsert

;check if scheduler is started. If scheduler is not started
;then runningThreadObjectPtr = 0.

LDR    R0, =runningThreadObjectPtr
              ;R0=&runningThreadObjectPtr
```

```
        LDR    R0, [R0]         ;R0=runningThreadObjectPtr

        CMP    R0, #0           ;if(runningThreadObjectPtr == 0)

        BEQ    schuduler_is_not_started
                        ;if(runningThreadObjectPtr == 0)
                        ;then just return.

;if called from the interrupt service routine, then just return.
        MRS    R1, CPSR         ;get the current status

        AND    R1, R1, #0x1F    ;keep only mode bits.

        CMP    R1, #IRQ_MODE    ;check whether we are in kernel mode.

        BEQ    called_from_interrupt_service_routine
                        ;This function is called from
                        ;interrupt service routine.
                        ;So just return.

        BL    is_thread_switch_needed

        CMP    R0, #0

        BEQ    context_switch_not_needed

        INTERRUPTS_RESTORE oldCPSR, R1
                        ;restore the original interrupts
                        ;status.

        BL    block            ;context switch is needed.
                        ;Just call block
                        ;block function keep the
                        ;running thread into readyList
                        ;and start the highest priority
                        ;thread available in the readyList.

        LDMFD  SP!, {PC}        ;return

schuduler_is_not_started
called_from_interrupt_service_routine
context_switch_not_needed

        INTERRUPTS_RESTORE oldCPSR, R1
                        ;get original interrupts status.
```

```
LDMFD   SP!, {PC}        ;return

END
```

9.1.5 mutexObjectAsm.s

```
        INCLUDE rtosAsm.h

        IMPORT  runningThreadObjectPtr
        IMPORT  listObjectInsert
        IMPORT  listObjectDelete
        IMPORT  readyList
        IMPORT  scheduler
        IMPORT  oldCPSR

        EXPORT  mutexObjectLock
        EXPORT  mutexObjectRelease

;The below code section implement the mutexObjectLock() and
;mutexObjectRelease() functions.

        AREA mutexObjectCode, CODE

;The mutexObjectLock function lock the mutex. The pseduo code for
;mutexObjectLock() is shown below.
;int32 mutexObjectLock(mutexObject_t *mutexObjectPtr, int32 waitFlag)
;{
;  if(swap(0, &mutexObjectPtr->mutex))
;  {
;     return 1;
;  }
;  else
;  {
;     if(waitFlag)
;     {
;       interruptsDisable();
;       get the context which should be functionally equivalent to starting
;       of this function and store that context in the running
;       threadObject i.e. context space of running thread.
;       listObjectInsert(&mutexObjectPtr->waitList,
;       runningThreadObjectPtr);
;       jump to scheduler();
;     }
;     else
;     {
;       return 0;
;     }
;  }
;}
```

;Note : This function should not be called from interrupt service
;routinie non zero waitFlag.

     ;R0 = mutexObjectPtr, R1 = waitFlag according to the calling
     ;convention.
mutexObjectLock

```
    MOV    R2, #0        ;R2=0;

    ASSERT  mutexObject_t_mutex_offset = 0

    SWP    R2, R2, [R0]  ;R2 = mutex

    CMP    R2, #1        ;if(mutex == 1)

    MOVEQ  R0, #1        ;if(mutex == 1) returnValue = 1.

    BXEQ   LR            ;if(mutex == 1) return returnValue.

    CMP    R1, #0        ;if(waitFlag == 0)

    MOVEQ  R0, #0        ;if(mutex == 0 and waitFlag == 0)
                         ;then returnValue = 0

    BXEQ   LR            ;if(mutex == 0 and waitFlag == 0)
                         ;then return returnValue.
```

;waitFlag > 0 and mutex is locked by some other thread.
;So keep the current thread in waitList of the mutexObject
;and jump to scheduler.

;interruptDisable()
INTERRUPTS_SAVE_DISABLE oldCPSR, R2, R3

;creating thread object for the current thread.
```
LDR    R3, =runningThreadObjectPtr
               ;R3=&runningThreadObjectPtr

LDR    R3, [R3]

ASSERT  threadObject_t_R_offset = 0

STMIA  R3, {R0-R14}       ;save all registers R0-R14 in
                          ;the running threadObject
```

```
ADR    R4, mutexObjectLock    ;get the address of this function.
                               ;(to start this thread later).
                               ;R4=mutexObjectLock

STR    R4, [R3, #(15*4)]      ;save it as the PC to start later.

LDR    R4, =oldCPSR

LDR    R4, [R4]              ;get original status of the thread
                             ;before masking interrupts.

STR    R4, [R3, #threadObject_t_cpsr_offset]
                             ;save the status of the thread.

;insert the running thread into waitList of mutexObject.

ADD    R0, R0, #mutexObject_t_waitList_offset
                             ;R0=&mutexObject->waitList.

MOV    R1, R3
                             ;R1=&runningThreadObjectPtr

BL     listObjectInsert;

;jump to scheduler

B      scheduler
```

```
;The below code implement mutexObjectRelease() function. mutexObjectRelease()
;function release the mutex and do context switch if necessary. The high level
;pseudo code for mutexObjectRelease() is shown below.
;void mutexObjectRelease(mutexObject_t *mutexObjectPtr)
;{
;  threadObject_t *waitingThreadObjectPtr;
;  interruptsDisable();
;  mutexObjectPtr->mutex = 1;
;  if(listObjectCount(&mutexObjectPtr->waitList))
;  {
;    waitingThreadObjectPtr=listObjectDelete(&mutexObjectPtr->waitList);
;    listObjectInsert(&readyList,waitingThreadObjectPtr);
;    if(waitingThreadObjectPtr->priority < runningThreadObject.priority &&
;        this function not called from interrupt service routine)
;    {
;      get the context functionally equivalent to the end
```

230

```
;       this function and save that context into running
;       threadObject.
;       listObjectInsert(&readyList,&runningThreadObject);
;       jump to scheduler();
;   }
; }
; interruptRestore();
; return;
;}
```

;This function can be called from interrupt service routine
;with out any ristrictions.

```
        ;R0=mutexObjectPtr according to the calling convention.
mutexObjectRelease
        ;interruptsDisable

        INTERRUPTS_SAVE_DISABLE oldCPSR, R1, R2

        MOV    R1, #1  ;R1=1

        ASSERT mutexObject_t_mutex_offset = 0

        SWP    R1, R1, [R0]   ;mutexObject->mutex = 1;

        LDR    R1, [R0, #(mutexObject_t_waitList_offset+ \
                listObject_t_auxInfo_offset)]
                ;R1=listObjectCount(&mutexObjectPtr->waitList)

        CMP    R1, #0

        BEQ    no_thread_waiting_for_mutex;

        ;some thread is waiting for this mutex.

        ADD    R0, R0, #mutexObject_t_waitList_offset
                ;R0=&mutexObjectPtr->waitList.

        STMFD  SP!, {R14}  ;saving R14 to make function call.

        ;listObjectDelete(&mutexObjectPtr->waitList)
        BL     listObjectDelete
                ;After returning from the function,
                ;R0 contain waitingThreadObjectPtr

        MOV    R1, R0     ;R1=waitingThreadObjectPtr
```

```
LDR    R0, =readyList
              ;R0 = &readyList.

STMFD  SP!, {R1}  ;Save waitingThreadObjectPtr as we are
              ;going to make a function call.

BL     listObjectInsert
              ;insert waiting thread object into
              ;ready list.
```

;Now check if the waiting thread has higher priority than the
;current running thread. and switch to the waiting thread if
;that has high priority.

```
LDMFD  SP!, {R0, R14}
              ;R0=waitingThreadObjectPtr,
              ;R14=return address from this function.

LDR    R1, =runningThreadObjectPtr
              ;R1=&runningThreadObjectPtr

LDR    R1, [R1]

LDR    R2, [R0, #threadObject_t_priority_offset]
              ;R2=waitingThreadObjectPtr->priority

LDR    R3, [R1, #threadObject_t_priority_offset]
              ;R3=runningThreadObject.priority.

CMP    R2, R3     ;if(waitingThreadObjectPtr->priority <
              ;runningThreadObject.priority)

BHS    waiting_thread_does_not_have_high_priority;
```

;check whether we are coming from the interrupt service routine.
;If we are coming from the interrupt service routine we should
;not make context switch. IRQ_handler will do the context switch.

```
MRS    R2, CPSR

AND    R2, R2, #0x1F
              ;keep only mode bits.

CMP    R2, #IRQ_MODE
```

```
                    ;if(currentMode == IRQ_MODE)

        BEQ    called_from_interrupt_service_routine

        ;This function is called from user/system mode.
        ;waiting thread has higher priority.
        ;save running thread context to readyList and call scheduler.

        STMIA  R1, {R0-R14}
                    ;save registers for running thread.

        STR    R14, [R1, #(15*4)]
                    ;saving the return address as starting
                    ;program counter.

        LDR    R2, =oldCPSR

        LDR    R2, [R2]    ;get status.

        SET_STATE_OF_PC_IN_CPSR R14, R2
                    ;set the correct state in CPSR for the
                    ;starting the thread next time.
                    ;(add the state bit correctly).

        STR    R2, [R1, #threadObject_t_cpsr_offset]   ;save status.

        LDR    R0, =readyList
                    ;R0=&readyList.

        BL     listObjectInsert
                    ;Insert the running thread into readyList

        B      scheduler   ;Jump to scheduler.


no_thread_waiting_for_mutex
waiting_thread_does_not_have_high_priority
called_from_interrupt_service_routine

        ;interruptsRestore()
        INTERRUPTS_RESTORE oldCPSR, R1

        BX     LR

        END
```

9.1.6 semaphoreObjectAsm.s

```
        INCLUDE rtosAsm.h

        IMPORT  runningThreadObjectPtr
        IMPORT  listObjectInsert
        IMPORT  listObjectDelete
        IMPORT  readyList

        IMPORT  oldCPSR
        IMPORT  scheduler

        EXPORT  semaphoreObjectPend
        EXPORT  semaphoreObjectPost

;The below code section implement semaphoreObjectPost(), semaphoreObjectPend()
;functions.

        AREA semaphoreObjectCode, CODE

;The semaphoreObjectPend() function decrement the semaphoreCount by 1. The
;pseudo code for semaphoreObjectPend() function is shown below.
;int32 semaphoreObjectPend(semaphoreObject_t *semaphoreObjectPtr,
;                               int32 waitFlag)
;{
;  interruptsDisable();
;
;  if(semaphoreObjectPtr->count > 0)
;  {
;    semaphoreObjectPtr->count--;
;    returnValue = 1;
;  }
;  else
;  {
;    if(waitFlag)
;    {
;      get the context same as start of the thread into
;      runningThreadObject.
;      listObjectInsert(&semaphoreObjectPtr->waitList,
;                  &runningThreadObject);
;      jump to scheduler();
;    }
;    else
;    {
;      returnValue = 0;
```

234

```
;     }
; }
;  interruptsRestore();
;  return returnValue;
;}
;This function should not be called from interrupt service routine
;with nonzero waitFlag.

semaphoreObjectPend

        INTERRUPTS_SAVE_DISABLE oldCPSR, R2, R3

        LDR      R2, [R0, #semaphoreObject_t_count_offset]
                    ;R2=semaphoreObjectPtr->count

        CMP      R2, #0

        SUBGT    R2, R2, #1  ;R2=R2-1

        STRGT    R2, [R0, #semaphoreObject_t_count_offset]
                    ;semaphoreObjectPtr->count--;

        MOVGT    R0, #1     ;returnValue = 1;

        BGT      semaphore_count_greater_than_0

;semaphore count equal to zero here.

        CMP      R1, #0     ;if(waitFlag)

        MOVEQ    R0, #0     ;returnValue=0.

        BEQ      semaphore_wait_flag_is_zero

;waitFlag is non zero here. So insert the running thread into
;wait list and jump to scheduler.
;initialize the context equivalent to starting of the function
;into running threadObject.
        LDR      R3, =runningThreadObjectPtr

        LDR      R3, [R3]

        ASSERT   threadObject_t_R_offset = 0

        STMIA    R3, {R0-R14}   ;save current context.
```

```
ADR     R4, semaphoreObjectPend
                ;R4=semaphoreObjectPend

STR     R4, [R3, #(15*4)]
                ;save PC as beginning of this
                ;function.

LDR     R4, =oldCPSR

LDR     R4, [R4]    ;get the original status.

STR     R4, [R3, #threadObject_t_cpsr_offset]
                ;save the current status of the thread.

;insert the running thread into waiting list.

ADD     R0, R0, #semaphoreObject_t_waitList_offset
                ;R0=&semaphoreObjectPtr->waitList

MOV     R1, R3    ;R1=&runningThreadObjectPtr

BL      listObjectInsert
                ;listObjectInsert()


;jump to scheduler to start next thread.

B       scheduler


semaphore_wait_flag_is_zero

semaphore_count_greater_than_0

        INTERRUPTS_RESTORE oldCPSR, R2

BX      LR      ;return returnValue.
```

;The semaphoreObjectPost() function increment the semaphore count by 1.
;The High level pseudo code for semaphoreObjectPost() function is shown below.
;void semaphoreObjectPost(semaphoreObject_t *semaphoreObjectPtr)

```
;{
;   threadObject_t *waitingThreadObjectPtr;
;
;   interruptsDisable();
;   semaphoreObjectPtr->count++;
;   if(listObjectCount(&semaphoreObjectPtr->waitList) > 0)
;   {
;       waitingThreadObjectPtr =
;               listObjectDelete(semaphoreObjectPtr->waitList);
;       assert(waitingThreadObjectPtr != NULL);
;       listObjectInsert(readyList, waitingThreadObjectPtr);
;       if(waitingThreadObjectPtr->priority < runningThread.priority &&
;           this function is not called from interrupt service routine)
;       {
;           get the context same as the end of this function
;           and keep that into the running threadObject.
;           listObjectInsert(&readyList, &runningThreadObject);
;           jump to scheduler();
;       }
;   }
;   interruptsRestore();
;}
```

semaphoreObjectPost

```
        INTERRUPTS_SAVE_DISABLE oldCPSR, R1, R2

        LDR    R2, [R0, #semaphoreObject_t_count_offset]
                    ;R2=semaphoreObjectPtr->count

        ADD    R2, R2, #1    ;R2=R2+1

        STR    R2, [R0, #semaphoreObject_t_count_offset]
                    ;semaphoreObjectPtr->count++

        LDR    R1, [R0, #(semaphoreObject_t_waitList_offset+ \
                    listObject_t_auxInfo_offset)]
                ;R1=listObjectCount(&semaphoreObjectPtr->waitList)

        CMP    R1, #0 ;if(listObjectCount(&semaphoreObjectPtr->waitList) > 0)

        BLE    no_thread_waiting_for_semaphore

        ;some thread is waiting for the semaphore.
        ;remove the waiting thread from waitlist and put that into
```

```
;readyList.
ADD    R0, R0, #semaphoreObject_t_waitList_offset
          ;R0=&semaphoreObjectPtr->waitList.


STMFD  SP!, {R14} ;save return address of this function before
          ;making function call.


;waitingThreadObjectPtr =
;          listObjectDelete(semaphoreObjectPtr->waitList);
BL    listObjectDelete
          ;After this function call R0 holds
          ;waitingThreadObjectPtr.


STMFD  SP!, {R0}    ;save waitingThreadObjectPtr to make
          ;function call.


MOV    R1, R0        ;R1=waitingThreadObjectPtr


LDR    R0, =readyList ;R0=&readyList


;listObjectInsert(readyList, waitingThreadObjectPtr);
BL    listObjectInsert


LDMFD  SP!, {R0, R14} ;R0 = waitingThreadObjectPtr,
          ;R14=return address of this function.


LDR    R1, =runningThreadObjectPtr ;R1=&runningThreadObjectPtr


LDR    R1, [R1]


LDR    R2, [R0, #threadObject_t_priority_offset]
          ;R2=waitingThreadObjectPtr->priority


LDR    R3, [R1, #threadObject_t_priority_offset]
          ;R3=runningThread.priority.


CMP    R2, R3 ;if(waitingThreadObjectPtr->priority <
          ;          runningThread.priority)


BGE    waiting_thread_not_higer_priority


MRS    R2, CPSR


AND    R2, R2, #0x1F  ;keep the mode bits only.
```

```
        CMP    R2, #IRQ_MODE   ;if(mode == IRQ_MODE)

        BEQ    called_from_interrrupt_service_routine
        ;This function is from interrupt service routine.
        ;context switch should not be done when called from interrupt
        ;service routine. IRQ handler will do the context switch anyway.


        ;This function is called form user/system mode thread.
        ;waiting thread has higher priority. Insert running thread
        ;into ready list and call scheduler.

        STMIA  R1, {R0-R14}   ;save registers for running thread.

        STR    R14, [R1, #(15*4)] ;saving the new start point as
                         ;return address.

        LDR    R2, =oldCPSR

        LDR    R2, [R2]        ;get the original status.

        SET_STATE_OF_PC_IN_CPSR R14, R2 ;keep the correct mode of the
                         ;CPSR for the starting position
                         ;of the new PC.

        STR    R2, [R1, #threadObject_t_cpsr_offset]   ;save status.

        LDR    R0, =readyList        ;R0=&readyList.

        ;listObjectInsert(&readyList, &runningThread);
        BL     listObjectInsert

        B      scheduler


no_thread_waiting_for_semaphore
waiting_thread_not_higer_priority
called_from_interrrupt_service_routine

        INTERRUPTS_RESTORE oldCPSR, R2

        BX     LR

        END
```

9.1.7 mailboxObjectAsm.s

```
        INCLUDE rtosAsm.h

        IMPORT  runningThreadObjectPtr
        IMPORT  listObjectInsert
        IMPORT  listObjectDelete
        IMPORT  readyList

        IMPORT  scheduler
        IMPORT  oldCPSR

        EXPORT  mailboxObjectPend
        EXPORT  mailboxObjectPost


;The below code section implement mailboxObjectPost(), mailboxObjectPend()
;functions.

        AREA mailboxObjectCode, CODE

;mailboxObjectPend() function retieve a message from mailbox. The below pseudo
;code show the functionality of the mailboxObjectPend().
;int32 mailboxObjectPend(mailboxObject_t *mailboxObjectPtr,
;           int32 waitFlag,
;           void *message)
;{
;   int32 returnValue;
;
;   interruptsDisable();
;   if(mailboxObjectPtr->emptyBufferSize <=
;       mailboxObjectPtr->mailboxBufferSize - mailboxObjectPtr->messageSize)
;   {
;       //content is available in mailbox. take one message.
;       memcpy(message,
;           &mailboxObjectPtr->mailboxBuffer[readIndex],
;           mailboxObjectPtr->messageSize);
;
;       mailboxObjectPtr->readIndex += mailboxObjectPtr->messageSize;
;       mailboxObjectPtr->emptyBufferSize += mailboxObjectPtr->messageSize;
;
;       assert(mailboxObjectPtr->readIndex <=
;                   mailboxObjectPtr->mailboxBufferSize);
;       if(mailboxObjectPtr->readIndex == mailboxObjectPtr->mailboxBufferSize)
;       {
```

240

```
;            mailboxObjectPtr->readIndex = 0;
;        }
;    returnValue = 1;
;
;    //if any thread waiting for this mailbox to become empty.
;    if(listObjectCount(&mailboxObjectPtr->waitList) > 0)
;    {
;        waitingThreadObjectPtr =
;                listObjectDelete(&mailboxObjectPtr->waitList);
;        assert(waitingThreadObjectPtr != NULL);
;        listObjectInsert(readyList, waitingThreadObjectPtr);
;        if(waitingThreadObjectPtr->priority < runningThread.priority &&
;            this function not called from interrupt service routine)
;        {
;            get the context same as the end of this function
;            and insert into the running threadObject.
;            listObjectInsert(&readyList, &runningThreadObject);
;            jump to scheduler();
;        }
;    }
; }
; else
; {
;    if(waitFlag)
;    {
;        get the context of starting of the function into running
;        threadObject.
;        listObjectInsert(mailboxObjectPtr->waitList, &runningThreadObject);
;        jump to scheduler();
;    }
;    else
;    {
;        returnValue = 0;
;    }
; }
; interruptsRestore();
; return returnValue;
;}
;This function should not be called from interrupt service routine
;with non zero waitFlag (i.e. TRUE).
mailboxObjectPend

        INTERRUPTS_SAVE_DISABLE oldCPSR, R3, R12

        LDR     R12, [R0, #mailboxObject_t_mailboxBufferSize_offset]
```

```
                      ;R12=mailboxObjectPtr->mailboxBufferSize

LDR       R3, [R0, #mailboxObject_t_messageSize_offset]
                  ;R3=mailboxObjectPtr->messageSize

SUB       R12, R12, R3
;R12=mailboxObjectPtr->mailboxBufferSize-
;                   mailboxObjectPtr->messageSize

LDR       R3, [R0, #mailboxObject_t_emptyBufferSize_offset]
                  ;R3=mailboxObjectPtr->emptyBufferSize

CMP       R3, R12
;if(mailboxObjectPtr->emptyBufferSize <=
;mailboxObjectPtr->mailboxBufferSize - mailboxObjectPtr->messageSize)

BGT       message_not_available_in_the_mailbox

;message available in the mailbox.
ADD       R12, R0, #mailboxObject_t_mailboxBuffer_offset
                  ;R12=&&mailboxObjectPtr->mailboxBuffer[0]

LDR       R12, [R12]  ;R12=&mailboxObjectPtr->mailboxBuffer[0]

LDR       R3, [R0, #mailboxObject_t_readIndex_offset]
                  ;R3=mailboxObjectPtr->readIndex

ADD       R12, R12, R3
;R12=&mailboxObjectPtr->mailboxBuffer[mailboxObjectPtr->readIndex]

LDR       R3, [R0, #mailboxObject_t_messageSize_offset]
                  ;R8=mailboxObjectPtr->messageSize

;memcpy(message,
;     &mailboxObjectPtr->mailboxBuffer[readIndex],
;     mailboxObjectPtr->messageSize);
MEMCPY    R2, R12, R3, R1

LDR       R2, [R0, #mailboxObject_t_readIndex_offset]
                  ;R2=mailboxObjectPtr->readIndex

LDR       R1, [R0, #mailboxObject_t_messageSize_offset]
                  ;R1=mailboxObjectPtr->messageSize

ADD       R2, R2, R1
```

```
                ;R2=mailboxObjectPtr->readIndex+mailboxObjectPtr->messageSize

LDR      R3, [R0, #mailboxObject_t_emptyBufferSize_offset]
                ;R3=mailboxObjectPtr->emptyBufferSize

ADD      R3, R3, R1
;R3=mailboxObjectPtr->emptyBufferSize+mailboxObjectPtr->messageSize

STR      R3, [R0, #mailboxObject_t_emptyBufferSize_offset]
;mailboxObjectPtr->emptyBufferSize += mailboxObjectPtr->messageSize

LDR      R3, [R0, #mailboxObject_t_mailboxBufferSize_offset]
;R3=mailboxObjectPtr->mailboxBufferSize

CMP      R2, R3
;if(mailboxObjectPtr->readIndex+mailboxObjectPtr->messageSize ==
;mailboxObjectPtr->mailboxBufferSize)

MOVEQ    R2, #0
;if(mailboxObjectPtr->readIndex+mailboxObjectPtr->messageSize ==
;mailboxObjectPtr->mailboxBufferSize) then R2=0

STR      R2, [R0, #mailboxObject_t_readIndex_offset]
;mailboxObjectPtr->readIndex += mailboxObjectPtr->messageSize
;(with modulo buffer size)

;check if any thread is waiting for the mailbox to become empty
LDR      R3, [R0, #(mailboxObject_t_waitList_offset+ \
                listObject_t_auxInfo_offset)]
;R3=listObjectCount(&mailboxObjectPtr->waitList)

CMP      R3, #0
;if(listObjectCount(&mailboxObjectPtr->waitList) > 0)

MOVLE    R0, #1  ;returnValue=1.

BLE      no_thread_is_waiting

;some thread is waiting for the space in mailbox.

ADD    R0, R0, #mailboxObject_t_waitList_offset
                ;R0=&mailboxObjectPtr->waitList

STMFD  SP!, {R14}      ;save the return address of this function
                ;first to make function call from here.
```

```
;waitingThreadObjectPtr =
;              listObjectDelete(&mailboxObjectPtr->waitList);
BL     listObjectDelete
          ;After this function R0 = waitingThreadObjectPtr

STMFD  SP!, {R0}
          ;save waitingThreadObjectPtr to make function call.

MOV    R1, R0 ;R1=waitingThreadObjectPtr

LDR    R0, =readyList ;R0=&readyList

;listObjectInsert(readyList, waitingThreadObjectPtr);
BL     listObjectInsert

LDMFD  SP!, {R0, R14}
          ;R0=waitingThreadObjectPtr,
          ;R14=return address of this function.

LDR    R2, =runningThreadObjectPtr

LDR    R2, [R2]

LDR    R1, [R0, #threadObject_t_priority_offset]
                ;R1=waitingThreadObjectPtr->priority

LDR    R3, [R2, #threadObject_t_priority_offset]
                ;R3=runningThread.priority

CMP    R1, R3
;if(waitingThreadObjectPtr->priority < runningThread.priority)

MOVGE  R0, #1   ;returnValue = 1

BGE    waiting_thread_is_not_of_higher_priority;

MRS    R1, CPSR

AND    R1, R1, #0x1F     ;keep mode bits only.

CMP    R1, #IRQ_MODE

MOVEQ  R0, #1           ;returnValue=1.
```

```
BEQ    called_from_interrupt_service_routine
;This function is called from interrupt service routine.
;context switch should not be done when called from interrupt service
;routine. IRQ handler will do the context switch.

;This functin is called from user/system mode thread.
;waiting thread is of higher priority.
;insert the running thread into readyList and call scheduler.
MOV    R0, #1        ;This is the returnValue of the function.

ASSERT  threadObject_t_R_offset = 0

STMIA  R2, {R0-R14}   ;save R0-R14 of running thread.

STR    R14, [R2, #(15*4)]  ;set PC as the return address of
                    ;this function.

LDR    R1, =oldCPSR

LDR    R1, [R1]   ;get original status.

SET_STATE_OF_PC_IN_CPSR R14, R1
            ;make correct CPSR value (with state of PC stored).

STR    R1, [R2, #threadObject_t_cpsr_offset]   ;save status.

LDR    R0, =readyList  ;R0=&readyList.

MOV    R1, R2        ;R1=&runningThreadObject

;listObjectInsert(&readyList, &runningThread);
BL     listObjectInsert

B      scheduler


message_not_available_in_the_mailbox

CMP    R1, #0

MOVEQ  R0, #0        ;returnValue is zero.

BEQ    waitFlag_is_zero

;waitFlag is non zero
```

```
LDR    R3, =runningThreadObjectPtr

LDR    R3, [R3]

ASSERT  threadObject_t_R_offset = 0

STMIA  R3, {R0-R14}    ;save the context of running thread.

ADR    R1, mailboxObjectPend
;R1=program counter to start the thread.

STR    R1, [R3, #(15*4)] ;save PC.

LDR    R1, =oldCPSR

LDR    R1, [R1]      ;get original status.

STR    R1, [R3, #threadObject_t_cpsr_offset]   ;save status.

MOV    R1, R3        ;R1=runningThread

ADD    R0, R0, #mailboxObject_t_waitList_offset
               ;R0=&mailboxObjectPtr->waitList.

;listObjectInsert(&mailboxObjectPtr->waitList, &runningThreadObject);
BL     listObjectInsert


B      scheduler


waiting_thread_is_not_of_higher_priority
called_from_interrupt_service_routine
no_thread_is_waiting
waitFlag_is_zero

    INTERRUPTS_RESTORE     oldCPSR, R3

    BX    LR           ;return returnValue.
```

;mailboxObjectPost() function keep a message into the mailbox. The
;pseudo code of mailboxObjectPost() function is shown below.

```
;int32 mailboxObjectPost(mailboxObject_t *mailboxObjectPtr,
;             int32 waitFlag,
;             void *message)
;{
;  int32 returnValue;
;
;  interruptsDisable();
;  if(mailboxObjectPtr->emptyBufferSize >= mailboxObjectPtr->messageSize)
;  {
;     //content will fit into mailbox. keep the message.
;     memcpy(&mailboxObjectPtr->mailboxBuffer[writeIndex],
;          message,
;          mailboxObjectPtr->messageSize);
;
;     mailboxObjectPtr->writeIndex += mailboxObjectPtr->messageSize;
;     mailboxObjectPtr->emptyBufferSize -= mailboxObjectPtr->messageSize;
;
;     assert(mailboxObjectPtr->writeIndex <=
;                  mailboxObjectPtr->mailboxBufferSize);
;
;     if(mailboxObjectPtr->writeIndex ==
;                  mailboxObjectPtr->mailboxBufferSize)
;     {
;        mailboxObjectPtr->writeIndex = 0;
;     }
;     returnValue = 1;
;
;     //if any thread waiting for this mailbox to become full.
;     if(listObjectCount(&mailboxObjectPtr->waitList) > 0)
;     {
;        waitingThreadObjectPtr =
;             listObjectDelete(&mailboxObjectPtr->waitList);
;        assert(waitingThreadObjectPtr != NULL);
;        listObjectInsert(readyList, waitingThreadObjectPtr);
;        if(waitingThreadObjectPtr->priority < runningThread.priority &&
;           this function is not called from interrupt service routine)
;        {
;           get the context same as the end of this function and keep it
;           into running threadObject.
;           listObjectInsert(&readyList, &runningThreadObject);
;           jump to scheduler();
;        }
;     }
;  }
;  else
```

```
;  {
;     if(waitFlag)
;     {
;        get the context same as the starting of this function and keep
;        it into running threadObject
;        listObjectInsert(&mailboxObjectPtr->waitList, &runningThreadObject);
;        jump to scheduler();
;     }
;     else
;     {
;        returnValue = 0;
;     }
;  }
;  interruptsRestore();
;  return returnValue;
;}
;This function should not be called from interrupt service routine
;with non zero waitFlag

mailboxObjectPost

     INTERRUPTS_SAVE_DISABLE    oldCPSR, R3, R12

     LDR      R3, [R0, #mailboxObject_t_emptyBufferSize_offset]
               ;R3=mailboxObjectPtr->emptyBufferSize

     LDR      R12, [R0, #mailboxObject_t_messageSize_offset]
               ;R12=mailboxObjectPtr->messageSize

     CMP      R3, R12
;if(mailboxObjectPtr->emptyBufferSize >=
;               mailboxObjectPtr->messageSize)

     BLT      enough_space_not_available_in_the_mailbox

;enough space available for the message to keep.

     ADD      R12, R0, #mailboxObject_t_mailboxBuffer_offset
               ;R12=&&mailboxObjectPtr->mailboxBuffer[0]

     LDR      R12, [R12]

     LDR      R3, [R0, #mailboxObject_t_writeIndex_offset]
               ;R3=writeIndex
```

```
ADD       R12, R12, R3
;&mailboxObjectPtr->mailboxBuffer[writeIndex]

LDR       R3, [R0, #mailboxObject_t_messageSize_offset]
          ;R3=mailboxObjectPtr->messageSize

;memcpy(&mailboxObjectPtr->mailboxBuffer[writeIndex],
;    message,
;    mailboxObjectPtr->messageSize)

mailboxObjectPostCopy   MEMCPY     R12, R2, R3, R1

LDR       R2, [R0, #mailboxObject_t_writeIndex_offset]
          ;R2=mailboxObjectPtr->writeIndex

LDR       R1, [R0, #mailboxObject_t_messageSize_offset]
          ;R1=mailboxObjectPtr->messageSize

LDR       R3, [R0, #mailboxObject_t_emptyBufferSize_offset]
          ;R3=mailboxObjectPtr->emptyBufferSize

LDR       R12, [R0, #mailboxObject_t_mailboxBufferSize_offset]
          ;R12=mailboxObjectPtr->mailboxBufferSize

ADD       R2, R2, R1
;R2=mailboxObjectPtr->writeIndex+mailboxObjectPtr->messageSize

CMP       R2, R12

MOVEQ     R2, #0
;if(mailboxObjectPtr->writeIndex+mailboxObjectPtr->messageSize ==
;mailboxObjectPtr->mailboxBufferSize) then R2=0

STR       R2, [R0, #mailboxObject_t_writeIndex_offset]
;mailboxObjectPtr->writeIndex += mailboxObjectPtr->messageSize
;(with modulo bufferSize)

SUB       R3, R3, R1
;R3=mailboxObjectPtr->emptyBufferSize - mailboxObjectPtr->messageSize;

STR       R3, [R0, #mailboxObject_t_emptyBufferSize_offset]
;mailboxObjectPtr->emptyBufferSize -= mailboxObjectPtr->messageSize

;check if any thread is waiting for the mailbox to become filled.
LDR       R3, [R0, #(mailboxObject_t_waitList_offset+ \
```

```
                    listObject_t_auxInfo_offset)]
;R3=listObjectCount(&mailboxObjectPtr->waitList)

CMP       R3, #0
;if(listObjectCount(&mailboxObjectPtr->waitList) > 0)

MOVLE     R0, #1        ;returnValue=1

BLE       mailboxObjectPost_no_thread_is_waiting

;some thread(s) is waiting for contents in mailbox.
ADD    R0, R0, #mailboxObject_t_waitList_offset
                ;R0=&mailboxObjectPtr->waitList

STMFD  SP!, {R14}      ;Save the return address of this function
                ;to make function call from here.

;waitingThreadObjectPtr =
;          listObjectDelete(&mailboxObjectPtr->waitList);
BL     listObjectDelete   ;After this function R0 =
                ;waitingThreadObjectPtr

STMFD  SP!, {R0}        ;save waitingThreadObjectPtr to make
                ;function call.

MOV    R1, R0          ;R1=waitingThreadObjectPtr

LDR    R0, =readyList     ;R0=&readyList

;listObjectInsert(readyList, waitingThreadObjectPtr);
BL     listObjectInsert


LDMFD  SP!, {R0, R14}     ;R0=waitingThreadObjectPtr.
                ;R14=return address of this function.

LDR    R2, =runningThreadObjectPtr

LDR    R2, [R2]

LDR    R1, [R0, #threadObject_t_priority_offset]
                ;R1=waitingThreadObjectPtr->priority

LDR    R3, [R2, #threadObject_t_priority_offset]
                ;R3=runningThread.priority
```

```
CMP    R1, R3
;if(waitingThreadObjectPtr->priority < runningThread.priority)

MOVGE  R0, #1          ;returnValue=1

BGE    mailboxObjectPost_waiting_thread_is_not_of_higher_priority;

MRS    R1, CPSR

AND    R1, R1, #0x1F    ;keep only mode bits.

CMP    R1, #IRQ_MODE

MOVEQ  R0, #1          ;returnValue=1

BEQ    mailboxObjectPost_called_from_interrupt_service_routine


;This thread is called form user/system mode thread.
;waiting thread is of higher priority.
;insert the running thread into readyList and jump to scheduler.
MOV    R0, #1     ;returnValue=1

STMIA  R2, {R0-R14}    ;save R0-R12 of running thread.

STR    R14, [R2, #(15*4)]
               ;save PC as return address of this function.

LDR    R1, =oldCPSR

LDR    R1, [R1]       ;get original status.

SET_STATE_OF_PC_IN_CPSR R14, R1
               ;make correct CPSR for the PC stored.

STR    R1, [R2, #threadObject_t_cpsr_offset]
               ;save status.

LDR    R0, =readyList    ;R0=&readyList.

MOV    R1, R2          ;R1=&runningThread

;listObjectInsert(&readyList, &runningThreadObject);
BL     listObjectInsert
```

```
        B       scheduler


enough_space_not_available_in_the_mailbox

        CMP     R1, #0

        MOVEQ   R0, #0          ;returnValue = 0

        BEQ     mailboxObjectPost_waitFlag_is_zero

        ;waitFlag is non zero
        LDR     R3, =runningThreadObjectPtr

        LDR     R3, [R3]

        STMIA   R3, {R0-R14}    ;save the context of running thread.

        ADR     R1, mailboxObjectPost
                        ;R1=program counter to start the thread.

        STR     R1, [R3, #(15*4)]   ;save PC.

        LDR     R1, =oldCPSR

        LDR     R1, [R1]        ;get original status.

        STR     R1, [R3, #threadObject_t_cpsr_offset]
                        ;save status.

        MOV     R1, R3          ;R1=runningThread

        ADD     R0, R0, #mailboxObject_t_waitList_offset
                        ;R0=&mailboxObjectPtr->waitList.

        ;listObjectInsert(&mailboxObjectPtr->waitList, &runningThreadObject);
        BL      listObjectInsert

        B       scheduler


mailboxObjectPost_waiting_thread_is_not_of_higher_priority
mailboxObjectPost_called_from_interrupt_service_routine
```

```
mailboxObjectPost_no_thread_is_waiting
mailboxObjectPost_waitFlag_is_zero

        INTERRUPTS_RESTORE  oldCPSR, R3

        BX     LR              ;return returnValue.


        END
```

9.2 SROS V2.0

9.2.1 rtos.h

```
#ifndef __rtos__
#define __rtos__

#include "typeDef.h"

#define    INITIAL_CPSR_ARM_FUNCTION   0x0000005F
#define    INITIAL_CPSR_THUMB_FUNCTION 0x0000007F
#define    INITIAL_CPSR_ARM_DISABLED_INTERRUPTS_FUNCTION 0x000000DF
#define    INITIAL_CPSR_THUMB_DISABLED_INTERRUPTS_FUNCTION 0x000000FF
```

extern int64 time; //This gloable variable is incremented after every timer tick. At the starting of the system this variable is initialized to 0.

```
//Work around to make sure that threadObject_t have *listObject_t inside it,
//and listObject_t has *threadObject_t inside it.
struct _threadObject_;
struct _listObject_;

typedef struct _listObject_
{
    struct _threadObject_ *element;
    int32 auxInfo;
    struct _listObject_ *nextListNode;
}listNode_t;

typedef listNode_t listObject_t;

typedef struct _threadObject_
{
    int32 R[16];
    uint32 cpsr;
    uint32 priority;
    struct _listObject_ *waitListResource;
    struct _listObject_ *waitListTimer;
    char   *threadObjectName;
}threadObject_t;


typedef struct
{
    int32 mutex;
```

```
    listObject_t waitList;
}mutexObject_t;

typedef struct
{
    uint32 count;
    listObject_t waitList;

}semaphoreObject_t;

typedef struct
{
    int8 *mailboxBuffer;
    int32 readIndex;
    int32 writeIndex;
    int32 mailboxBufferSize;
    int32 emptyBufferSize;
    int32 messageSize;
    listObject_t waitList;

}mailboxObject_t;


listNode_t *listNodeAlloc(void);

void listNodeFree(listNode_t *listNodePtr);

void listObjectModuleInit(void);

void listObjectInit(listObject_t *listObjectPtr);

void listObjectInsert(listObject_t *listNodePtr, threadObject_t *newThreadObject);

threadObject_t *listObjectDelete(listObject_t *listObjectPtr);

void listObjectDeleteMiddle(listObject_t *waitList, threadObject_t
*threadObjectToBeDeleted);

int32 listObjectCount(listObject_t *listObjectPtr);

void threadObjectCreate(threadObject_t *threadObjectPtr,
                void *functionPtr,
                int32 arg1,
                int32 arg2,
                int32 arg3,
```

```
                int32 arg4,
                int32* stackPointer,
                uint32 priority,
                uint32 cpsr,
                char   *threadObjectName);
```

```
void threadObjectDestroy(threadObject_t *threadObjectPtr);
```

```
void mutexObjectInit(mutexObject_t *mutexObjectPtr, int32 initialFlag);
```

```
int32 mutexObjectLock(mutexObject_t *mutexObjectPtr, int32 waitFlag);
```

```
void mutexObjectRelease(mutexObject_t *mutexObjectPtr);
```

```
void semaphoreObjectInit(semaphoreObject_t *semaphoreObjectPtr, uint32
initialCount);
```

```
int32 semaphoreObjectPend(semaphoreObject_t *semaphoreObjectPtr, int32 waitFlag);
```

```
void semaphoreObjectPost(semaphoreObject_t *semaphoreObjectPtr);
```

```
void mailboxObjectInit(mailboxObject_t *mailboxObjectPtr,
            int8 *mailboxBuffer,
            int32 mailboxBufferSize,
            int32 messageSize);
```

```
int32 mailboxObjectPend(mailboxObject_t *mailboxObjectPtr,
        int32 waitFlag,
        void *message);
```

```
int32 mailboxObjectPost(mailboxObject_t *mailboxObjectPtr,
        int32 waitFlag,
        void *message);
```

```
void scheduler(void);      //This function never returns.
void rtosInit(void);
void block(void);
void timerTick(void);
void sleep(int32 noOfTicks);
void timerTick(void);
```

```
#endif
```

9.2.2 rtos.c

```
#include "rtos.h"
#include "assert.h"

#define MAX_THREADS_IN_THE_SYSTEM   100
#define MAX_LIST_NODES          2*MAX_THREADS_IN_THE_SYSTEM
listNode_t listNodes[MAX_LIST_NODES];
uint32    listNodesAvailableCount;
listNode_t *listNodesAvailable[MAX_LIST_NODES];

listObject_t readyList;
listObject_t timerList;
int64      time;
threadObject_t *runningThreadObjectPtr;
threadObject_t idleThread;
int32      idleStack[5];

extern void rtosInitAsm(void);
extern void interrupt_disable(void);
extern void interrupt_restore(void);

/*
Description:
This function
initializes the pool unallocated listNodes in the
"listNodesAvailable" global array.
initializes the "listNodesAvailableCount" which count the number of
listNodes in the pool.
*/
void listObjectModuleInit(void)
{
   int32 i;

   assert(MAX_LIST_NODES > 0);

   listNodesAvailableCount = MAX_LIST_NODES;

   for(i=0; i<MAX_LIST_NODES; i++)
   {
      listNodesAvailable[i] = &listNodes[i];
   }
}

/*
```

Description:
This function just return the last available listNode from the
pool (i.e."listNodesAvailable" array) and decrement the counter
(i.e."listNodesAvailableCount")that count the number of listNodes in the pool.
*/
listNode_t *listNodeAlloc()
{
    assert(listNodesAvailableCount > 0);

    return listNodesAvailable[--listNodesAvailableCount];
}

/*
Description:
This function just add the freed listNode to the pool of available
listNodes and increment the counter(i.e."listNodesAvailableCount") that
count the number of listNodes in the pool.
*/
void listNodeFree(listNode_t *listNodePtr)
{
    listNodesAvailable[listNodesAvailableCount++] = listNodePtr;

    assert(listNodesAvailableCount <= MAX_LIST_NODES);
}

/*
Description:
This function initilizes the listObject. ListObject is the dummy listNode
in the beginning of list in the linked list data structure. The dummy node
contain number of list nodes in the "auxInfo" field. This function initializes the
listObject. (i.e. initializes the dummy first node in the linked list).
*/
void listObjectInit(listObject_t *listObjectPtr)
{
    //The list object is the dummy head at the beginning of the linked list.
    //It is an invalid node.
    //It holds the number of list nodes in auxInfo field.
    assert(listObjectPtr != 0);
    listObjectPtr->element = 0;
    listObjectPtr->auxInfo = 0;
    listObjectPtr->nextListNode = 0;
}

/*
Description:

This function insert a new listNode into the linked list. The linked
list hold the threadObjects as its elements. It take "newThreadObject"
and insert it at appropriate place in the list according to the priority.
All the threadObjects in the list are stored in the descending order of
priority. (Note lower the priority number, higher the priority).
In each list node, the "priority" field of threadObject is noted into
the auxInfo field of the listNode.
*/
```c
void listObjectInsert(listObject_t *listNodePtr,
           threadObject_t *newThreadObject)
{
   listNode_t *newListNodePtr;
   uint32 newThreadObjectPriority;

   assert(newThreadObject != 0);
   assert(newThreadObject->waitListResource == 0);
   assert(listNodePtr != 0);

   //note the list pointer into the threadObject.
   newThreadObject->waitListResource = listNodePtr;

   newThreadObjectPriority = newThreadObject->priority;
   //listObject first element is dummy head. Its auxInfo hold
   //the number of list nodes available in the list.
   //So the count is increased when inserting an element.
   listNodePtr->auxInfo++;

   //parse the list till we reach the correct place for the newThreadObject.
   while(listNodePtr->nextListNode != 0 &&
     listNodePtr->nextListNode->auxInfo <= newThreadObjectPriority)
   {
      listNodePtr = listNodePtr->nextListNode;
   }

   //allocate and initialize the new node.
   newListNodePtr = listNodeAlloc();
   newListNodePtr->element = newThreadObject;
   newListNodePtr->auxInfo = newThreadObjectPriority;

   //insert into the list.
   newListNodePtr->nextListNode = listNodePtr->nextListNode;
   listNodePtr->nextListNode = newListNodePtr;
}

/*
```

Description:
This function delete the first listNode from the linked list
and return the threadObject (i.e. "element") in the listNode.
*/
threadObject_t *listObjectDelete(listObject_t *listObjectPtr)
{
    threadObject_t *element;

    listNode_t *freedListNodePtr;

    assert(listObjectPtr != 0);
    assert(listObjectPtr->nextListNode != 0);
    assert(listObjectPtr->auxInfo > 0);

    //decrement the number of listNodes counter.
    listObjectPtr->auxInfo--;

    //Note the element to be freed.
    freedListNodePtr = listObjectPtr->nextListNode;
    element = freedListNodePtr->element;

    //adjust the link from dummy head to the second listNode
    //in the list (as first one is removed).
    listObjectPtr->nextListNode = freedListNodePtr->nextListNode;

    //free the removed listNode.
    listNodeFree(freedListNodePtr);

    assert(element->waitListResource == listObjectPtr);

    //make the waitListResource pointer in the thread object equal to null.
    element->waitListResource = 0;

    //return the threadObject (i.e. element) available
    //in the first listNode (which is deleted).

    return element;
}

/*
Description:
This function delete the node that is holding the threadObject given as input.
The node that is holding the threadObject can be anywhere in the listObject.
*/
void listObjectDeleteMiddle(listObject_t *waitList,

```
                    threadObject_t *threadObjectToBeDeleted)
{
  listObject_t *listNodePtr, *freedListNodePtr;
  int i;

  assert(threadObjectToBeDeleted != 0);
  assert(threadObjectToBeDeleted->waitListResource == waitList);
  assert(waitList->auxInfo > 0);

  listNodePtr = waitList;
  for(i=0; i<waitList->auxInfo; i++)
  {
    if(listNodePtr->nextListNode->element == threadObjectToBeDeleted)
    {
      freedListNodePtr = listNodePtr->nextListNode;

      listNodePtr->nextListNode = freedListNodePtr->nextListNode;

      listNodeFree(freedListNodePtr);

      waitList->auxInfo--;

      //make the waitListResource pointer in the thread object equal
      //to null.
      threadObjectToBeDeleted->waitListResource = 0;

      break;
    }
    else
    {
      listNodePtr = listNodePtr->nextListNode;
    }
  }


  return;
}

/*
Description:
This function just return the number of listNodes available in the linked list.
The number of listNodes in the list are maintained in the dummy header "auxInfo"
field. So this function just return the value in the "auxInfo" field of
the dummy head.
*/
```

```
int32 listObjectCount(listObject_t *listObjectPtr)
{
    return listObjectPtr->auxInfo;
}


/*
Description:
This function implement the idle loop to execute in the idle thread.
*/
void idleFunction(void)
{
    while(1)
    {
        ;
    }
}


/*
Description:
This function initializes the SROS.
It initializes the list module to create unallocated pool of listNodes.
Initalizes the "readyList" which hold the threadObjects waiting
for the CPU time.
Initializes the "timerList" that hold the threadObjects waiting for
timeout.
Intialize the system time to 0.
Initializes the "runningThreadObjectPtr" (which always hold the
running threadObject address) to NULL.
Create the Idle thread in the sytem.
*/
void rtosInit(void)
{
    listObjectModuleInit();

    listObjectInit(&readyList);

    listObjectInit(&timerList);

    time = 0;

    runningThreadObjectPtr = 0;

    rtosInitAsm();

    threadObjectCreate(&idleThread,
```

```
                    (void *)idleFunction,
                    0,
                    0,
                    0,
                    0,
                    &idleStack[5],
                    127,
                    INITIAL_CPSR_ARM_FUNCTION,
                    "idleThread"
                    );

    return;
}
```

```
/*
Description:
This function check whether a context switch is needed.
This function return 1 (denoting context switch is needed) when
the currently running thread in the system has lower priority than
highest priority thread available in the readyList. Otherwise this function
return 0. Note that lower the priority number higher the thread priority.
*/
int is_thread_switch_needed(void)
{
    //check if the runningThreadObject has less priority than
    //highest priority thread in the ready list. If so return 1
    //else return 0.

    int returnValue = 0;

    if(readyList.auxInfo > 0)   //if the number of threads in the ready list > 0
    {
        if((readyList.nextListNode)->auxInfo < runningThreadObjectPtr->priority)
        {
            returnValue = 1;
        }
    }

    return returnValue;
}
```

```
/*
Description:
This function inserts the given threadObject into new node of the timerList.
The threadObject should hold the timeout value in R1 register. The
```

threadObject is inserted at an appropriate place depending on the timeout value. (all the threadObjects with lower than the new threadObject timeout are preceding it in the timerList).
*/

```
void insertIntoTimerList(threadObject_t *newThreadObject,
            listObject_t *waitList)
{
    int32 waitTime;
    listNode_t *listNodePtr, *newListNodePtr;

    assert(newThreadObject != 0);
    assert(newThreadObject->waitListTimer == 0);

    //always the waitTime is in R1 register.
    waitTime = newThreadObject->R[1];

    assert(waitTime > 0);

    listNodePtr = &timerList;

    //note the timer list pointer into the threadObject.
    newThreadObject->waitListTimer = listNodePtr;

    //parse the list past the low waiting time nodes.
    while(listNodePtr->nextListNode != 0 && \
        listNodePtr->nextListNode->element->R[1] < waitTime)
    {
        waitTime = waitTime - listNodePtr->nextListNode->element->R[1];
        listNodePtr = listNodePtr->nextListNode;
    }

    //allocate and initialize the new node.
    newListNodePtr = listNodeAlloc();
    newThreadObject->R[1] = waitTime;
    newListNodePtr->element = newThreadObject;
    newListNodePtr->auxInfo = (int32)(waitList);
    //In the timer list each node auxInfo field hold the waitList of
    //mutexObject or semaphoreObject or mailboxObject.

    //insert into list
    newListNodePtr->nextListNode = listNodePtr->nextListNode;
    listNodePtr->nextListNode = newListNodePtr;

    //subtract the waiting time for the following list nodes after
    //newListNodePtr
```

```
  if(newListNodePtr->nextListNode != 0)
  {
     newListNodePtr->nextListNode->element->R[1] -= \
                newListNodePtr->element->R[1];
  }

  //listObject first element is dummy node. Its auxInfo field holds
  //the number of nodes in the list.
  timerList.auxInfo++;
}

/*
Description:
This function delete the node that is holding the given threadObject from the
timerList.
*/
void deleteFromTimerList(threadObject_t *threadObjectToBeDeleted)
{
  listObject_t *listNodePtr, *freedListNodePtr;
  int i;

  assert(threadObjectToBeDeleted != 0);
  assert(threadObjectToBeDeleted->waitListTimer == &timerList);

  listNodePtr = &timerList;
  for(i=0; i<timerList.auxInfo; i++)
  {
    if(listNodePtr->nextListNode->element == threadObjectToBeDeleted)
    {
       freedListNodePtr = listNodePtr->nextListNode;

       listNodePtr->nextListNode = freedListNodePtr->nextListNode;

       //add wait time for the next thread object.
       if(listNodePtr->nextListNode != 0)
       {
          listNodePtr->nextListNode->element->R[1] += \
                   freedListNodePtr->element->R[1];
       }

       listNodeFree(freedListNodePtr);

       timerList.auxInfo--;
       //decrease the count by 1.( auxInfo field hold the number of
       //elements in the list).
```

```
        //make the timerList pointer in the thread object equal to null.
        threadObjectToBeDeleted->waitListTimer = 0;

        break;
      }
      else
      {
        listNodePtr = listNodePtr->nextListNode;
      }
    }

    return;
}


/*
Description:
This function is the timer interrupt service routine. This function should be
called for every timer interrupt. (i.e. timer tick). This function updates
the timeouts of threads which are waiting for timeout at each timer tick.
When ever the number of ticks for timeout for a threadObject is finished,
then that threadObject will be moved to readyList (and the threadObject is
removed from any waitList if it is in).
*/
void timerTick(void)
{
    listObject_t *freedListNodePtr;

    time++;
    //decrease the waiting time by 1.
    if(timerList.auxInfo > 0)
    {
        timerList.nextListNode->element->R[1]--;
        while(timerList.auxInfo > 0)
        {
            if(timerList.nextListNode->element->R[1] <= 0)  //is waitTime == 0
            {
                //delete the threadObject from the list.
                freedListNodePtr = timerList.nextListNode;

                timerList.nextListNode = freedListNodePtr->nextListNode;

                //delete the threadObject from the waitList of resource
                //(mutex/semaphore/mailBox).
                if(freedListNodePtr->auxInfo != 0)
```

```
        {
            listObjectDeleteMiddle((listObject_t *)(freedListNodePtr->auxInfo),
                    freedListNodePtr->element);
        }

        assert(freedListNodePtr->element->waitListTimer == &timerList);

        //make the timerList pointer in the thread object equal to null.
        freedListNodePtr->element->waitListTimer = 0;

        //insert the threadObject into readyList.
        listObjectInsert(&readyList, freedListNodePtr->element);

        //free the listNode.
        listNodeFree(freedListNodePtr);

        timerList.auxInfo--;
        }
        else
        {
            break;
        }
        }
    }

    return;
}


/*
Description:
This function remove the threadObject from the system.
This function remove the threadObject from the any waitList or readyList if
it is waiting for a resource. This function remove the threadObject from
timerList if it is waiting for timeout.
*/
void threadObjectDestroy(threadObject_t *threadObjectPtr)
{
    interrupt_disable();

    assert((threadObjectPtr->waitListResource != 0) || \
            (threadObjectPtr->waitListTimer != 0));

    if(threadObjectPtr->waitListResource != 0)
    {
        assert(threadObjectPtr->waitListResource->auxInfo > 0);
```

```
        listObjectDeleteMiddle(threadObjectPtr->waitListResource, \
                threadObjectPtr);
    }

    if(threadObjectPtr->waitListTimer != 0)
    {
        assert(timerList.auxInfo > 0);

        deleteFromTimerList(threadObjectPtr);
    }

    interrupt_restore();
}


/*
Description:
This function initializes the mailboxObject.
"mailboxBuffer" is the memory space where messages are stored.
"mailboxBufferSize" is the size of the "mailboxBuffer"
"messageSize" is the size of each message.
*/
void mailboxObjectInit(mailboxObject_t *mailboxObjectPtr,
            int8 *mailboxBuffer,
            int32 mailboxBufferSize,
            int32 messageSize)
{
    mailboxObjectPtr->mailboxBuffer = mailboxBuffer;
    mailboxObjectPtr->readIndex = 0;
    mailboxObjectPtr->writeIndex = 0;
    mailboxObjectPtr->mailboxBufferSize = mailboxBufferSize;
    mailboxObjectPtr->emptyBufferSize = mailboxBufferSize;
    mailboxObjectPtr->messageSize = messageSize;

    listObjectInit(&mailboxObjectPtr->waitList);

    assert(mailboxObjectPtr->mailboxBufferSize % messageSize == 0);
}


/*
Description:
This function initializes the mutexObject. The initial status of mutex
is initialized with the "initialFlag" which can be either 0 or 1.
*/
void mutexObjectInit(mutexObject_t *mutexObjectPtr, int32 initialFlag)
```

```
{
    assert(initialFlag == 0 || initialFlag == 1);

    mutexObjectPtr->mutex = initialFlag;

    listObjectInit(&mutexObjectPtr->waitList);
}

/*
This funciton initializes the semaphoreObject. The initial count of the
semaphore is initialized with the "initialCount" passed to this function.
*/
void semaphoreObjectInit(semaphoreObject_t *semaphoreObjectPtr,
            uint32 initialCount)
{
    semaphoreObjectPtr->count = initialCount;

    listObjectInit(&(semaphoreObjectPtr->waitList));
}
```

9.2.3 rtosAsm.h

```
                    IF :LNOT::DEF: __rtosAsm_h__

            GBLS    __rtosAsm_h__
__rtosAsm_h__       SETS    "1"

USER_MODE           EQU    2_10000
SYSTEM_MODE          EQU    2_11111
FIQ_MODE            EQU    2_10001
IRQ_MODE            EQU    2_10010
SVC_MODE             EQU    2_10011
ABT_MODE             EQU    2_10111
UND_MODE             EQU    2_11011



        MACRO
$lable     INTERRUPTS_DISABLE $scratchRegister

        MRS    $scratchRegister, CPSR

        ;disable 6th (F), 7th (I)bits. (bit count starts from 0)
        ORR    $scratchRegister, $scratchRegister, #0x000000C0 ;set F, I bits.

        MSR    CPSR_c, $scratchRegister

        MEND

        MACRO
$lable     INTERRUPTS_SAVE_DISABLE $cpsrSaveMemoryAddress, $scratchRegister1,
$scratchRegister2

        MRS    $scratchRegister1, CPSR

        MOV    $scratchRegister2, $scratchRegister1

        ;disable 6th (F), 7th (I)bits. (bit count starts from 0)
        ORR    $scratchRegister1, $scratchRegister1, #0x000000C0   ;clear F, I bits.

        MSR    CPSR_c, $scratchRegister1

        LDR    $scratchRegister1, =$cpsrSaveMemoryAddress

        STR    $scratchRegister2, [$scratchRegister1]
```

```
        MEND

        MACRO
$lable    INTERRUPTS_RESTORE  $cpsrSaveMemoryAddress, $scratchRegister

        LDR    $scratchRegister, =$cpsrSaveMemoryAddress   ;get the oldCPSR address
into register.

        LDR    $scratchRegister, [$scratchRegister] ;load the old CPSR

        MSR    CPSR_c, $scratchRegister    ;restore the old CPSR.

        MEND

        MACRO
$label    MEMCPY  $destAddressRegister, $sourceAddressRegister, $noOfBytesRegister,
$scratchRegister

$label.loop
        LDRB   $scratchRegister, [$sourceAddressRegister], #1

        STRB   $scratchRegister, [$destAddressRegister], #1

        SUBS   $noOfBytesRegister, $noOfBytesRegister, #1

        BGT    $label.loop

        MEND

        MACRO
SET_IRQ_MODE   $scratchRegister

        MRS    $scratchRegister, CPSR

        BIC    $scratchRegister, $scratchRegister, #0x1F   ;keep only mode bits.

        ORR    $scratchRegister, $scratchRegister, #IRQ_MODE

        MSR    CPSR_c, $scratchRegister

        MEND


        MACRO
```

```
        SET_STATE_OF_PC_IN_CPSR $pcRegister, $cpsrRegister

    AND    $pcRegister, $pcRegister, #0x1      ;$pcRegister = the mode of the PC when
the thread starts next time (0-ARM, 1-Thumb)

    ORR    $cpsrRegister, $cpsrRegister, $pcRegister, LSL #5      ;set the appropriate
mode for the next PC.  5 is THUMB bit position in CPSR.

    MEND


listNode_t_element_offset      EQU 0
listNode_t_auxInfo_offset      EQU 4
listNode_t_nextListNode_offset EQU 8
listNode_t_size                EQU 12

listObject_t_element_offset    EQU 0
listObject_t_auxInfo_offset    EQU 4
listObject_t_nextListNode_offset   EQU 8
listObject_t_size              EQU 12


mutexObject_t_mutex_offset     EQU    0
mutexObject_t_waitList_offset  EQU    4
mutexObject_t_size             EQU    (4+listObject_t_size)

threadObject_t_R_offset            EQU    0
threadObject_t_cpsr_offset         EQU    64
threadObject_t_priority_offset     EQU    68
threadObject_t_waitListResource_offset EQU   72
threadObject_t_waitListTimer_offset    EQU    76
threadObject_t_threadObjectName_offset EQU    80
threadObject_t_size                EQU    84

mailboxObject_t_mailboxBuffer_offset   EQU    0
mailboxObject_t_readIndex_offset       EQU    4
mailboxObject_t_writeIndex_offset      EQU    8
mailboxObject_t_mailboxBufferSize_offset EQU   12
mailboxObject_t_emptyBufferSize_offset EQU   16
mailboxObject_t_messageSize_offset     EQU    20
mailboxObject_t_waitList_offset        EQU    24
mailboxObject_t_size                   EQU    (24+listObject_t_size)

semaphoreObject_t_count_offset         EQU    0
semaphoreObject_t_waitList_offset      EQU    4
semaphoreObject_t_size                 EQU    (4+listObject_t_size)
```

272

ENDIF
END

9.2.4 rtosAsm.s

```
        INCLUDE rtosAsm.h

        IMPORT  runningThreadObjectPtr
        IMPORT  listObjectInsert
        IMPORT  listObjectDelete
        IMPORT  readyList
        IMPORT  irq_interrupt_service_routine
        IMPORT  is_thread_switch_needed
        IMPORT  __main

        IMPORT  insertIntoTimerList
        IMPORT  deleteFromTimerList

        EXPORT  scheduler
        EXPORT  rtosInitAsm
        EXPORT  block
        EXPORT  sleep
        EXPORT  irq_interrupt_handler
        EXPORT  interrupt_disable
        EXPORT  interrupt_restore
        EXPORT  threadObjectCreate
        EXPORT  oldCPSR


        AREA srosData, DATA

oldCPSR DCD 0


        GBLS    R13_irq
        GBLS    R14_irq
        GBLS    SPSR_irq

R13_irq    SETS    "R13"
R14_irq    SETS    "R14"
SPSR_irq   SETS    "SPSR"

;The below section is vector table of ARM processor.
;This code section has to be placed at 0x00000000 for low vectors
;or at 0xFFFF0000 for high vectors.

        AREA    vectorTable, CODE
```

```
        B     reset_interrupt_handler
                    ;0x0000 for reset interrupt
        B     reset_interrupt_handler
                    ;0x0004 for Undefined instructions interrupt
        B     reset_interrupt_handler
                    ;0x0008 for SWI interrupts.
        B     reset_interrupt_handler
                    ;0x000c for instruction fetchabort.
        B     reset_interrupt_handler
                    ;0x0010 for data abort.
        B     reset_interrupt_handler
                    ;0x0014 reserved.
        B     irq_interrupt_handler
                    ;0x0018 for irq interrupts.
        B     reset_interrupt_handler
                    ;0x001c for fiq interrupts.



        AREA    interrupt_disable_code, CODE

interrupt_disable
        INTERRUPTS_SAVE_DISABLE oldCPSR, R0, R1

        BX  LR

        AREA    interrupt_restore_code, CODE

interrupt_restore
        INTERRUPTS_RESTORE  oldCPSR, R0

        BX  LR

;The below code section changes the processor mode to IRQ mode
;i.e (kernel mode).
;This code section also initializes the current mode (superviser mode)
;stack pointer to IRQ mode stack pointer. This function copies the
;return address in superviser mode to IRQ mode LR so that it can use
;it for returning.

        AREA    rtosInitAsm_code, CODE
rtosInitAsm
        ;This function changes the processor mode to IRQ mode.
        MRS     R0, CPSR        ;get the status.
```

```
BIC     R0, R0, #0x1F      ;remove mode bits.

ORR     R0, R0, #IRQ_MODE  ;make mode as IRQ mode.

;before writing the mode into CPSR, save R13, R14 and keep
;the same R13, R14 into IRQ mode.
MOV     R1, R13            ;get the stack pointerof superviser
                          ;mode.

MOV     R2, R14            ;save the return address to return
                          ;later.

MSR     CPSR_c, R0         ;write the status register to change
                          ;the processor mode.

MOV     R13, R1            ;initialize the stack pointer for IRQ
                          ;mode.

MOV     R14, R2            ;Get the return address into LR.

BX      LR                 ;return using the return address.
```

;This code section is code section for block() function. This block function
;keep the runnning threadObject into the readyList and jump to scheduler to
;start the highest priority ready thread. If the running thread is the highest
;priority ready thread then calling block() function does not result in
;context switch and do not have any effect in the system.
;Note: As interrupt service routine is not a thread, this function should
;not be called from interrupt service routine.

```
        AREA    block_code, CODE
block
        INTERRUPTS_SAVE_DISABLE oldCPSR, R2, R3    ;disable interrupts

        ;creating context for the current running thread.
        ;take the context as the end of the block() function.

        LDR     R1, =runningThreadObjectPtr
                        ;R1=&runningThreadObjectPtr

        LDR     R1, [R1]        ;R1=&runningThreadObject

        ASSERT  threadObject_t_R_offset = 0
```

```
STMIA   R1, {R0-R14}
                ;saved registers R0-R14 in
                ;the running threadObject.

STR     R14, [R1, #(15*4)]
                ;save the return address as the
                ;starting point (i.e. PC) when the
                ;thread starts later.

LDR     R4, =oldCPSR

LDR     R4, [R4]
                ;get current status of the thread
                ;when it enters this function.

SET_STATE_OF_PC_IN_CPSR R14, R4
                ;This macro keep the correct state of
                ;later starting point of the thread
                ;in R4

STR     R4, [R1, #threadObject_t_cpsr_offset]
                ;save the correct status of the
                ;thread into the threadObject CPSR

;insert the running thread into readyList.

LDR     R0, =readyList

BL      listObjectInsert
                ;insert the running threadObject
                ;into the readyList.

;jump to scheduler

B       scheduler
```

```
;The below code section implement sleep() function. This function should not
;be called from interrupt servicer routine. The pseudo code of the sleep()
;function is shown below.
;void sleep(int waitTime)
;{
;   interrupts_disable();
;   collect context equivalent to end of the function into the
;   running threadObject and keep it into the timerList;
;   Jump to Scheduler();
```

;}

```
        AREA    sleep_code, CODE

sleep
        INTERRUPTS_SAVE_DISABLE oldCPSR, R2, R3
                        ;disable interrupts.

        ;keep the context of the running thread into the
        ;running threadObject.

        MOV    R1, R0           ;R1=waitTime. waitTime should be
                        ;always in R1 register
                        ;(similar to mutex, semaphore,
                        ;mailbox function calls).

        LDR    R0, =runningThreadObjectPtr
                        ;R0=&runningThreadObjectPtr

        LDR    R0, [R0]

        ASSERT  threadObject_t_R_offset = 0

        STMIA  R0, {R0-R14}        ;saved all registers R0-R14 in the
                        ;ready thread.

        STR    R14, [R0, #(15*4)]    ;save the return address as the
                        ;starting point of the PC when the
                        ;thread starts.

        LDR    R4, =oldCPSR

        LDR    R4, [R4]            ;get current status of the thread.

        SET_STATE_OF_PC_IN_CPSR R14, R4 ;This macro keep the state of
                        ;PC in R4

        STR    R4, [R1, #threadObject_t_cpsr_offset]
                        ;save the current status of the
                        ;thread.

        ;insert the running thread into timerList.

        MOV    R1, #0           ;wait list is null.
```

```
                            ;Running thread will only wait in
                            ;timer list.

            BL      insertIntoTimerList
            ;insertIntoTimerList(&runningThread, NULL);

            ;jump to scheduler

            B       scheduler
```

```
;The below code section is code for scheduler. The scheduler first disables
;interrupts and set the mode to kernel mode (irq mode)
;and loads the context of the highest priority ready thread in the system.
;As starting of the highest priority read thread is also done in the
;interrupt handler code, the below code section just jump to interrupt
;handler code section to reuse the code in interrupt handler.
;The pseudo code of the scheduler is shown below.
;void scheduler(void)
;{
;   threadObject_t *threadObjectPtr;
;
;   disableInterrupts();
;   change the processor mode to kernel mode; (if it is not in kernel mode).
;   threadObjectPtr = listObjectDelete(&readyList);
;
;   load the context in the threadObjectPtr.
;   start running from the PC in the threadObjectPtr.
;}

        AREA    schuduler_code, CODE

scheduler
scheduler INTERRUPTS_DISABLE R0     ;disable interrupts.

        ;change to kernel mode.
        ;This is necessary as we do not have SPSR in system mdoe.
        ;So go to IRQ mode to load SPSR and copy that into CPSR.
        SET_IRQ_MODE   R0

        ;make a jump to the interrupt handler code section which has
        ;the functionality of starting the highest priority thread
        ;from readyList.
        B       start_high_priority_thread
```

;The below code section is the reset interrupt handler code section.
;The reset interrupt handler just jump to the entry point of the embedded
;application.

    AREA   reset_interrupt_handler_code, CODE

reset_interrupt_handler

    B   __main   ;branch to entry point. If the embedded
                     ;application entry point is not __main
                     ;__main has to be replaced by the entry
                     ;point.

;The below code section implement the irq_interrupt_handler.
;The irq interrupt handler just call irq_interrupt_service_routine().
;Note that irq_interrupt_service_routine() should not use interrupt
;key word of C language. The irq_interrupt_service_routine() should
;be developed like normal C function. The saving and restoring of
;callee preserve register in the calling convention i.e.R0-R3, R12
;are done by the interrupt handler.
;The irq_interrupt_handler do context switch if needed after the
;irq_interrupt_service_routine() returns. Note that any SROS call that
;can block should not be called in irq_interrupt_service_routine().
;After the irq_interrupt_service_routine() returns, irq_interrupt_handler
;do context switch if needed. Note that instead of jumping to schuduler()
;irq_interrupt_handler() implemented the code to start the highest priority
;ready thread in the system. (Infact schuduler() function is also using the
;same code that is irq_interrupt_handler_code section.
;The pseudo code of the irq_interrupt_handler() is shown below.
;void irq_interrupt_handler(void)
;{
; irq_interrupt_service_routine();
; if (running thread priority higher than highest
;   thread priority in the readyList)
; {
;   return to the interrupted thread.
; }
; else
; {
;   Get the context exactly equal to the position when
;   interrupt happened in the running thread, Save that
;   context into the running threadObject.
;   Insert the running threadObject into readyList.
;   jump to scheduler tostart the highest priority ready thread.

```
;  }
;}

        AREA   irq_interrupt_handler_code, CODE

irq_interrupt_handler

        ;R13_irq, R14_irq, spsr_irq are active here. cpsr of the interrupted
        ;thread is stored in spsr_irq.
        ;So we are operating on irq stack here.

        SUB    $R14_irq, $R14_irq, #4
                        ;calculate the actual address to be returned.

        STMFD  $R13_irq!, {R0-R3, R12, $R14_irq}
                        ;save the interrupted thread registers.
                        ;This step is necessary as the
                        ;irq_interrupt_service_routine() may destroy
                        ;those registers.

        BL     irq_interrupt_service_routine
                        ;call the user defined
                        ;irq_interrupt_service_routine().

        BL     is_thread_switch_needed
                        ;check if context switch is necessary.
                        ;If irq_interrupt_service_routine() has
                        ;triggered a higher priority thread than
                        ;running thread to ready state,
                        ;then context switch will become necessary.

        CMP R0, #0          ;if(is_thread_switch_needed()==0)

        LDMEQFD $R13_irq!, {R0-R3, R12, PC}^
                        ;thread switch is not needed. So returning
                        ;to the interrupted (i.e. running) thread.
                        ;SPSR_irq copied to CPSR. This is LDM (3)
                        ;instruction.

        ;context switch is necessary. So
        ;save the current thread context first
        LDR    R0, =runningThreadObjectPtr

        LDR    R0, [R0]     ;R0=&runningThreadObject
```

```
MRS    R1, $SPSR_irq   ;interrupted thread CPSR is on SPSR_irq.
                       ;So get that.

ASSERT  threadObject_t_R_offset = 0

STR    R1, [R0, #threadObject_t_cpsr_offset]
                       ;save interrupted thread CPSR.

LDMFD  $R13_irq!, {R2, R3}
                       ;get interrupted thread R0, R1 into R2, R3
                       ;respectively.

STMIA  R0!, {R2, R3}   ;save interrupted thread R0, R1.
                       ;R0=&runningThread+8

LDMFD  $R13_irq!, {R2, R3, R12, $R14_irq}
                       ;load the interrupted thread registers that
                       ;we have saved on the stack.
                       ;(NOTE:R14 loaded is R14_irq as we are in
                       ;IRQ mode).

STR    $R14_irq, [R0, #(15*4-8)]
                       ;save the R14_irq as the starting point of
                       ;execution of the interrupted thread.

STMIA  R0, {R2-R14}^
                       ;Save the interrupted thread registers.
                       ;save user/system mode registers.
                       ;This instruction
                       ;loads always user mode registers even though
                       ; we are in IRQ mode. (STM (2) instruction).
                       ;Note that previously R0=&runningThread.R[2]

;now insert the runningThread into readyList.
;listObjectInsert(listObject_t *listNodePtr, void *newElement)

SUB    R1, R0, #(2*4)
                       ;R1=&runningThread

LDR    R0, =readyList
                       ;R0=&readyList.

BL     listObjectInsert
                       ;insert the interrupted threadObject into the
                       ;readyList.
```

;Now we are ready to load the context of the highest priority
;threadObject from the readyList.

start_high_priority_thread

;get the new thread object to be started.
;threadObject = void *listObjectDelete(listObject_t *listObjectPtr);

```
LDR     R0, =readyList

BL      listObjectDelete
                ;get the high priority thread to be run.
                ;After this function R0 holds the
                ;&threadObject

LDR     R1, =runningThreadObjectPtr

STR     R0, [R1]      ;store runninThreadObject pointer.

LDR     R12, [R0, #threadObject_t_cpsr_offset]
                ;get the cpsr of the threadObject.

MSR     $SPSR_irq._fsxc, R12
                ;save the cpsr into SPSR (SPSR will be copied
                ;into CPSR at exit of this function).

ASSERT  threadObject_t_R_offset = 0

LDR     $R14_irq, [R0, #(15*4)]
                ;get PC value into R14_irq (R14_irq will be
                ;copied into PC at exit of this function).

LDMIA   R0, {R0-R14}^  ;load saved R0-R14 of high priority thread
                ;into user mode R0-R14 registers. (LDM (2)
                ;instruction)

NOP             ;can not use banked registers after user
                ;mode LDM.


MOVS    PC, $R14_irq  ;PC=R14_irq, CPSR=SPSR_irq
                ;After this instruction the highest priority
                ;ready thread in the system will start running
```

```
;The below code section create a new thread in the system. The new thread
;creation is done by saving appropriate context for the new thread in to the
;readyList.
;If the new thread created has higher priorty than running thread, context
;switch will happen. (if context switch is allowed).
;The pseudo code of the threadObjectCreate() function is shown below.
;void threadObjectCreate(threadObject_t *threadObjectPtr,
;               void (*functionPtr)(void*, ...),
;               int32 arg1,
;               int32 arg2,
;               int32 arg3,
;               int32 arg4,
;               int32* stackPointer,
;               uint32 priority,
;               uint32 cpsr,
;               int8 *threadObjectName)
;{
;  threadObjectPtr->R[15] = (int32)(functionPtr);
;  threadObjectPtr->R[0] = arg1;
;  threadObjectPtr->R[1] = arg2;
;  threadObjectPtr->R[2] = arg3;
;  threadObjectPtr->R[3] = arg4;
;  threadObjectPtr->R[13] = (int32)(stackPointer);
;  threadObjectPtr->R[14] = scheduler;
;  threadObjectPtr->priority = priority;
;  threadObjectPtr->threadObjectName = threadObjectName;
;  interruptDisable();
;
;  listObjectInsert(&readyList, threadObjectPtr);
;
;  if(priority < runningThreadObjectPtr->priority &&
;       context switch is allowed)
;  {
;    get the context of running thread functionally equivalent to end of
;    this function.
;    listObjectInsert(&readyList,
;             runningThreadObjectPtr);
;    jump to scheduler().
;  }
;
;  interruptsRestore();
;}

    AREA   threadObjectCreate_code, CODE
```

threadObjectCreate

```
        GBLS    threadObjectPtrR0
        GBLS    functionPtrR1
        GBLS    arg1R2
        GBLS    arg2R3

threadObjectPtrR0  SETS   "R0"
functionPtrR1      SETS   "R1"
arg1R2             SETS   "R2"
arg2R3             SETS   "R3"
arg3_offset        EQU    0
arg4_offset        EQU    4
stackPointer_offset EQU    8
priority_offset    EQU    12
cpsr_offset        EQU    16
threadObjectName_offset EQU 20

        ASSERT  threadObject_t_R_offset = 0

        STR    $functionPtrR1, [$threadObjectPtrR0, #(15*4)]
                    ;threadObjectPtr->R[15]=functionPtr

        STR    $arg1R2, [$threadObjectPtrR0, #(0*4)]
                    ;threadObjectPtr->R[0] = arg1

        STR    $arg2R3, [$threadObjectPtrR0, #(1*4)]
                    ;threadObjectPtr->R[1] = arg2

        LDR    R12, [SP, #arg3_offset]
                    ;R12=arg3

        STR    R12, [$threadObjectPtrR0, #(2*4)]
                    ;threadObjectPtr->R[2]=arg3

        LDR    R12, [SP, #arg4_offset]
                    ;R12=arg4

        STR    R12, [$threadObjectPtrR0, #(3*4)]
                    ;threadObjectPtr->r[3]=arg4

        LDR    R12, [SP, #stackPointer_offset]
                    ;R12=stackPointer

        STR    R12, [$threadObjectPtrR0, #(13*4)]
```

```
                        ;threadObjectPtr->R[13]=stackPointer.

LDR    R12, =scheduler

STR    R12, [$threadObjectPtrR0, #(14*4)]
                  ;threadObjectPtr->R[14]=scheduler

LDR    R12, [SP, #priority_offset]
                  ;R12=priority.

STR    R12, [$threadObjectPtrR0, #threadObject_t_priority_offset]
                  ;threadObjectPtr->priority=priority.

LDR    R1, [SP, #cpsr_offset]
                  ;R1=cpsr

STR    R1, [$threadObjectPtrR0, #threadObject_t_cpsr_offset]
                  ;save CPSR

LDR    R1, [SP, #threadObjectName_offset]
                  ;R1=threadObjectName

STR    R1, [$threadObjectPtrR0, \
           #threadObject_t_threadObjectName_offset]
                  ;save name pointer.

MOV    R1, #0    ;R1=0

STR    R1, [$threadObjectPtrR0, #threadObject_t_waitListTimer_offset]
;waitListTimer=0 as the current thread object is not in timer list.

STR    R1, [$threadObjectPtrR0, #threadObject_t_waitListResource_offset]
;waitListResource should be 0 before inserting into any list.

INTERRUPTS_SAVE_DISABLE oldCPSR, R1, R2

MOV    R1, R0           ;R1=threadObjectPtr

LDR    R0, =readyList    ;R0=readyList

STMFD  SP!, {LR}

;listObjectInsert(&readyList, threadObject);
BL     listObjectInsert
```

;check if scheduler is started. If scheduler is not started
;then runningThreadObjectPtr = 0.

```
LDR    R0, =runningThreadObjectPtr
                ;R0=&runningThreadObjectPtr

LDR    R0, [R0]        ;R0=runningThreadObjectPtr

CMP    R0, #0          ;if(runningThreadObjectPtr == 0)

BEQ    schuduler_is_not_started
                ;if(runningThreadObjectPtr == 0)
                ;then just return
```

;if called from the interrupt service routine, then just return.
```
MRS    R1, CPSR        ;get the current status

AND    R1, R1, #0x1F    ;keep only mode bits.

CMP    R1, #IRQ_MODE    ;check whether we are in kernel mode.

BEQ    called_from_interrupt_service_routine
                ;This function is called from
                ;interrupt service routine.
                ;So just return.

BL    is_thread_switch_needed

CMP    R0, #0

BEQ    context_switch_not_needed

INTERRUPTS_RESTORE oldCPSR, R1
                ;restore the original interrupts
                ;status.

BL    block           ;context switch is needed.
                ;Just call block
                ;block function keep the
                ;running thread into readyList
                ;and start the highest priority
                ;thread available in the readyList.

LDMFD  SP!, {PC}        ;return
```

schuduler_is_not_started
called_from_interrupt_service_routine
context_switch_not_needed

```
        INTERRUPTS_RESTORE oldCPSR, R1
                    ;get original interrupts status.


        LDMFD  SP!, {PC}        ;return



        END
```

9.2.5 mutexObjectAsm.s

```
INCLUDE rtosAsm.h

IMPORT  runningThreadObjectPtr
IMPORT  listObjectInsert
IMPORT  listObjectDelete
IMPORT  readyList
IMPORT  scheduler
IMPORT  oldCPSR

IMPORT  insertIntoTimerList
IMPORT  deleteFromTimerList

EXPORT  mutexObjectLock
EXPORT  mutexObjectRelease
```

;The below code section implement the mutexObjectLock() and
;mutexObjectRelease() functions.

```
AREA mutexObjectCode, CODE
```

;The mutexObjectLock function lock the mutex. The pseduo code for
;mutexObjectLock() is shown below.
;int32 mutexObjectLock(mutexObject_t *mutexObjectPtr, int32 waitTime)
;{
; if(swap(0, &mutexObjectPtr->mutex))
; {
;   return 1;
; }
; else
; {
;   if(waitTime)
;   {
;   interruptsDisable();
;   get the context which should be functionally equivalent to starting
;   of this function and store that context in the running
;   threadObject i.e. context space of running thread.
;   listObjectInsert(&mutexObjectPtr->waitList,
;   runningThreadObjectPtr);
;   if(waitTime > 0)
;   {
;   insertIntoTimerList(&runningThreadObject,
;   mutexObjectPtr->waitList);
;   }
```
```

```
;        jump to scheduler();
;      }
;    else
;      {
;        return 0;
;      }
;  }
;}
;Note : This function should not be called from interrupt service
;routinie with nonzero waitTime.

        ;R0 = mutexObjectPtr, R1 = waitTime according to the calling
        ;convention.
mutexObjectLock

        MOV    R2, #0        ;R2=0;

        ASSERT  mutexObject_t_mutex_offset = 0

        SWP    R2, R2, [R0]   ;R2 = mutex

        CMP    R2, #1         ;if(mutex == 1)

        MOVEQ  R0, #1         ;if(mutex == 1) returnValue = 1.

        BXEQ   LR             ;if(mutex == 1) return returnValue.

        CMP    R1, #0         ;if(waitTime == 0)

        MOVEQ  R0, #0         ;if(mutex == 0 and waitTime == 0)
                      ;then returnValue = 0

        BXEQ   LR             ;if(mutex == 0 and waitTime == 0)
                      ;then return returnValue.

    ;waitTime > 0 and mutex is locked by some other thread.
    ;So keep the current thread in waitList of this mutex
    ;If waiting for a limited time, keep the threadObject
    ;in timerList too
    ;and jump to scheduler.

    ;interruptDisable()
    INTERRUPTS_SAVE_DISABLE oldCPSR, R2, R3

    ;creating thread object for the current thread.
```

```
LDR    R3, =runningThreadObjectPtr
              ;R3=&runningThreadObjectPtr

LDR    R3, [R3]

ASSERT  threadObject_t_R_offset = 0

STMIA  R3, {R0-R14}         ;save all registers R0-R14 in
              ;the running threadObject

ADR    R4, mutexObjectLock    ;get the address of this function.
              ;(to start this thread later).
              ;R4=mutexObjectLock

STR    R4, [R3, #(15*4)]      ;save it as the PC to start later.

LDR    R4, =oldCPSR

LDR    R4, [R4]          ;get original status of the thread
              ;before masking interrupts.

STR    R4, [R3, #threadObject_t_cpsr_offset]
              ;save the status of the thread.

;insert the running thread into waitList of mutexObject.

ADD    R0, R0, #mutexObject_t_waitList_offset
              ;R0=&mutexObject->waitList.

MOV    R1, R3
              ;R1=&runningThreadObjectPtr

BL     listObjectInsert;

;insert the running thread into the waitList of timerList.

LDR    R0, =runningThreadObjectPtr
              ;R0 =&&runningThreadObject

LDR    R0, [R0]          ;R0=&runningThreadObject

LDR    R1, [R0, #threadObject_t_R_offset]
              ;R1=R0 of running
              ;threadObject=mutexObjectPtr
```

```
        ADD    R1, R1, #mutexObject_t_waitList_offset
                        ;R1=mutexObjectPtr->waitList

        LDR    R2, [R0, #(threadObject_t_R_offset+4)]
                        ;R2=waitTime

        CMP    R2, #0              ;if(waitTime > 0)

        ;insertIntoTimerList(&runningThread, waitList).
        ;R1 register of threadObject alwasy holds the waitTime.
        BLGT   insertIntoTimerList

        ;jump to scheduler

        B      scheduler


;The below code implement mutexObjectRelease() function. mutexObjectRelease()
;function release the mutex and do context switch if necessary. The high level
;pseudo code for mutexObjectRelease() is shown below.
;void mutexObjectRelease(mutexObject_t *mutexObjectPtr)
;{
;   threadObject_t *waitingThreadObjectPtr;
;   interruptsDisable();
;   mutexObjectPtr->mutex = 1;
;   if(listObjectCount(&mutexObjectPtr->waitList))
;   {
;     waitingThreadObjectPtr=listObjectDelete(&mutexObjectPtr->waitList);
;     listObjectInsert(&readyList,waitingThreadObjectPtr);
;     if(waitingThreadObjectPtr->waitTime >= 0)
;     {
;       deleteFromTimerList(waitingThreadObjectPtr);
;     }
;     if(waitingThreadObjectPtr->priority < runningThreadObject.priority &&
;          this function not called from interrupt service routine)
;     {
;       get the context functionally equivalent to the end
;       this function and save that context into running
;       threadObject.
;       listObjectInsert(&readyList,&runningThreadObject);
;       jump to scheduler();
;     }
;   }
;   interruptRestore();
;   return;
```

```
;}
;This function can be called from interrupt service routine
;with out any ristrictions.

        ;R0=mutexObjectPtr according to the calling convention.
mutexObjectRelease
        ;interruptsDisable

        INTERRUPTS_SAVE_DISABLE oldCPSR, R1, R2

        MOV    R1, #1  ;R1=1

        ASSERT mutexObject_t_mutex_offset = 0

        SWP    R1, R1, [R0]   ;mutexObject->mutex = 1;

        LDR    R1, [R0, #(mutexObject_t_waitList_offset+ \
                 listObject_t_auxInfo_offset)]
                 ;R1=listObjectCount(&mutexObjectPtr->waitList)

        CMP    R1, #0

        BEQ    no_thread_waiting_for_mutex;

        ;some thread is waiting for this mutex.

        ADD    R0, R0, #mutexObject_t_waitList_offset
                 ;R0=&mutexObjectPtr->waitList.

        STMFD  SP!, {R14}  ;saving R14 to make function call.

        ;listObjectDelete(&mutexObjectPtr->waitList)
        BL     listObjectDelete
                 ;After returning from the function,
                 ;R0 contain waitingThreadObjectPtr

        MOV    R1, R0     ;R1=waitingThreadObjectPtr

        LDR    R0, =readyList
                 ;R0 = &readyList.

        STMFD  SP!, {R1}   ;Save waitingThreadObjectPtr as we are
                 ;going to make a function call.

        BL     listObjectInsert
```

```
                    ;insert waiting thread object into
                    ;ready list.

LDR    R0, [SP]        ;We get R0=waitingThreadObjectPtr

LDR    R1, [R0, #(threadObject_t_R_offset+4)]  ;R1=waitTime

CMP    R1, #0        ;if(waitTime >= 0)

BLGE    deleteFromTimerList
;deleteFromTimerList(waitingThreadObjectPtr)
;(when waitTime greater than or equal to 0, this threadObject will
;be in timerList).

;Now check if the waiting thread has higher priority than the
;current running thread. and switch to the  waiting thread if
;that has high priority.

LDMFD  SP!, {R0, R14}
            ;R0=waitingThreadObjectPtr,
            ;R14=return address from this function.

LDR    R1, =runningThreadObjectPtr
            ;R1=&runningThreadObjectPtr

LDR    R1, [R1]

LDR    R2, [R0, #threadObject_t_priority_offset]
            ;R2=waitingThreadObjectPtr->priority

LDR    R3, [R1, #threadObject_t_priority_offset]
            ;R3=runningThreadObject.priority.

CMP    R2, R3    ;if(waitingThreadObjectPtr->priority <
            ;runningThreadObject.priority)

BHS    waiting_thread_does_not_have_high_priority;

;check whether we are coming from the interrupt service routine.
;If we are coming from the interrupt service routine we should
;not make context switch. IRQ_handler will do the context switch.

MRS    R2, CPSR

AND    R2, R2, #0x1F
```

;keep only mode bits.

```
CMP    R2, #IRQ_MODE
            ;if(currentMode == IRQ_MODE)
```

```
BEQ    called_from_interrupt_service_routine
```

;This function is called from user/system mode.
;waiting thread has higher priority.
;save running thread context to readyList and call scheduler.

```
STMIA  R1, {R0-R14}
            ;save registers for running thread.
```

```
STR    R14, [R1, #(15*4)]
            ;saving the return address as starting
            ;program counter.
```

```
LDR    R2, =oldCPSR
```

```
LDR    R2, [R2]   ;get status.
```

```
SET_STATE_OF_PC_IN_CPSR R14, R2
            ;set the correct state in CPSR for the
            ;starting the thread next time.
            ;(add the state bit correctly).
```

```
STR    R2, [R1, #threadObject_t_cpsr_offset]   ;save status.
```

```
LDR    R0, =readyList
            ;R0=&readyList.
```

```
BL     listObjectInsert
            ;Insert the running thread into readyList
```

```
B      scheduler   ;Jump to scheduler.
```

```
no_thread_waiting_for_mutex
waiting_thread_does_not_have_high_priority
called_from_interrupt_service_routine
```

```
            ;interruptsRestore()
            INTERRUPTS_RESTORE oldCPSR, R1
```

```
        BX    LR

        END
```

9.2.6 semaphoreObjectAsm.s

```
        INCLUDE rtosAsm.h

        IMPORT  runningThreadObjectPtr
        IMPORT  listObjectInsert
        IMPORT  listObjectDelete
        IMPORT  readyList
        IMPORT  oldCPSR
        IMPORT  scheduler

        IMPORT  insertIntoTimerList
        IMPORT  deleteFromTimerList

        EXPORT  semaphoreObjectPend
        EXPORT  semaphoreObjectPost

;The below code section implement semaphoreObjectPost(), semaphoreObjectPend()
;functions.

        AREA semaphoreObjectCode, CODE

;The semaphoreObjectPend() function decrement the semaphoreCount by 1. The
;pseudo code for semaphoreObjectPend() function is shown below.
;int32 semaphoreObjectPend(semaphoreObject_t *semaphoreObjectPtr,
;                               int32 waitTime)
;{
;   interruptsDisable();
;
;   if(semaphoreObjectPtr->count > 0)
;   {
;       semaphoreObjectPtr->count--;
;       returnValue = 1;
;   }
;   else
;   {
;       if(waitTime)
;       {
;           get the context same as start of the thread into
;           runningThreadObject.
;           listObjectInsert(&semaphoreObjectPtr->waitList,
;                       &runningThreadObject);
;           if(waitTime > 0)
;           {
;               insertIntoTimerList(&runningThread,
```

```
;                        semaphoreObjectPtr->waitList);
;        }
;        jump to scheduler();
;     }
;     else
;     {
;        returnValue = 0;
;     }
;  }
;  interruptsRestore();
;  return returnValue;
;}
;This function should not be called from interrupt service routine
;with nonzero waitTime.


semaphoreObjectPend

        INTERRUPTS_SAVE_DISABLE oldCPSR, R2, R3

        LDR      R2, [R0, #semaphoreObject_t_count_offset]
                    ;R2=semaphoreObjectPtr->count

        CMP      R2, #0

        SUBGT    R2, R2, #1  ;R2=R2-1

        STRGT    R2, [R0, #semaphoreObject_t_count_offset]
                    ;semaphoreObjectPtr->count--;

        MOVGT    R0, #1     ;returnValue = 1;

        BGT      semaphore_count_greater_than_0

;semaphore count equal to zero here.

        CMP      R1, #0     ;if(waitTime)

        MOVEQ    R0, #0     ;returnValue=0.

        BEQ      semaphore_wait_flag_is_zero

;waitTime is non zero here. So insert the running thread into
;wait list and jump to scheduler.
;initialize the context equivalent to starting of the function
;into running threadObject.
```

```
LDR       R3, =runningThreadObjectPtr

LDR       R3, [R3]

ASSERT    threadObject_t_R_offset = 0

STMIA     R3, {R0-R14}   ;save current context.

ADR       R4, semaphoreObjectPend
                ;R4=semaphoreObjectPend

STR       R4, [R3, #(15*4)]
                ;save PC as beginning of this
                ;function.

LDR       R4, =oldCPSR

LDR       R4, [R4]      ;get the original status.

STR       R4, [R3, #threadObject_t_cpsr_offset]
                ;save the current status of the thread.

;insert the running thread into waiting list.

ADD       R0, R0, #semaphoreObject_t_waitList_offset
                ;R0=&semaphoreObjectPtr->waitList

MOV       R1, R3     ;R1=&runningThreadObjectPtr

BL        listObjectInsert
                ;listObjectInsert()

LDR       R0, =runningThreadObjectPtr
                ;R0=&&runningThreadObject

LDR       R0, [R0]   ;R0=&runningThreadObject.

LDR       R1, [R0, #threadObject_t_R_offset]
                ;R1=R0 of running thread i.e.
                ;R1=semaphoreObjectPtr

ADD       R1, R1, #semaphoreObject_t_waitList_offset
                ;R1=&waitList of semaphoreObject.

LDR       R2, [R0, #(threadObject_t_R_offset+4)]
```

```
                          ;R2=waitTime

     CMP      R2, #0     ;if(waitTime > 0)

     BLGT     insertIntoTimerList
                        ;insertIntoTimerList(&runningThread).
                        ;R1 register of threadObject alwasy holds
                        ;the waitTime.
     ;jump to scheduler to start next thread.

     B        scheduler



semaphore_wait_flag_is_zero

semaphore_count_greater_than_0

     INTERRUPTS_RESTORE oldCPSR, R2

     BX       LR       ;return returnValue.
```

```
;The semaphoreObjectPost() function increment the semaphore count by 1.
;The High level pseudo code for semaphoreObjectPost() function is shown below.
;void semaphoreObjectPost(semaphoreObject_t *semaphoreObjectPtr)
;{
;   threadObject_t *waitingThreadObjectPtr;
;
;   interruptsDisable();
;   semaphoreObjectPtr->count++;
;   if(listObjectCount(&semaphoreObjectPtr->waitList) > 0)
;   {
;      waitingThreadObjectPtr =
;            listObjectDelete(semaphoreObjectPtr->waitList);
;      assert(waitingThreadObjectPtr != NULL);
;      listObjectInsert(readyList, waitingThreadObjectPtr);
;      if(waitingThreadObjectPtr->waitTime >= 0)
;      {
;         deleteFromTimerList(waitingThreadObjectPtr);
;      }
;      if(waitingThreadObjectPtr->priority < runningThread.priority &&
;           this function is not called from interrupt service routine)
;      {
;         get the context same as the end of this function
```

```
;       and keep that into the running threadObject.
;       listObjectInsert(&readyList, &runningThreadObject);
;       jump to scheduler();
;    }
; }
; interruptsRestore();
;}
```

semaphoreObjectPost

```
        INTERRUPTS_SAVE_DISABLE oldCPSR, R1, R2

        LDR    R2, [R0, #semaphoreObject_t_count_offset]
                    ;R2=semaphoreObjectPtr->count

        ADD    R2, R2, #1     ;R2=R2+1

        STR    R2, [R0, #semaphoreObject_t_count_offset]
                    ;semaphoreObjectPtr->count++

        LDR    R1, [R0, #(semaphoreObject_t_waitList_offset+ \
                    listObject_t_auxInfo_offset)]
                  ;R1=listObjectCount(&semaphoreObjectPtr->waitList)

        CMP    R1, #0  ;if(listObjectCount(&semaphoreObjectPtr->waitList) > 0)

        BLE    no_thread_waiting_for_semaphore

        ;some thread is waiting for the semaphore.
        ;remove the waiting thread from waitlist and put that into
        ;readyList.
        ADD    R0, R0, #semaphoreObject_t_waitList_offset
                    ;R0=&semaphoreObjectPtr->waitList.

        STMFD  SP!, {R14} ;save return address of this function before
                    ;making function call.

        ;waitingThreadObjectPtr =
        ;       listObjectDelete(semaphoreObjectPtr->waitList);
        BL     listObjectDelete
                    ;After this function call R0 holds
                    ;waitingThreadObjectPtr.

        STMFD  SP!, {R0}     ;save waitingThreadObjectPtr to make
                    ;function call.
```

```
MOV    R1, R0        ;R1=waitingThreadObjectPtr

LDR    R0, =readyList ;R0=&readyList

;listObjectInsert(readyList, waitingThreadObjectPtr);
BL     listObjectInsert

LDR    R0, [SP]      ;We get R0=waitingThreadObjectPtr

LDR    R1, [R0, #(threadObject_t_R_offset+4)] ;R1=waitTime

CMP    R1, #0        ;if(waitTime >= 0)

BLGE   deleteFromTimerList
;deleteFromTimerList(waitingThreadObjectPtr)
;(when waitTime greater than 0, this threadObject will be in
;timerList).

LDMFD  SP!, {R0, R14} ;R0 = waitingThreadObjectPtr,
              ;R14=return address of this function.

LDR    R1, =runningThreadObjectPtr ;R1=&runningThreadObjectPtr

LDR    R1, [R1]

LDR    R2, [R0, #threadObject_t_priority_offset]
            ;R2=waitingThreadObjectPtr->priority

LDR    R3, [R1, #threadObject_t_priority_offset]
            ;R3=runningThread.priority.

CMP    R2, R3 ;if(waitingThreadObjectPtr->priority <
       ;            runningThread.priority)

BGE    waiting_thread_not_higer_priority

MRS    R2, CPSR

AND    R2, R2, #0x1F   ;keep the mode bits only.

CMP    R2, #IRQ_MODE   ;if(mode == IRQ_MODE)

BEQ    called_from_interrrupt_service_routine
;This function is from interrupt service routine.
```

```
;context switch should not be done when called from interrupt
;service routine. IRQ handler will do the context switch anyway.


;This function is called form user/system mode thread.
;waiting thread has higher priority. Insert running thread
;into ready list and call scheduler.

STMIA  R1, {R0-R14}   ;save registers for running thread.

STR    R14, [R1, #(15*4)]  ;saving the new start point as
                           ;return address.

LDR    R2, =oldCPSR

LDR    R2, [R2]          ;get the original status.

SET_STATE_OF_PC_IN_CPSR R14, R2 ;keep the correct mode of the
                           ;CPSR for the starting position
                           ;of the new PC.

STR    R2, [R1, #threadObject_t_cpsr_offset]   ;save status.

LDR    R0, =readyList        ;R0=&readyList.

;listObjectInsert(&readyList, &runningThread);
BL     listObjectInsert

B      scheduler


no_thread_waiting_for_semaphore
waiting_thread_not_higer_priority
called_from_interrrupt_service_routine

       INTERRUPTS_RESTORE oldCPSR, R2

BX     LR



END
```

9.2.7 mailboxObjectAsm.s

```
        INCLUDE rtosAsm.h

        IMPORT  runningThreadObjectPtr
        IMPORT  listObjectInsert
        IMPORT  listObjectDelete
        IMPORT  readyList
        IMPORT  scheduler
        IMPORT  oldCPSR

        IMPORT  insertIntoTimerList
        IMPORT  deleteFromTimerList

        EXPORT  mailboxObjectPend
        EXPORT  mailboxObjectPost


;The below code section implement mailboxObjectPost(), mailboxObjectPend()
;functions.

        AREA mailboxObjectCode, CODE

;mailboxObjectPend() function retieve a message from mailbox. The below pseudo
;code show the functionality of the mailboxObjectPend().
;int32 mailboxObjectPend(mailboxObject_t *mailboxObjectPtr,
;           int32 waitTime,   //Second parameter should be
;                   //waitTime for HROS implementation.
;                   //(similar to mutex, semaphore functions).
;           void *message)
;{
;   int32 returnValue;
;
;   interruptsDisable();
;   if(mailboxObjectPtr->emptyBufferSize <=
;       mailboxObjectPtr->mailboxBufferSize - mailboxObjectPtr->messageSize)
;   {
;       //content is available in mailbox. take one message.
;       memcpy(message,
;           &mailboxObjectPtr->mailboxBuffer[readIndex],
;           mailboxObjectPtr->messageSize);
;
;       mailboxObjectPtr->readIndex += mailboxObjectPtr->messageSize;
;       mailboxObjectPtr->emptyBufferSize += mailboxObjectPtr->messageSize;
;
```

```
;    assert(mailboxObjectPtr->readIndex <=
;                  mailboxObjectPtr->mailboxBufferSize);
;    if(mailboxObjectPtr->readIndex == mailboxObjectPtr->mailboxBufferSize)
;    {
;      mailboxObjectPtr->readIndex = 0;
;    }
;    returnValue = 1;
;
;    //if any thread waiting for this mailbox to become empty.
;    if(listObjectCount(&mailboxObjectPtr->waitList) > 0)
;    {
;      waitingThreadObjectPtr =
;            listObjectDelete(&mailboxObjectPtr->waitList);
;      assert(waitingThreadObjectPtr != NULL);
;      listObjectInsert(readyList, waitingThreadObjectPtr);
;      if(waitingThreadObjectPtr->waitTime >= 0)
;      {
;        deleteFromTimerList(waitingThreadObjectPtr);
;      }
;      if(waitingThreadObjectPtr->priority < runningThread.priority &&
;        this function not called from interrupt service routine)
;      {
;        get the context same as the end of this function
;        and insert into the running threadObject.
;        listObjectInsert(&readyList, &runningThreadObject);
;        jump to scheduler();
;      }
;    }
;  }
;  else
;  {
;    if(waitTime)
;    {
;      get the context of starting of the function into running
;      threadObject.
;      listObjectInsert(mailboxObjectPtr->waitList, &runningThreadObject);
;      if(waitTime > 0)
;      {
;        insertIntoTimerList(&runningThread, mailboxObjectPtr->waitList);
;      }
;      jump to scheduler();
;    }
;    else
;    {
;      returnValue = 0;
```

```
;    }
;  }
;  interruptsRestore();
;  return returnValue;
;}
;This function should not be called from interrupt service routine
;with non zero waitTime
mailboxObjectPend


        INTERRUPTS_SAVE_DISABLE oldCPSR, R3, R12


        LDR       R12, [R0, #mailboxObject_t_mailboxBufferSize_offset]
                      ;R12=mailboxObjectPtr->mailboxBufferSize


        LDR       R3, [R0, #mailboxObject_t_messageSize_offset]
                      ;R3=mailboxObjectPtr->messageSize


        SUB       R12, R12, R3
        ;R12=mailboxObjectPtr->mailboxBufferSize-
        ;                  mailboxObjectPtr->messageSize


        LDR       R3, [R0, #mailboxObject_t_emptyBufferSize_offset]
                      ;R3=mailboxObjectPtr->emptyBufferSize


        CMP       R3, R12
        ;if(mailboxObjectPtr->emptyBufferSize <=
        ;mailboxObjectPtr->mailboxBufferSize - mailboxObjectPtr->messageSize)


        BGT       message_not_available_in_the_mailbox


        ;message available in the mailbox.
        ADD       R12, R0, #mailboxObject_t_mailboxBuffer_offset
                      ;R12=&&mailboxObjectPtr->mailboxBuffer[0]


        LDR       R12, [R12]  ;R12=&mailboxObjectPtr->mailboxBuffer[0]


        LDR       R3, [R0, #mailboxObject_t_readIndex_offset]
                      ;R3=mailboxObjectPtr->readIndex


        ADD       R12, R12, R3
        ;R12=&mailboxObjectPtr->mailboxBuffer[mailboxObjectPtr->readIndex]


        LDR       R3, [R0, #mailboxObject_t_messageSize_offset]
                      ;R8=mailboxObjectPtr->messageSize
```

```
;memcpy(message,
;      &mailboxObjectPtr->mailboxBuffer[readIndex],
;      mailboxObjectPtr->messageSize);
MEMCPY    R2, R12, R3, R1

LDR       R2, [R0, #mailboxObject_t_readIndex_offset]
              ;R2=mailboxObjectPtr->readIndex

LDR       R1, [R0, #mailboxObject_t_messageSize_offset]
              ;R1=mailboxObjectPtr->messageSize

ADD       R2, R2, R1
;R2=mailboxObjectPtr->readIndex+mailboxObjectPtr->messageSize

LDR       R3, [R0, #mailboxObject_t_emptyBufferSize_offset]
              ;R3=mailboxObjectPtr->emptyBufferSize

ADD       R3, R3, R1
;R3=mailboxObjectPtr->emptyBufferSize+mailboxObjectPtr->messageSize

STR       R3, [R0, #mailboxObject_t_emptyBufferSize_offset]
;mailboxObjectPtr->emptyBufferSize += mailboxObjectPtr->messageSize

LDR       R3, [R0, #mailboxObject_t_mailboxBufferSize_offset]
;R3=mailboxObjectPtr->mailboxBufferSize

CMP       R2, R3
;if(mailboxObjectPtr->readIndex+mailboxObjectPtr->messageSize ==
;mailboxObjectPtr->mailboxBufferSize)

MOVEQ     R2, #0
;if(mailboxObjectPtr->readIndex+mailboxObjectPtr->messageSize ==
;mailboxObjectPtr->mailboxBufferSize) then R2=0

STR       R2, [R0, #mailboxObject_t_readIndex_offset]
;mailboxObjectPtr->readIndex += mailboxObjectPtr->messageSize
;(with modulo buffer size)

;check if any thread is waiting for the mailbox to become empty
LDR       R3, [R0, #(mailboxObject_t_waitList_offset+ \
                    listObject_t_auxInfo_offset)]
;R3=listObjectCount(&mailboxObjectPtr->waitList)

CMP       R3, #0
;if(listObjectCount(&mailboxObjectPtr->waitList) > 0)
```

```
MOVLE    R0, #1  ;returnValue=1.

BLE      no_thread_is_waiting

;some thread is waiting for the space in mailbox.

ADD    R0, R0, #mailboxObject_t_waitList_offset
            ;R0=&mailboxObjectPtr->waitList

STMFD  SP!, {R14}      ;save the return address of this function
                    ;first to make function call from here.

;waitingThreadObjectPtr =
;        listObjectDelete(&mailboxObjectPtr->waitList);
BL    listObjectDelete
        ;After this function R0 = waitingThreadObjectPtr

STMFD  SP!, {R0}
        ;save waitingThreadObjectPtr to make function call.

MOV    R1, R0  ;R1=waitingThreadObjectPtr

LDR    R0, =readyList  ;R0=&readyList

;listObjectInsert(readyList, waitingThreadObjectPtr);
BL    listObjectInsert

LDR    R0, [SP]      ;We get R0=waitingThreadObjectPtr

LDR    R1, [R0, #(threadObject_t_R_offset+4)]
            ;R1=waitTime

CMP    R1, #0      ;if(waitTime >= 0)

BLGE   deleteFromTimerList
            ;deleteFromTimerList(waitingThreadObjectPtr)
            ;(when waitTime greater than or equal to 0,
            ;this threadObject will be in timerList).


LDMFD  SP!, {R0, R14}
        ;R0=waitingThreadObjectPtr,
        ;R14=return address of this function.
```

```
LDR    R2, =runningThreadObjectPtr

LDR    R2, [R2]

LDR    R1, [R0, #threadObject_t_priority_offset]
              ;R1=waitingThreadObjectPtr->priority

LDR    R3, [R2, #threadObject_t_priority_offset]
              ;R3=runningThread.priority

CMP    R1, R3
;if(waitingThreadObjectPtr->priority < runningThread.priority)

MOVGE  R0, #1   ;returnValue = 1

BGE    waiting_thread_is_not_of_higher_priority;

MRS    R1, CPSR

AND    R1, R1, #0x1F      ;keep mode bits only.

CMP    R1, #IRQ_MODE

MOVEQ  R0, #1          ;returnValue=1.

BEQ    called_from_interrupt_service_routine
;This function is called from interrupt service routine.
;context switch should not be done when called from interrupt service
;routine. IRQ handler will do the context switch.

;This functin is called from user/system mode thread.
;waiting thread is of higher priority.
;insert the running thread into readyList and call scheduler.
MOV    R0, #1        ;This is the returnValue of the function.

ASSERT  threadObject_t_R_offset = 0

STMIA  R2, {R0-R14}    ;save R0-R14 of running thread.

STR    R14, [R2, #(15*4)] ;set PC as the return address of
                ;this function.

LDR    R1, =oldCPSR

LDR    R1, [R1]   ;get original status.
```

```
    SET_STATE_OF_PC_IN_CPSR R14, R1
            ;make correct CPSR value (with state of PC stored).

    STR    R1, [R2, #threadObject_t_cpsr_offset]  ;save status.

    LDR    R0, =readyList  ;R0=&readyList.

    MOV    R1, R2        ;R1=&runningThreadObject

    ;listObjectInsert(&readyList, &runningThread);
    BL     listObjectInsert

    B      scheduler


message_not_available_in_the_mailbox

    CMP    R1, #0

    MOVEQ  R0, #0        ;returnValue is zero.

    BEQ    waitTime_is_zero

    ;waitTime is non zero

    LDR    R3, =runningThreadObjectPtr

    LDR    R3, [R3]

    ASSERT  threadObject_t_R_offset = 0

    STMIA  R3, {R0-R14}    ;save the context of running thread.

    ADR    R1, mailboxObjectPend
    ;R1=program counter to start the thread.

    STR    R1, [R3, #(15*4)]  ;save PC.

    LDR    R1, =oldCPSR

    LDR    R1, [R1]      ;get original status.

    STR    R1, [R3, #threadObject_t_cpsr_offset]  ;save status.
```

```
MOV    R1, R3        ;R1=runningThread

ADD    R0, R0, #mailboxObject_t_waitList_offset
               ;R0=&mailboxObjectPtr->waitList.

;listObjectInsert(&mailboxObjectPtr->waitList, &runningThreadObject);
BL     listObjectInsert

;insert the running thread into the timerList if waitTime>0

LDR    R0, =runningThreadObjectPtr    ;R0 =&&runningThreadObject

LDR    R0, [R0]                ;R0=&runningThreadObject

LDR    R1, [R0, #threadObject_t_R_offset]
;R1=R0 of running thread=mailboxObjectPtr

ADD    R1, R1, #mailboxObject_t_waitList_offset
                  ;R1=&mailboxObjectPtr->waitList

LDR    R2, [R0, #(threadObject_t_R_offset+4)]
                  ;R2=waitTime

CMP    R2, #0              ;if(waitTime > 0)

BLGT   insertIntoTimerList
;insertIntoTimerList(&runningThread, waitList).
;R1 register of threadObject alwasy holds the waitTime.



B      scheduler




waiting_thread_is_not_of_higher_priority
called_from_interrupt_service_routine
no_thread_is_waiting
waitTime_is_zero

    INTERRUPTS_RESTORE     oldCPSR, R3

    BX    LR          ;return returnValue.
```

;mailboxObjectPost() function keep a message into the mailbox. The

```
;pseudo code of mailboxObjectPost() function is shown below.
;int32 mailboxObjectPost(mailboxObject_t *mailboxObjectPtr,
;             int32 waitTime,
;             void *message)
;{
;   int32 returnValue;
;
;   interruptsDisable();
;   if(mailboxObjectPtr->emptyBufferSize >= mailboxObjectPtr->messageSize)
;   {
;       //content will fit into mailbox. keep the message.
;       memcpy(&mailboxObjectPtr->mailboxBuffer[writeIndex],
;           message,
;           mailboxObjectPtr->messageSize);
;
;       mailboxObjectPtr->writeIndex += mailboxObjectPtr->messageSize;
;       mailboxObjectPtr->emptyBufferSize -= mailboxObjectPtr->messageSize;
;
;       assert(mailboxObjectPtr->writeIndex <=
;                   mailboxObjectPtr->mailboxBufferSize);
;
;       if(mailboxObjectPtr->writeIndex ==
;                   mailboxObjectPtr->mailboxBufferSize)
;       {
;           mailboxObjectPtr->writeIndex = 0;
;       }
;       returnValue = 1;
;
;       //if any thread waiting for this mailbox to become full.
;       if(listObjectCount(&mailboxObjectPtr->waitList) > 0)
;       {
;           waitingThreadObjectPtr =
;               listObjectDelete(&mailboxObjectPtr->waitList);
;           assert(waitingThreadObjectPtr != NULL);
;           listObjectInsert(readyList, waitingThreadObjectPtr);
;           if(waitingThreadObjectPtr->waitTime >= 0)
;           {
;               deleteFromTimerList(waitingThreadObjectPtr);
;           }
;           if(waitingThreadObjectPtr->priority < runningThread.priority &&
;               this function is not called from interrupt service routine)
;           {
;               get the context same as the end of this function and keep it
;               into running threadObject.
;               listObjectInsert(&readyList, &runningThreadObject);
```

```
;          jump to scheduler();
;       }
;     }
;   }
; else
; {
;   if(waitTime)
;   {
;     get the context same as the starting of this function and keep
;     it into running threadObject
;     listObjectInsert(&mailboxObjectPtr->waitList, &runningThreadObject);
;     if(waitTime > 0)
;     {
;       insertIntoTimerList(&runningThread,
;           &mailboxObjectPtr->waitList);
;     }
;     jump to scheduler();
;   }
;   else
;   {
;     returnValue = 0;
;   }
; }
; interruptsRestore();
; return returnValue;
;}
;This function should not be called from interrupt service routine
;with non zero waitTime

mailboxObjectPost

    INTERRUPTS_SAVE_DISABLE    oldCPSR, R3, R12

    LDR     R3, [R0, #mailboxObject_t_emptyBufferSize_offset]
                ;R3=mailboxObjectPtr->emptyBufferSize

    LDR     R12, [R0, #mailboxObject_t_messageSize_offset]
                ;R12=mailboxObjectPtr->messageSize

    CMP     R3, R12
    ;if(mailboxObjectPtr->emptyBufferSize >=
    ;           mailboxObjectPtr->messageSize)

    BLT     enough_space_not_available_in_the_mailbox
```

;enough space available for the message to keep.

```
ADD     R12, R0, #mailboxObject_t_mailboxBuffer_offset
            ;R12=&&mailboxObjectPtr->mailboxBuffer[0]

LDR     R12, [R12]

LDR     R3, [R0, #mailboxObject_t_writeIndex_offset]
            ;R3=writeIndex

ADD     R12, R12, R3
;&mailboxObjectPtr->mailboxBuffer[writeIndex]

LDR     R3, [R0, #mailboxObject_t_messageSize_offset]
            ;R3=mailboxObjectPtr->messageSize

;memcpy(&mailboxObjectPtr->mailboxBuffer[writeIndex],
;     message,
;     mailboxObjectPtr->messageSize)

mailboxObjectPostCopy  MEMCPY   R12, R2, R3, R1

LDR     R2, [R0, #mailboxObject_t_writeIndex_offset]
            ;R2=mailboxObjectPtr->writeIndex

LDR     R1, [R0, #mailboxObject_t_messageSize_offset]
            ;R1=mailboxObjectPtr->messageSize

LDR     R3, [R0, #mailboxObject_t_emptyBufferSize_offset]
            ;R3=mailboxObjectPtr->emptyBufferSize

LDR     R12, [R0, #mailboxObject_t_mailboxBufferSize_offset]
            ;R12=mailboxObjectPtr->mailboxBufferSize

ADD     R2, R2, R1
;R2=mailboxObjectPtr->writeIndex+mailboxObjectPtr->messageSize

CMP     R2, R12

MOVEQ   R2, #0
;if(mailboxObjectPtr->writeIndex+mailboxObjectPtr->messageSize ==
;mailboxObjectPtr->mailboxBufferSize) then R2=0

STR     R2, [R0, #mailboxObject_t_writeIndex_offset]
;mailboxObjectPtr->writeIndex += mailboxObjectPtr->messageSize
```

;(with modulo bufferSize)

SUB   R3, R3, R1
;R3=mailboxObjectPtr->emptyBufferSize - mailboxObjectPtr->messageSize;

STR   R3, [R0, #mailboxObject_t_emptyBufferSize_offset]
;mailboxObjectPtr->emptyBufferSize -= mailboxObjectPtr->messageSize

;check if any thread is waiting for the mailbox to become filled.
LDR   R3, [R0, #(mailboxObject_t_waitList_offset+ \
                    listObject_t_auxInfo_offset)]
;R3=listObjectCount(&mailboxObjectPtr->waitList)

CMP   R3, #0
;if(listObjectCount(&mailboxObjectPtr->waitList) > 0)

MOVLE   R0, #1   ;returnValue=1

BLE   mailboxObjectPost_no_thread_is_waiting

;some thread(s) is waiting for contents in mailbox.
ADD   R0, R0, #mailboxObject_t_waitList_offset
          ;R0=&mailboxObjectPtr->waitList

STMFD SP!, {R14}   ;Save the return address of this function
          ;to make function call from here.

;waitingThreadObjectPtr =
;   listObjectDelete(&mailboxObjectPtr->waitList);
BL   listObjectDelete   ;After this function R0 =
          ;waitingThreadObjectPtr

STMFD SP!, {R0}   ;save waitingThreadObjectPtr to make
          ;function call.

MOV   R1, R0   ;R1=waitingThreadObjectPtr

LDR   R0, =readyList   ;R0=&readyList

;listObjectInsert(readyList, waitingThreadObjectPtr);
BL   listObjectInsert

LDR   R0, [SP]   ;We get R0=waitingThreadObjectPtr

LDR   R1, [R0, #(threadObject_t_R_offset+4)]

```
                    ;R1=waitTime

CMP    R1, #0          ;if(waitTime >= 0)

BLGE   deleteFromTimerList ;deleteFromTimerList(waitingThreadObjectPtr)
                    ;(when waitTime greater or equal to 0, this
                    ;threadObject will be in timerList).


LDMFD  SP!, {R0, R14}    ;R0=waitingThreadObjectPtr.
                    ;R14=return address of this function.

LDR    R2, =runningThreadObjectPtr

LDR    R2, [R2]

LDR    R1, [R0, #threadObject_t_priority_offset]
               ;R1=waitingThreadObjectPtr->priority

LDR    R3, [R2, #threadObject_t_priority_offset]
               ;R3=runningThread.priority

CMP    R1, R3
;if(waitingThreadObjectPtr->priority < runningThread.priority)

MOVGE  R0, #1          ;returnValue=1

BGE    mailboxObjectPost_waiting_thread_is_not_of_higher_priority;

MRS    R1, CPSR

AND    R1, R1, #0x1F     ;keep only mode bits.

CMP    R1, #IRQ_MODE

MOVEQ  R0, #1          ;returnValue=1

BEQ    mailboxObjectPost_called_from_interrupt_service_routine


;This thread is called form user/system mode thread.
;waiting thread is of higher priority.
;insert the running thread into readyList and jump to scheduler.
MOV    R0, #1    ;returnValue=1
```

```
STMIA   R2, {R0-R14}      ;save R0-R12 of running thread.

STR     R14, [R2, #(15*4)]
                    ;save PC as return address of this function.

LDR     R1, =oldCPSR

LDR     R1, [R1]       ;get original status.

SET_STATE_OF_PC_IN_CPSR R14, R1
                    ;make correct CPSR for the PC stored.

STR     R1, [R2, #threadObject_t_cpsr_offset]
                    ;save status.

LDR     R0, =readyList     ;R0=&readyList.

MOV     R1, R2         ;R1=&runningThread

;listObjectInsert(&readyList, &runningThreadObject);
BL      listObjectInsert

B       scheduler



enough_space_not_available_in_the_mailbox

CMP     R1, #0

MOVEQ   R0, #0         ;returnValue = 0

BEQ     mailboxObjectPost_waitTime_is_zero

;waitTime is non zero
LDR     R3, =runningThreadObjectPtr

LDR     R3, [R3]

STMIA   R3, {R0-R14}      ;save the context of running thread.

ADR     R1, mailboxObjectPost
                    ;R1=program counter to start the thread.

STR     R1, [R3, #(15*4)]  ;save PC.
```

```
LDR     R1, =oldCPSR

LDR     R1, [R1]        ;get original status.

STR     R1, [R3, #threadObject_t_cpsr_offset]
                ;save status.

MOV     R1, R3          ;R1=runningThread

ADD     R0, R0, #mailboxObject_t_waitList_offset
                ;R0=&mailboxObjectPtr->waitList.
```

;listObjectInsert(&mailboxObjectPtr->waitList, &runningThreadObject);
```
BL      listObjectInsert
```

;insert the running thread into the timerList if waitTime>0

```
LDR     R0, =runningThreadObjectPtr
                ;R0 =&&runningThreadObject

LDR     R0, [R0]        ;R0=&runningThreadObject

LDR     R1, [R0, #threadObject_t_R_offset]
                ;R1=R0 of running thread=mailboxObjectPtr

ADD     R1, R1, #mailboxObject_t_waitList_offset
                ;R1=&mailboxObjectPtr->waitList

LDR     R2, [R0, #(threadObject_t_R_offset+4)]
                ;R2=waitTime

CMP     R2, #0          ;if(waitTime > 0)
```

```
BLGT    insertIntoTimerList
```
;insertIntoTimerList(&runningThread, waitList).
;R1 register of threadObject alwasy holds the waitTime.

```
B       scheduler
```


mailboxObjectPost_waiting_thread_is_not_of_higher_priority
mailboxObjectPost_called_from_interrupt_service_routine
mailboxObjectPost_no_thread_is_waiting
mailboxObjectPost_waitTime_is_zero

```
        INTERRUPTS_RESTORE  oldCPSR, R3

        BX    LR            ;return returnValue.


        END
```

Index

A

B

C

D

E

F

H

I

J

L

Printed in the United States
By Bookmasters